Governance of the European Monetary Union

The crisis in the euro area is a defining moment in the history of European integration. It has revealed major flaws in the architecture of the European Union; it has challenged European institutions to shape an appropriate response; and it has tested the patience of a European public that is eager to see their economic prospects improve again. This volume brings together some of the world's top economists and policymakers to explain how this crisis came about and what is to be done. The policy agenda these chapters establish is going to be difficult to implement, not least because of popular misunderstanding and political opposition. This book argues, that it is essential that European policymakers push forward this agenda or they run the risk of seeing Europe's economies fall back into crisis.

This book was previously published as a special issue of the *Journal of European Integration*.

Erik Jones is Professor of European Studies and International Political Economy and Director of European and Eurasian Studies at the Johns Hopkins School of Advanced International Studies, USA, and Senior Research Fellow at Nuffield College, Oxford, UK.

Francisco Torres is Visiting Senior Fellow in European Political Economy at the European Institute, London School of Economics and a Senior Member and PEFM Associate at St Antony's College, Oxford, UK. He is also Adjunct Professor at the Catholic University in Lisbon and an EU Steering Committee Member of the ECPR.

Governance of the European Monetary Union

Recasting political, fiscal and financial integration

Edited by

Erik Jones and Francisco Torres

Routledge
Taylor & Francis Group
LONDON AND NEW YORK

First published 2016 by Routledge

2 Park Square, Milton Park, Abingdon, Oxfordshire OX14 4RN
711 Third Avenue, New York, NY 10017

Routledge is an imprint of the Taylor & Francis Group, an informa business

First issued in paperback 2018

British Library Cataloguing in Publication Data
A catalogue record for this book is available from the British Library

ISBN 13: 978-1-138-67312-0 (hbk)
ISBN 13: 978-1-138-39218-2 (pbk)

Typeset in Sabon
by RefineCatch Limited, Bungay, Suffolk

Publisher's Note
The publisher accepts responsibility for any inconsistencies that may have arisen during the conversion of this book from journal articles to book chapters, namely the possible inclusion of journal terminology.

Contents

Citation Information

The chapters in this book were originally published in the *Journal of European Integration*, volume 37, issue 7 (November 2015). When citing this material, please use the original page numbering for each article, as follows:

Chapter 1
An 'Economics' Window on an Interdisciplinary Crisis
Erik Jones & Francisco Torres
Journal of European Integration, volume 37, issue 7 (November 2015)
pp. 713–722

Chapter 2
EMU: Old Flaws Revisited
Francesco Giavazzi & Charles Wyplosz
Journal of European Integration, volume 37, issue 7 (November 2015)
pp. 723–737

Chapter 3
Correcting for the Eurozone Design Failures: The Role of the ECB
Paul De Grauwe & Yuemei Ji
Journal of European Integration, volume 37, issue 7 (November 2015)
pp. 739–751

Chapter 4
Governance and Conditionality: Toward a Sustainable Framework?
Lorenzo Bini Smaghi
Journal of European Integration, volume 37, issue 7 (November 2015)
pp. 755–768

Chapter 5
Responses to the Euro Area Crisis: Measuring the Path of European Institutional Integration
Francesco Paolo Mongelli, Ettore Dorrucci, Demosthenes Ioannou & Alessio Terzi
Journal of European Integration, volume 37, issue 7 (November 2015)
pp. 769–786

Chapter 6
Avoiding Another Crisis in the Euro Area: Public and Private Imbalances and National Policy Responses
Russell Kincaid & Max Watson
Journal of European Integration, volume 37, issue 7 (November 2015)
pp. 787–801

Chapter 7
EMU and Sustainable Integration
Iain Begg, Annette Bongardt, Kalypso Nicolaïdis & Francisco Torres
Journal of European Integration, volume 37, issue 7 (November 2015)
pp. 803–816

Chapter 8
Getting the Story Right: How You Should Choose between Different Interpretations of the European Crisis (And Why You Should Care)
Erik Jones
Journal of European Integration, volume 37, issue 7 (November 2015)
pp. 817–832

Chapter 9
At Cross-purposes: Commercial versus Technocratic Governance of Sovereign Debt in the EU
Zsófia Barta & Waltraud Schelkle
Journal of European Integration, volume 37, issue 7 (November 2015)
pp. 833–846

Chapter 10
The Making of a Continental Financial System: Lessons for Europe from Early American History
Vítor Gaspar
Journal of European Integration, volume 37, issue 7 (November 2015)
pp. 847–859

Chapter 11
Impossible Macroeconomic Trinity: The Challenge to Economic Governance in the Eurozone
David Vines
Journal of European Integration, volume 37, issue 7 (November 2015)
pp. 861–874

Chapter 12
Using Interdisciplinary Analysis to Shape a Policy Agenda
Erik Jones & Francisco Torres
Journal of European Integration, volume 37, issue 7 (November 2015)
pp. 875–880

Notes on Contributors

Zsófia Barta is Assistant Professor in Politics at Rockefeller College of Public Affairs & Policy, State University of New York, Albany, USA.

Iain Begg is Professional Research Fellow at the European Institute, London School of Economics and Political Science, London, UK.

Lorenzo Bini Smaghi is a Visiting Scholar at WCIA, Harvard University, Cambridge, USA, and Senior Research Fellow at the School of European Political Economy, LUISS, Rome, Italy.

Annette Bongardt is Visiting Senior Fellow in European Political Economy at the European Institute, London School of Economics and Political Science, London, UK.

Paul De Grauwe is Professor in International Economics, European Institute, London School of Economics and Political Science, London, UK.

Ettore Dorrucci is Head of the Convergence and Competitiveness Division, Directorate General Economics, European Central Bank, Frankfurt am Main, Germany.

Vitor Gaspar is Director of the Fiscal Affairs Department of the International Monetary Fund, Washington, DC, USA.

Francesco Giavazzi is Professor of Economics at IGIER-Universitá Bocconi, Italy, Research Associate of the National Bureau of Economic Research (NBER), USA, and Research Fellow of the Centre for Economic Policy Research (CEPR), UK.

Demosthenes Ioannou is Principal Economist at the European Central Bank, Frankfurt am Main, Germany.

Yuemei Ji, PhD, is a Lecturer in Economics at University College London, UK.

Erik Jones is Professor of European Studies and International Political Economy and Director of European and Eurasian Studies at the Johns Hopkins School of Advanced International Studies, USA, and Senior Research Fellow at Nuffield College, Oxford, UK.

Russell Kincaid is a senior member of the European Studies Centre, St Antony's College, University of Oxford, Oxford, UK.

Francesco Paolo Mongelli is Senior Adviser in the European Central Bank, Frankfurt am Main, Germany, and honorary Professor at the Johann Wolfgang Goethe University, Frankfurt am Main, Germany.

Kalypso Nicolaïdis is Professor of International Relations in the Department of Politics and International Relations, University of Oxford, Oxford, UK.

Waltraud Schelkle is Associate Professor of Political Economy at the European Institute, London School of Economics and Political Science, London, UK.

Alessio Terzi is an Affiliate Fellow at Bruegel, Brussels, Belgium, and PhD candidate at the Hertie School of Governance, Berlin, Germany.

Francisco Torres is Visiting Senior Fellow in European Political Economy at the European Institute, London School of Economics and a Senior Member and PEFM Associate at St Antony's College, Oxford, UK.

David Vines is Professor of Economics in the Economics Department, Balliol College, Oxford University, Oxford, UK.

Max Watson was Director of the Political Economy of Financial Markets programme in the European Studies Centre, St Antony's College, University of Oxford, Oxford, UK.

Charles Wyplosz is Professor in International Economics at the The Graduate Institute, Geneva, Switzerland.

Dedication

In honour of the memory of Max Watson, a great scholar and policymaker who showed us the true value of interdisciplinary research and cross-disciplinary conversation.

An 'Economics' Window on an Interdisciplinary Crisis

ERIK JONES*,** & FRANCISCO TORRES***,****

*Johns Hopkins University SAIS, USA;
**Nuffield College, Oxford, UK;
***European Institute, London School of Economics and Political Science, London, UK;
****European Studies Centre, St. Antony's College, Oxford University, Oxford, UK

ABSTRACT The euro area crisis cannot be understood without combining insights from a variety of disciplines — economics and political science first and foremost. This introduction aims at explaining how the essays in this collection map onto a number of important debates in political science. We sketch four well-known areas for the political science community: the framework for multilevel governance, the role of ideas in policymaking, the interaction between power politics and distributive bargaining, and the challenge of popular legitimation. These critical themes in the current crisis are important areas of overlap in economic and political analysis. Hence, the aim of this introduction is to show how these themes emerge in the essays that follow.

Introduction

The euro area crisis cannot be understood without combining insights from a variety of disciplines — economics and political science first and foremost. Nevertheless, most conversations about European integration, and monetary integration in particular, take place within disciplinary boundaries. This is true even when the participants hope to speak to a wider audience in the public and private sectors. A few academic outlets, like the Journal of European Integration, do their best to create a forum for scholars from different disciplines to interact, Nevertheless, more often than not the contributors wind up having parallel conversations — citing the work of their disciplinary colleagues, using the same jargon, and ignoring the rest.

This lack of engagement across disciplines is a problem insofar as the different voices in the debate about the origins of and remedies for the European crisis have so much to offer one another. This is perhaps easiest to see when political scientists rely on economic analysis as in the recent debate about austerity (Blyth 2012). There are important examples that go in the other direction with economists drawing upon political science, as in the recent debates about democracy and development (Acemoglu and Robinson 2005) or income inequality (Piketty 2014). Nevertheless, it is a harsh reality that in a world indexed by Google and narrated by Twitter, the barriers to entry in any disciplinary conversation are large. There is simply too much material out there that is too accessible. Just keeping abreast with the pace of analysis and commentary within a given discipline is enough of a challenge to occupy the time of any academic, analyst or researcher. As a consequence, much value added is lost.

The purpose of this special issue is help redress the balance. In doing so, we hope to honour the memory of Max Watson, who was an academic, analyst and policymaker who showed the true value of interdisciplinary research and cross-disciplinary conversation. Organizing a series of seminars and a workshop on these very issues were among his last scholarly endeavours. We are privileged to be able to complete a project started with him and that he so generously supported.

Our contribution with this collection is two-fold. First, we make available the insights of some of the most accomplished economists and policymakers working on the crisis in the euro area to a wider research community from cognate disciplines. With few exceptions that will be easy to spot from the notes on contributors, these are not 'interdisciplinary' scholars. They work within the economics discipline, where they have achieved the highest level of recognition. We have asked these contributors to write in accessible language and to focus on questions of broad significance. They have responded with a wealth of insight about opportunities missed, flaws uncovered, data misinterpreted, experience ignored and politics trumping economics. Each of these arguments sheds light on a different aspect of the European dilemma and each reveals an agenda for positive action. Some of this action is conceptual and shows how we can better understand the dynamics at work both in the current crisis and looking to the future; some is more practical and suggests how we can reshape European institutions to make them more resilient — and integration more sustainable — looking to the future. The abstracts to the different essays provide a quick survey of the material they contain, and so, we do not repeat that information here.

The success of that contribution should be measured in terms of the breadth of appeal — both for the individual papers and for the collection as a whole. Hence, the goal of these essays is not to push forward scientific knowledge in the 'normal' manner described by Kuhn (1970). Strict disciplinary journals would be more appropriate for such arguments. But then, our ambition to foster cross-disciplinary exchange would be thwarted. Hence, we encouraged our contributors to challenge fundamental assumptions and to look across disciplinary boundaries. In doing so, we asked them to work outside their comfort zones and to develop arguments that are more familiar to those working in other disciplines. This should create multiple avenues for engagement.

This explains our second contribution, which is to show how the essays in this collection map onto a number of important debates in political science. We use the introduction and conclusion to achieve that objective. This allows us to highlight areas we believe are of particular concern. It also makes it easy for us to show how this kind of cross-disciplinary engagement can take place. We offer a gateway not a finished product. There are other themes from political science that recur in these essays. We leave these for the reader to discover. Moreover, the value added to draw from this type of collection will always be a work in progress. If we can introduce these arguments to a new audience and show how they can be folded into existing debates with which that audience is likely to be familiar, we can begin the cross-disciplinary conversation.

The introduction sets the stage by sketching four areas for attention that are well known within the political science community: the framework for multilevel governance, the role of ideas in policymaking, the interaction between power politics and distributive bargaining, and the challenge of popular legitimation. These are critical themes in the current crisis and important areas of overlap in economic and political analysis. Hence, the aim of the introduction is to show how these themes emerge in the essays that follow.

The goal of the conclusion is to suggest how both economists and political scientists can use shared themes to foster a coherent and productive cross-disciplinary conversation. That conversation should help us move towards a two-fold objective: it should improve the quality of the answers we provide to important questions in the scholarly literature and should also help to shape recommendations for strengthening public policy. Clearly, the European Union needs to make progress on both dimensions. There is a wealth of insight and analysis out there to be exploited offering a variety of solutions to the wide array of pressing problems. At the moment, though, the interaction between economics and politics is working against effective public policymaking. The solutions that are acceptable are not effective, and many of the measures that could improve the situation are unpopular (if not simply unacceptable). It is times like these that we need to start thinking outside of disciplinary boxes.

Multilevel Governance

At its core, the euro area crisis is a crisis in the framework for multilevel governance. For political scientists, this is territory made familiar both through the study of federal systems and through analysis of the European Union itself. Hooghe and Gary (2001) have brought together the various strands of argument in the multilevel governance literature in a synthetic framework and Scharpf (1999, 2001) has provided invaluable insights on the unique challenges that multilevel governance arrangements face in terms of decision-making and legitimation. These insights are fundamental to understanding the crisis of the euro area.

Consider, for example the theory of optimum currency areas (OCA). In abstract terms, the question is how large or small of an economy domain should be encompassed by a single currency. In more practical terms, the question is whether the currency domain and the political domain should be the same. The OCA literature exists because economists questioned the necessity of subjugating economic institutions to a political logic — one sovereign and so one currency. Yet if you break that link, then it is unclear how many governance institutions need to coordinate at the same level of aggregation as the currency and how many can be allowed to operate at levels that are either larger or smaller. This is an age-old problem and, as Vitor Gaspar shows, it lies at the heart of American experience with federal state building. Gaspar focuses on the financial system and the crucial role played by Alexander Hamilton in structuring both federal budgets and private finances. The story he tells is progressive insofar as the US federal state continues to amass authority. It is a non-linear story; Hamilton's financial institutions were largely dismantled by Andrew Jackson. Nevertheless, Hamilton anticipated much of what is required in a modern multilevel financial economy like the one you find in the United States today.

The process of European integration is only very loosely analogous to the US experience. Nevertheless, there are certain insights about multilevel governance in the areas of money and finance that resonate in both places. You can see this in the essay by Francesco Giavazzi and Charles Wyplosz. The story they tell is about design features that should have been included in European efforts and yet were omitted either because they were unpopular or because they were simply ignored. Fiscal union falls in the unpopular category; financial union should be filed under neglect. Implicitly, this shows the importance of learning from the experience of other cases. The United States tried to manage a currency without a financial union and nearly failed. That is why Hamilton's original insights are so important. Hamilton had a more lasting impact on federal finances. Yet if pooling finances is necessary for successful monetary integration, it is an open question why the architects of the single currency went ahead with their project without securing political support for fiscal centralization first.

The easy answer is to assume that monetary policy could operate at the European level while fiscal policy could operate at the national level. This assumption works under certain conditions. But it does not work when national economies are allowed to accumulate essentially unlimited public or private sector liabilities. This is the point made in the paper by Russel Kincaid and Max Watson. What it reveals are the externalities of policy action (or inaction) at the mid-range of a multilevel governance structure. Their point is that these externalities accumulate to such an extent that they can threaten the viability of the multilevel governance framework as a whole. Moreover, there are strong incentives at the Member State level to allow these imbalances to accumulate into a source of systemic stability. As

Scharpf (and many others in the political science community) anticipated, there are gaps in the decision-making framework that no level of government and no specific actor have the authority to fill. The consequences can be seen in the essay by Lorenzo Bini Smaghi. He shows how attempts to impose conditionality on governments in distress have failed to achieve a desired reaction. Worse, they have engendered widespread discontent — both among those countries that have been subjected to conditionality and among those countries that have provided resources for European bailouts against what they now perceive as 'empty' promises of 'meaningful' reform. This is a challenge that Iain Begg and his colleagues recognize as well. In fact, an alternative to an improbable full-fledged fiscal integration would be to improve both the current model of conditionality and make it more sustainable (Bini Smaghi) and complementing it with an integrated economic policy framework (Begg et al.; Kincaid and Watson; Sapir and Wolff 2015).

The problem of imbalances focuses on the negative interaction between a large currency union and smaller fiscal authorities. A further concern is the interaction between policymakers in the monetary and fiscal domains that does not take place because they are not working at the same level of aggregation. Here, the issue is not perverse incentives that give rise to excessive indebtedness, it is the lack of coordination necessary for effective macroeconomic adjustment. This theme would be anachronistic in the paper by Gaspar; macroeconomic demand stabilization was not a consideration for the founding fathers of the American Republic. It was not anachronistic for the founders of the euro area. Indeed, the importance of coordinating makes an appearance in Giavazzi and Wyplosz and features prominently in the essays by Paul De Grauwe and Yuemei Ji and by David Vines. Implicitly, the contributors appeal to a set of economic models where macroeconomic policy coordination is useful in stabilizing the evolution of inflation and unemployment. Such models assume a level of aggregation — both for policymaking and for data collection. Hence, they also assume some connection between the domains for political control and for relevant economic activity. This creates an important tension in the theory of OCAs — and hence also a tension in the architecture of the euro. A currency should encompass efficient markets (Mundell 1961) but it should also encompass effective macroeconomic demand stabilization (McKinnon 1963), and where the scale for effective macroeconomic demand stabilization is larger than the domain of market efficiency, then appropriately designed fiscal institutions can make up the difference through automatic flows in taxes and transfers across regions within the currency area (Kenen 1969). In other words, multilevel governance is both the problem and the solution.

The Role of Ideas

Of course, it is also possible that the shared assumption about the importance of coordinating macroeconomic policy instruments is flawed because aggregate demand stabilization is not a valid policy objective. Economists do not all accept models derived from the neoclassical synthesis. Indeed, those models are hotly contested in Europe. This observation is fundamental in the political science literature. It lies at the heart of virtually every major contribution to the role of ideas in comparative political economy from Hall's (1989) edited volume on Keynesianism across nations to McNamara's (1998) study of monetary integration and Blyth's (2002) work on the monetarist revolution. Economists are more comfortable trying to assert their own ideas in the policy process than trying to understand how ideas influence policy more generally. Nevertheless, they are well aware that such influence exists and that contestation has an impact on policy outcomes. This is clearly shown in the collection of papers on joining Europe's monetary club, which we published in the phase of convergence towards EMU (Jones et al. 1998).

Vines' essay is perhaps the strongest expression of concern about the role of ideas in European policymaking. He focuses his attention on the German economic establishment, but his real concern is not 'Germany' but what he brands as poor thinking. Hence, his essay is both an attempt to diagnose the problem at the heart of the European crisis and to explain how we might think about it more fruitfully. Erik Jones has a similar agenda in his essay. Ironically, the two disagree on both the most appropriate set of ideas for addressing the crisis and the appropriate strategy for choosing between them. There is a certain reassurance that emerges from the debate between them. No view has a monopoly on the truth. Hence, the contestation over ideas is not without reason.

That is not the same as saying that all ideas deserve equal merit. Some ideas work better than others — in helping policymakers to influence the world around them, but also in helping politicians to mobilize political support. This is one of the fundamental insights in the political science literature and it is on full display here as well. It connects the stories about institutional design features adopted and ignored by the architects of the single currency in the Giavazzi and Wyplosz essay to the conditionality and reform debates in the Bini Smaghi and Begg et al. papers and to the macroeconomic policies analysed by De Grauwe and Ji.

Ideas can take us further as well. As Blyth (2002) argues, ideas are a focal point for coordination. What De Grauwe and Ji show is how this coordination expresses in European financial markets. What they reveal is the extent to which actual financial market performance is inconsistent with what we would expect from ideational constructs like the efficient markets hypothesis. Instead of responding smoothly and consistently to assessments of fiscal solvency and sovereign creditworthiness, markets tend to ignore fiscal variables until suddenly they find them to be of interest. Ideas do not fit the rationality of perfect information, in that sense. They are heuristic or signalling devices used by market participants (as an aside, there is a growing literature on voters and elections that comes to similar conclusions in a more explicitly political context). Moreover, market participants are not the only economic agents who are fickle in their treatment of fiscal ideas. Zsofia Barta and Waltraud Schelkle show similar inconsistencies in the behaviour of credit ratings agencies and supranational institutions. These organizations do not have a monolithic sense of what is good and what is bad in the fiscal domain; rather, they operate with contested concepts and changing conventions.

Differences in ideas within a multilevel governance framework make for an added complication. This is another insight that Barta and Schelkle reveal. Once again, moreover, we are confronted with the disjuncture between the policy domain and the scope of relevant economic activity. This time, however, the supranational institutions are smaller than the economic actors (credit ratings agencies) that are the focus for attention. Hence, at least part of the challenge is to bring the credit ratings agencies into the policy domain. This challenge is not straightforward. Having validated the credit ratings agencies as sources of policy relevant data by writing ratings requirements into European legislation, European policymakers may have made matters worse rather than better.

Striking an appropriate balance is not easy. This is true partly because of the influence of unintended consequences and partly due to the lack of adequate measurement. Francesco Mongelli and his colleagues tackle the measurement problem by creating an indicator for capturing the evolution of the European Union as a framework for multilevel governance. The indicator they develop tracks the four unions that are central to the 'Five Presidents Report' (2015) to improve the architecture of the European Union. We return to this report in the conclusion. For now, what Mongelli et al. reveal is how much judgement is involved in assessing progress in institution building. Ideas factor into every aspect of the measurement process and so weave contention into the very fabric of our understanding of European integration.

Distributive Bargaining and Power Politics

Contention over the nature of European integration cannot be resolved through reference to objective principles. The European federalists recognized that early on. Worse, there are no ironclad or ineluctable causal mechanisms underpinning the process of institution building. Early neo-functionalists like Haas (1968) were disillusioned. Their historical institutionalist successors have been no more successful. This is not to say that neo-functionalist spillover or historical path dependence have no relevance. On the contrary, each of the essays in this collection shows how the crisis 'spills' across discrete policy areas, they illustrate the need for more coordinated intervention, and they highlight the challenge of working with and through those institutions that actually exist (as opposed to imagining some alternative universe). Nevertheless, even the most elegant framework for understanding European integration — or economics — has to allow space for distributive bargaining and power politics.

In many of the essays collected here, these forces show up as a kind of political hidden hand. They explain why the architects of the single currency did not pursue fiscal federalism and how they came to ignore the advantages of pooling financial market supervision. On a deeper level, they explain how macroeconomic imbalances arose, why they were allowed to grow to unsustainable dimensions and why national politicians have been so reluctant to undertake the reforms necessary to prevent their recurrence. Distributive bargaining and power politics explain the very negative dynamics at work in the application of 'conditionality', they explain the suspicion that often greets the promulgation of German ideas about the virtues of fiscal austerity and the ineffectiveness of macroeconomic demand stabilization, and they explain the difficulty of forging some kind of effective European discretion in responding to crisis imperatives.

The question is whether any pattern lies buried in all this negativity. If that pattern is 'might makes right', then the goal should be to persuade the most powerful or influential policy actors. If the pattern is 'right makes might', then the goal should be to speak truth to power. It is interesting in this sense to look at the tone of the different essays to see where they fall in that spectrum and what this implies about underlying assumptions. Here again, the contrast between Jones and Vines is of interest. There are, however, many more than just two points on the spectrum. Hence, it is useful to look at each of the essays to assess both the audience and the objective of the authors. It is also useful to judge which is likely to have any measure of success in influencing either the scholarly community or the policy process.

Popular Legitimation

By considering these contributions as part of a larger conversation, it becomes easier to fold them into the mechanism of European integration itself. That is an important step in the process of engagement. The point here is not that these essays will revolutionize how we understand Europe or how Europe is organized. Rather it is that each in its own way tackles a problem of multilevel governance, offers an idea about how that problem can be resolved and addresses that idea to a particular audience that hopefully will have some influence over the situation. Whether that influence is whispered directly into the ear of the most powerful person in the room or filters its way up through the cacophony of contemporary academic discourse is irrelevant. In the long run, 'Keynes' long-defunct economists' have as much influence as Keynes himself. Indeed, Keynes worries (not unreasonably) that he is outmatched.

For such a broad assessment to work, however, it must take questions of popular legitimation into account. These questions are front and centre in the chapter by Begg and his colleagues. That explains why they are so focused on the sustainability of integration as a multi-dimensional problem. If we are to take the long term into account, it is not enough simply to address the current crisis; it is not even enough to avoid the dilemma where the solutions of today become the problems of tomorrow. Here, it is worth recalling that Padoa-Schioppa *et al.* (1987) foresaw irrevocably fixed exchange rates as the first-best response to the challenge of currency market volatility even as politicians in France and Germany believed that monetary union would cement the reconciliation of their two countries (Dyson and Featherstone 1999).

Hence, the key to long-term sustainability requires doing more than just addressing the current crisis; it depends upon policymakers developing institutions and practices that will make it easier to address other future crises as well. The solution to the current problems of the euro area must help us deal with population ageing and climate change. This may seem far-fetched; once we take into account the impact of current reforms on public expenditures and market structures, however, it is easy to see how they are all connected. These connections exist in the eye of the public as well. Policymakers are not alone in having ideas about how the world works, and they are not unique in realizing the multilevel structure of governance. The people are active participants in politics as well as in the markets. Moreover, their actions play a critical role in validating or vitiating the assumptions that underpin European institutions. When De Grauwe and Ji focus their analysis on the behaviour of markets, this is what they mean.

The challenge for analysis is to understand how people are organized and what are the relevant levels of aggregation. That notion of relevance hinges on the principle of legitimacy. Where legitimacy is greatest, policymakers have the most effective control over collective action. This is what Begg and his colleagues reveal. Drawing upon the work of Nicolaïdis (2010, 2013), they show how units of political legitimation — *demoi* — operate as the political equivalent of OCAs. These units are not equal in scale or scope to the currency itself. That is the fundamental challenge. Hence, it is necessary for these different units to engage in power politics and distributive bargaining in order to influence how their common currency is governed. Along the way, they fight over different ideas about how the economy works and what institutions offer the most control over economic performance. And they reserve the right to act as sovereign even within a multilevel governance framework. This political analysis is not so different from the economic analysis in other chapters. Nevertheless, it operates at the other end of the prism with economic rationality on one end and political legitimation on the other. In fact, as put by Begg et al. and Mongelli et al., economic integration would have to be pursued along the lines of creating stronger incentives for structural reforms in low-productivity countries, thereby improving the overall stability of EMU to macroeconomic shocks by making the Eurozone better meet the economic requirements for a currency union.

Between these two points is a large and complicated set of dynamics. Currently, those dynamics are in crisis. Any attempt to resolve that crisis must take account of both the economic and political forces at work. The purpose of this collection is to shed light on the economic side of the problem. Doing so, however, only reveals the political dimensions that warrant complementary analysis. We hope that readers will use these essays as a source of inspiration to generate new questions. We cannot anticipate how those questions will be answered but we can imagine that the answers will operate across traditional academic disciplines.

Acknowledgements

This special issue benefited a lot from the very helpful comments of an anonymous referee and from the willingness of the authors to take up the challenge to engage with the other chapters and domains. We are also grateful to the editors of JEI for their comments and suggestions and the patience with which they accompanied the making of this special issue.

Disclosure statement

No potential conflict of interest was reported by the authors.

References

Acemoglu, Daron and James, Robinson. 2005. *The economic origins of dictatorship and democracy*. Cambridge: Cambridge University Press.

Blyth, Mark. 2002. *Great transformations*. Cambridge: Cambridge University Press.

Blyth, Mark. 2012. *Austerity: the history of a dangerous idea*. Oxford: Oxford University Press.

Dyson, Kenneth, and Kevin Featherstone. 1999. *The road to Maastricht: negotiating economic and monetary union*. Oxford: Oxford University Press.

Haas, Ernst. 1968. *The uniting of Europe: political, social, and economic forces 1950–1957*. Stanford, CA: Stanford University Press.

Hall, Peter, ed. 1989. *The political power of economic ideas: keynesianism across nations*. Princeton, NJ: Princeton University Press.

Hooghe, Liebeth, and Gary Marks. 2001. *Multilevel governance and European integration*. Lanham, MD: Rowman & Littlefield.

Jones, Erik, Jeffry Frieden, and Francisco Torres. 1998. *Joining Europe's monetary club: the challenges for smaller member states*. New York: St. Martin's Press.

Kenen, Peter. 1969. The optimum currency area: an eclectic view. In *Monetary problems of the international economy*, eds. R. Mundell and A. Swoboda, 41–60. Chicago, IL: University of Chicago Press.

Kuhn, Thomas. 1970. *The structure of scientific revolutions*, 2nd edn, enlarged. Chicago, IL: University of Chicago Press.

McKinnon, Ronald. 1963. Optimum currency areas. *American Economic Review* 53: 717–25.

McNamara, Kathleen. 1998. *The currency of ideas: monetary politics in the European Union*. Ithaca, NY: Cornell University Press.

Mundell, Robert. 1961. A theory of optimum currency areas. *American Economic Review* 51: 657–65.

Nicolaïdis, Kalypso. 2010. Sustainable integration: towards EU 2.0? *The JCMS Annual Review Lecture, Journal of Common Market Studies* 48: 21–54.

Nicolaïdis, Kalypso. 2013. European demoicracy and its crisis. *JCMS: Journal of Common Market Studies* 51, no. 2: 351–69.

Padoa-Schioppa, Tommaso, Michael Emerson, Mervin King, Jean-Claude Milleron, Jean Paelink, Lucas Papademos, Alfredo Pastor, and Fritz Scharf. 1987. *Efficiency, stability and equity: a strategy for the evolution of the economic system of the European community*. Oxford: Oxford University Press.

Piketty, Thomas. 2014. *Capital in the twenty-first century*. Cambridge, MA: Harvard University Press.

Sapir, André, and Guntram Wolff. 2015. *Euro-area governance: what to reform and how to do it*. Bruegel Policy Brief 2015/01, February.

Scharpf, Fritz. 1999. *Governing in Europe. Effective and democratic?* Oxford: Oxford University Press.

Scharpf, Fritz. 2001. Notes toward a theory of multilevel governing in Europe. *Scandinavian Political Studies* 24, no. 1: 1–26.

EMU: Old Flaws Revisited

FRANCESCO GIAVAZZI*,**,*** & CHARLES WYPLOSZ**,****

*IGIER-Università Bocconi, Milan, Italy;
**CEPR, London, UK;
***NBER, Cambridge, MA, USA;
****The Graduate Institute, Geneva, Switzerland

ABSTRACT Economic and monetary union (EMU) started with serious flaws. Those flaws had been carefully diagnosed and yet no attempts were made to deal with them. As an original experiment, it would have been extraordinary that its design be perfect from the start. The fact that these flaws came together to generate the euro-area crisis is an indictment of the denial that has characterized the first decade of the monetary union. The costs of this denial have been enormous, including lost incomes, unemployment, bankruptcies, and dangerous political under-currents. We revisit three main flaws: the lack of planning to deal with financial instability, the lack of transparency of the ECB, and the poor articulation between monetary policy and national fiscal policies.

Introduction

Economic and monetary union (EMU) started with serious flaws. Those flaws had been carefully diagnosed and yet no attempts were made to deal with them.[1] As an original experiment, it would have been extraordinary that its design be perfect from the start.[2] The fact that these flaws came together to generate the Euro-area crisis is an indictment of the denial that has characterized the first decade of the monetary union. The costs of this denial have been enormous, including lost incomes, unemployment, bankruptcies, and dangerous political under-currents.

Building on Begg *et al.* (1998), this article revisits three main flaws: the lack of planning to deal with financial instability, the lack of transparency of the ECB, and the poor articulation between monetary policy and national fiscal policies. As we take up these issues, we ask two questions: (i) what did we miss? For instance, we warned that the ECB might be ill-prepared to face a financial crisis, but our examples (admittedly in 1998) were backward looking pointing to the SouthEast Asian crisis as an example; (ii) what progress has been made in the areas that we had indicated as yet incomplete? Is this progress satisfactory?

EMU and Financial Stability

In the decade preceding the start of EMU, many researchers worried about the ability of the ECB to deliver financial stability. Three concerns had been raised:

- in the event of a sudden increase in the demand for liquidity, the ECB might be unable to provide such liquidity rapidly enough (see also *Jones* 2015);
- EMU might not be able to deal effectively with the insolvency of a large financial institution — either closing it down or using tax-payers' money tore capitalize it — so that such a default might reverberate throughout the Euro area;
- the new Euro-wide payment system run by the ECB (TARGET) may not takeoff, and transactions might use private and more fragile payment systems.

The ECB has dealt surprisingly well with the first and last of these concerns. The issue of how to face a bank insolvency has been put aside for over a decade: now it has emerged as the 'banking union'.

The Provision of Liquidity

We worried that limiting the ECB to lend only if adequate collateral was posted, might curb its ability to provide emergency liquidity. This did not happen, on the contrary. When the crisis started, in the summer of 2007, the ECB intervened faster than the Fed because at that time, the Fed only accepted a narrow range of collateral. The ECB instead maintained an extensive list of Tier 1 collateral. This was not smart anticipation, however, simply the fact that the ECB took on board all types of collateral previously accepted by the NCBs. In the event, when even this large list turned out to be too narrow for the task, it was expanded, even to include bank loans (or pools of loans). Collateral has never been a limitation to the provision of liquidity.

Differently from the Fed, however, the ECB did not intend to engage in outright purchases of the assets sitting in the balance sheets of banks. It provided liquidity under the assumption that the banks were solvent, only momentarily illiquid. In this way, the ECB protected its balance sheet, but did not have to face the issue of bank soundness. It is only in late 2011 that the ECB engaged in outright purchases and triggered the process that lead to the Banking Union and credible stress tests (see also *De Grauwe and Ji* 2015).

Banking Supervision and the Ability to Distinguish Between Illiquidity and Insolvency

As early as 1991, Begg *et al* (1991) noted that banking supervision was receiving only scant attention. ECB supervisory functions were not developed in its statutes,[3] yet the Treaty Protocol on the ECB (articles 25.1 and 25.2) left the door open for a role in the prudential supervision of banks and other financial institutions (with the surprising exclusion of insurance companies) and in guaranteeing financial stability.

Initially, the ECB did not think that a single supervisor might be necessary. The view was that banking supervision could rely on co-operation among national banking supervisors (Padoa Schioppa 1999). We were skeptical that cooperation might be sufficient. We worried that effective supervision might be hampered by excessive bargaining, high communication costs, and lobbying from pressure groups on national authorities. We argued for keeping separate illiquid and in solvent banks assigning liquidity and lender of last resort to the ECB and insolvency to a separate regulatory agency.

It took a crisis to break political and intellectual opposition to a single supervisory authority. However, although we correctly identified the problem, we only scratched its surface. Some issues that have come to the forefront as the ECB takes over its new responsibility were largely overlooked in our analysis. They are examined next.

Current Burning Issues for the Banking Union

- How should supervisors determine the appropriate amount of a bank's equity? Since many Euro-area banks hold large quantities of domestic sovereign bonds, the answer depends, importantly, on the way such bonds are treated. Pretending that all government bonds are safe is not satisfactory.
- As a prerequisite to assuming its supervisory role, the ECB has run stress tests. The bank should have enough capital to absorb the losses to face severe shocks. The first round of late 2014 was a significant improvement over earlier exercises. More and different tests will be required to establish the credibility of the Banking Union. The definition of what is a severe shock remains too vague for comfort.
- It has been agreed that in the case of a bank resolution, uninsured bank stakeholders will be bailed in, which is an important step forward. But many questions remain open.
- The availability of a 'backstop' — that is a way to keep a bank alive in case of a bad shock — is critical. The plan is to gradually raise a common fund, but no fund is ever large enough to deal with a large systemic crisis. The usual default option, then, is lending in last resort by

the central bank. The ECB resists to accept this role because it feels that it would pushed into fiscal policy territory. We return to this question in the next Section.

The Wrong Sequence

The decision to postpone for over a decade the choice of who should be responsible for banking supervision has had a serious consequence. It induced the Euro area to address the financial crisis in the wrong sequence. This is one of the reasons why the recession is lasting so much longer in the Euro area than in the US. The US government first cleaned up the banks, through the TARP (Troubled Asset Relieve Program) and then, once the credit channel was repaired, used macroeconomic policies. These policies worked because the credit channel was functioning again. In Europe, where banks are much more central than in the US in the financing of firms, monetary policy (right or wrong) was made ineffective by a non-functioning credit channel.

Financial Stability in Post-crisis Central Banking

A common view before the crisis was that central banks had a single objective: price stability. As Jean-Claude Trichet used to say: 'The best contribution of monetary policy to financial stability is price stability'. In Begg *et al.* (1998), we did not accept that reasoning. The view that central banks must take responsibility for financial stability is now accepted by most central bankers but the ECB resists accepting the role of lender of last resort because it could result in a fiscal transfer: imposing costs on taxpayers of Country A because a bank in Country B has failed. This position is understandable if the bank failure in A is the result of poor supervision by Country A's supervisor.

However, as the Single Supervisor, the ECB must accept responsibility for a bank failure. To intervene as lender of last resort, however, it must trust the Resolution Authority that will determine whether and which taxpayers will be made to bear the burden. Indeed, it is the relevant Resolution Authority that will set the conditions under which a failing bank is recapitalized with public money. In other words, a bank resolution determines the risks taken on behalf of the taxpayers by the institution that provides resources. In the particular context of EMU, where there are no European taxpayers, only national ones, the ECB needs to be fully reassured that bank resolution will minimize the risk of a residual cost to taxpayers and that eventual losses will be borne by national taxpayers — since taxes cannot be imposed by a 'foreign' entity. Either the Single Resolution Authority can be depended upon to tilt the risks toward the bank stakeholders, or resolution will remain in national hands where capture by national champions is the rule, in effect undermining the authority of the single supervisor.

Interplay Between the ECB and Member Governments

Coordination: The Old Debate Comes True

In our 1998 article, we were not convinced that the Stability and Growth Pact would deliver fiscal discipline.[4] We used the theory of policy coordination to think about the macroeconomic relationship between one central bank and n governments, and we concluded that this would lead governments to be excessively lax and the ECB to be excessively tight. Many governments indeed relaxed their fiscal stance after joining the Eurozone and monetary policy has not been unduly tight except, maybe, occasionally. Fiscal profligacy arose in various countries for two different reasons that were mentioned in some early works but not fully exploited. First, came the temptation by some governments to hide behind the monetary union to be profligate, guessing that the no-bailout clause would be relinquished if needed.[5] Second, Euro-area membership provided an aura of credibility that would ensure low or inexistent risk premia on national public bonds. As noted by Dornbusch, Favero, and Giavazzi (1998), this would imply a rapid decline in interest costs and an incentive to adopt larger primary deficits. One or both of these factors came to play in many countries and the Stability and Growth Pact failed to impose the fiscal discipline that was necessary to uphold the monetary union, avoiding undue pressure on the ECB.[6]

The lack of fiscal discipline and the implications for the ECB are further examined below. Here, we raise the issue to note that the relationship between the ECB and member governments has remained unsatisfactory (see also *Bini Smaghi* 2015 and *Vines* 2015).[7] While the Euro group assumed increasing responsibility to coordinate fiscal policies, it did not really seek to apply peer pressure on stray members and never developed the instruments to examine the overall fiscal policy stance of the monetary union. The European Commission tried to use the Stability and Growth Pact to constrain deficits but its legalistic approach failed in the face of occasional slowdowns or 'special circumstances'.

The absence of a fiscal authority at Eurozone level is a well-recognized inherent characteristic of EMU, in fact the reason why this experiment is both an innovation and a threat, as argued by Feldstein (1997). The political constraint is that there is no chance that national authorities (governments and parliaments) will give up sovereignty in fiscal policy matters. During the sovereign debt crisis, when speed and effectiveness became of the essence, the void was filled by the re-emergence of the German–French leadership, which soon turned into a German leadership.[8] This extreme form of coordination is not just politically explosive and an aggravation of the famed democratic deficit, it is also inefficient. In many respects, the crisis could have been mitigated and shortened had proper decisions been made. Examples of politically induced procrastination include the rejection of a Greek debt reduction that was finally enacted as the private sector involvement — which, however, failed to reduce the debt — or the long-lasting refusal to move to a single bank supervisor and a single resolution mechanism. Examples of misguided policies include the imposition of austerity policies on countries in depression, failure to make clear the distinction between austerity implemented by cutting spending or by raising taxes, and opposition to the ECB's role as lender in last resort.

Unfortunately, there is no easy solution. Democratic legitimacy lies with national governments and parliaments, which are constitutionally required to uphold national interests. Even though the collective goods may justify compromises in the name of national interest, in crisis situations national interests may diverge too far for enlightened coordination. The European Commission is ultimately a reflection of this political situation. The creation of a European Presidency and of a permanent Chair of the Euro group merely added new bureaucratic layers designed to obfuscate political deadlocks.

The single monetary authority itself had to forge its own identity out of equally disparate inherited traditions. The mantra that the Euro system makes decision by consensus sometimes cannot conceal deep differences of opinion within the Executive Board (until its latest renewal in 2011–2012) and within the Governing Council. This was anticipated in our 1998 article as we wrote that 'problems are created when the central Executive Committee is weak in relation to the chairmen of its constituent banks. [ ] How quickly the ECB achieves effective centralization may be one of the keys to its eventual success' (4–5). Recently, this centralization appears to have been accelerated, but much remains to be done.

We suggested that lessons be learned from the difficult early years of the Fed. Nowadays, no President of a regional Federal Reserve Bank, who sits on the policy-making bodies, even hails from the region, except by pure coincidence. They represent their respective regions in the sense that they report on local economic conditions, but they are unencumbered by local interests. Within the ECB Governing Council, instead, the views of the national governors are invariably shaped by national interests and prejudices.[9] The solution is to reduce the power of national governors, which can be easily done by reducing the frequency of Governing Council meetings, currently scheduled twice a month. A more audacious solution would be to move to the US model as recently suggested by Burda (2013).

Fiscal Discipline

The need for fiscal discipline was clearly identified by the Delors Committee. The adopted solution, unfortunately, has clearly failed. As noted above, lower interest rates and the belief (correct, as it turned out) that over-indebted governments would be bailed out have provided irresistible temptations. Not all governments have been fiscally undisciplined, however, which shows that domestic institutions can be effective if well designed. A key conclusion of Hallerberg, Rainer Strauch, and von Hagen (2009) is that, to be effective, institutions for fiscal discipline must be well adapted to political institutions. Two major conclusions follow. First, the one-size-fits-all Stability and Growth Pact is unlikely to be effective in all member countries. Second, any Euro area-wide arrangement must be compatible with EU political institutions.

This is where another lesson can be borrowed from the early US experience. Upon independence, the federal government was small and weak relative to the preexisting states, not unlike the European Commission today. In his famed effort to build up a federal Treasury, Alexander Hamilton offered to assume the state public debts that had grown large — by the standards of the late eighteenth century. This seminal bailout encouraged many more bailouts and the growth of the federal Treasury. Fiscal indiscipline at state level flourished until the 1840s when Congress created a precedent by refusing one more bailout. US states responded by adopting various forms of balanced budget rules.[10] The precedent still applies today and fiscal discipline is firmly established at the state level. Wyplosz (2013) argues that this model is relevant to the Euro area, in contrast to the Stability and Growth Pact, which is inspired by Germany's own arrangements based on a powerful federal government.

Another lesson can be learned from the Euro-area crisis. Ireland and Spain had a good record of fiscal discipline before the crisis and, yet, they were drawn into it. The reason is that both countries had to bail out their banking systems. In the absence of a domestic central bank, the lender of last resort function had to be assumed by the government through massive borrowing, including indirectly from ECB through the emergency liquidity assistance program. The implication is that either the ECB has to fully assume the role of lender of last resort, including the risk of suffering losses, or other governments must be ready to bail out a government that faces a banking crisis.

Policy Dominance

The Euro area provides a stark example of policy dominance. On paper, the ECB's independence status is as hard as can be. It is enshrined in no uncertain words in an international treaty that is very unlikely to ever be modified in this respect. Yet, a highly reticent ECB was pushed into contributing to the Greek bailout. Since then, it has joined the Troika, which goes way beyond its mission. It has provided banks with massive amounts of liquidity because it had no choice but to act as lender of last resort. It has been led to buy large amounts of public debts and to backstop the prices of debts from crisis countries through its OMT program. Monetary dominance ends when a central bank is somehow led to finance deficits and/or buy public debts.

Given the circumstances, these actions of the ECB were justified. Indeed, other major central banks (e.g., the Federal Reserve and the Bank of England) have carried out similar actions, often earlier, on a larger scale and without the safeguards that the ECB has sometimes obtained, e.g., the OMT program's conditionality.

All central banks now wonder about the policy dominance issue. As explained in Leeper (1991), no formal independence status can protect a central bank from financing the government one way or another, if refraining from doing so can have dramatic consequences — for example a breakup of the monetary union in our context.

When discussing this issue in our 1998 article, we made a number of suggestions that, we think, remain valid today:

- it is essential that the ECB achieves and retains a high degree of support from the broad public. The polarizing nature of the sovereign debt crisis, broadly separating the north and the south, represents a major challenge for the ECB. The massive expansion of the ECB's balance sheet has implied the acquisition of large quantities of collateral. Even though it was already large before of the crisis, the list of eligible collaterals has been expanded. This has meant a deterioration of the quality of the central bank's assets. The ECB applies haircuts on risky collaterals; even so, it takes risk, including on officially riskless public bonds. Any loss would have to be distributed among its shareholders, the national central banks. Ultimately these potential losses will be borne by the taxpayers. Enlisting the support of taxpayers, a key necessity for upholding the central bank' ability to resist pressure from governments, is no easy task. The countries not in crisis fear that they may have to bear the burden of ECB losses. The countries in crisis see the ECB as a hawkish member of the Troika that has imposed highly unpopular policies;
- we argued that the ECB needs to be as transparent as possible. The better its policy is understood, the less controversial it will be. We shall discuss transparency in the next section;
- we called for the adoption of a policy rule. A clear rule not only allows for more transparency, it also takes the edge off criticism when taking controversial actions. We suggested adopting the flexible inflation targeting strategy that many other central banks have pursued with evident success. We still believe that this is a desirable step. But the flexible inflation targeting strategy is designed for normal times. The ECB, and several other central banks as well, now needs to redefine their monetary policy strategy. As suggested in Blinder *et al.* (2013), this will require adopting the flexible inflation targeting strategy but making it explicitly conditional on the occurrence of major shocks, mostly financial shocks. While markets and observers can understand conditionality, the task of explaining the strategy to the broader public will be hard sale. Recently, the ECB has started to provide its own version of forward guidance, a step that may heralda more open approach to communication in the next Section develops this issue.

Like several other central banks, the ECB is now involved in banking supervision and cannot extricate itself fully from bank resolution. These activities do not belong to monetary policy proper. They involve decisions that have redistributive effects and are therefore normally in the realm of governments, which have the required democratic legitimacy. In many countries, these functions have been transferred, partly at least, to the central bank because the government agencies in charge of bank supervision and/or resolution have failed during the crisis. An additional reason to do so in the Euro area, as noted above, is that bank stability carries important externalities that are not properly internalized when supervision and resolution is carried out at the national level. By accepting these tasks, central banks take risks, which can reduce their effective independence if they come under pressure from politicians.

The ECB has already announced its intention to establish a Chinese wall between its monetary policy functions and its banking supervision branch. The new Supervisory Board (SB) will be a committee whose chair will have a non-renewable term of five years. The first Chair is Ms Danièle Nouy who is not a member of the Governing Council. A vice-chair, Sabine Lautenschläger, was chosen from among the members of the ECB's Executive Board. These two are accompanied by four ECB representatives and one representative of the national competent authority of each participating country. To resist national pressures, the SB will need to evolve rapidly towards a committee where the chair and the five ECB representatives make the important decisions. But this will bring the two functions dangerously close to one another.

ECB Transparency

Changing Theory and Practice

Central bank transparency is one issue that has undergone profound changes over the last twenty years, both in theory and practice. Using the Barro–Gordon model with rational expectations, Cukierman and Metzler (1986) showed that central banks must maintain a veil of secrecy for monetary policy to be effective. This conclusion was based on the 'only unanticipated money matters' assumption of the then-workhorse macroeconomic model, and on the assumption that central banks are better informed than the private sector. This theory provided support for the highly ambiguous, often purposely secretive behavior of most central banks at the time. Blinder (1998) challenged this orthodoxy. As formally established by Woodford (2005), central bank transparency is desirable when monetary policy affects the economy through interest rates of a longer maturity than the policy rate. In this case, providing information about future policy rates allows the central bank to shape the longer term interest rates and therefore gives more power to policy actions. This effect is reinforced when the central bank has an information advantage over the private sector, but this assumption is not needed to establish the usefulness of transparency. A number of central banks, following the lead of the Reserve Bank of New Zealand, of the Norges Bank and of the Riksbank, have moved to become increasingly more transparent.

Until now, the ECB has strenuously resisted providing information on future interest rates, except in the days immediately preceding a change, a practice that it calls 'market preparation'. The ECB has recently changed its approach, adopting 'forward guidance'. Forward guidance is a way of providing information about the level of future policy rates which, however, is less transparent then publishing a path for interest rates (as done, e.g., by the Riksbank)and clearly explaining why that path needs to be changed if new information becomes available.

The ECB Approach to Communication

The issue of transparency was raised critically by CEPR researchers. In the 2008 Monitoring the ECB report by Gerats, Giavazzi, and Wyplosz, we recalled the Blinder–Woodford arguments in favor of a high degree of transparency. We further argued that the process of decision-making itself is a source of opaqueness since the press conference invariably states that the decision has been reached by consensus. This makes it impossible for interested observers to detect whether the decision has been 'obvious' and therefore that future policies will be a mere continuation of the current policy stance, or whether the Council has been split, which could herald shifting majorities. Finally, the report observed that, in a democracy, central bank independence must be constantly defended. The only way of protecting independence is by acquiring and maintaining wide popular support, which calls for better communication, and not just towards financial markets.

The implications of these observations run deep. First, our report asked that decisions be made by formal vote. This is a requirement of the European treaty, which the ECB has presented as unnecessary given the existing consensus. This argument is surprising given that the Governing Council includes $6 + n$ members, n being the number of member countries. With n starting at 11 and 19 since January 2015, the Council is a large body where the probability of achieving (near) unanimity is extremely small. Consensus, therefore, is likely to allow a majority, possibly a narrow one, to silence a minority. Second, the report asked that the results of votes be made public, maybe without mentioning the names of Council members if it is believed that doing so could be exploited for nationalistic reasons. Third, the report called for the rapid publication of minutes, possibly unattributed for the same reason, so that observers can understand the arguments that led to each decision.

Until recently, the ECB has denied that such transparency was needed.[11] It has also long refused publishing minutes, claiming to be highly transparent.[12] Fortunately, this has changed since early 2015.

The crisis has shown the shortcomings of this approach. The ECB contribution to the bailout of Greece has triggered strong opposition within the Governing Council, too strong to be hidden, especially as the leading opponent was the Governor of the Bundesbank. Further nonstandard policies, especially the SMP and OMT programs, have met with criticism from the next Governor of the Bundesbank and a few colleagues. Although the ECB has not explicitly mentioned it, it seems that some form of voting, explicit or not, has taken place. The 'team spirit' has evaporated, assuming that it ever existed.

The votes of individual Governing Council members in divisive decisions are often eventually revealed, as exemplified by some of the cases discussed above. It would have been better if those votes, instead of being leaked to the press, had been acknowledged in a transparent way through the publication of minutes.

The ECB published its first minutes on 19 February 2015. Voting records, however, remain clouded in secrecy.

Communication and Strategy

We have so far discussed the 'how' of the ECB communication strategy, but the 'what' is intimately linked to the 'how'. Communicating intentions and doubts is difficult when the monetary policy strategy is not spelled out precisely. Very transparent central banks like the Norges Bank or the Riksbank accept that, at least in normal times, their strategies can be interpreted as minimizing a quadratic loss function that measures deviations of expected inflation from target and of unemployment from its natural rate. They even provide information on the weights that they attach on these deviations. In this case, communication amounts to publishing forecasts and explaining how these forecasts map into current and future interest rates.

The ECB strategy is far less clear-cut. In our 1998 report, we expressed concern about the two elements of the announced strategy. First, the lexicographic ordering of objectives — price stability above all, the rest if possible — is not just vague, it is unrealistic. It is vague because price stability is not a precise concept and because 'the rest' remains to be detailed. The ECB has given its definition of price stability (close to but below 2% inflation) but has always refused to provide information about 'the rest'.[13] The absolute priority given to price stability is not realistic because no central bank can ignore the state of the economy (GDP growth, unemployment), not to mention financial stability as explained in the next Section. In fact, there is convincing evidence that the ECB has behaved like other central banks, broadly following a Taylor rule. This means that the ECB does not do what it says it intends to do and that it does not say what it is trying to achieve. Communicating such an approach is mission impossible.

Second, the ECB has adopted its well-known two-pillar strategy. It analyzes the overall economic situation (inflation and the rest) and monitors the evolution of monetary trends. The second pillar, inherited from the Bundesbank, is a vestige of the times when the German central bank had developed a strategy based on the quantity theory of money. As we noted in our 1998 report, the Bundesbank had long abandoned this approach de facto but insisted that it remains faithful to the quantity theory. The reason is that the quantity theory assumes a constant velocity of money while this velocity has been varying, following both a trend and cyclical fluctuations around the trend. Indeed, most central banks have abandoned the monetary pillar. Insisting that the second pillar is useful for 'cross checking', the information obtained under the first pillar unnecessarily clouds the analysis that lies behind policy decisions. It also makes the communication of the analysis confusing.

There is no indication that the ECB is ready to jettison either the presentation of its strategy or the second pillar. The statement by the President after each policymaking meeting of the Governing Council continues the ritual of explaining decisions on the basis of the primary price stability objective and of referring to the two pillars. Recently, the President has been much more open during the Q&A session that follows the formal presentation of the decision of the day. Keen ECB observers have long learned to read in between the lines of this ritual but that does not make for transparency. It could even preclude hard-nosed debates within the Governing Council if the discussion is effectively structured along the lines of a strategy that is ill conceived.[14]

Appointments to the Executive Board

Finally, transparency also concerns the appointment of members of the ECB Executive Board. Even though it does not make policy decisions, the Board is arguably shaping them, so its composition is crucial. As befits the 'federal' nature of the ECB, these appointments are made by the European Council, and are not, therefore, a responsibility of the ECB itself. Unfortunately, the process has been clouded by political maneuvering so that it has been anything but transparent.[15]

To start with, four of the six positions have been informally attributed to the largest countries, although Spain recently lost its seat. The implicit logic, that larger countries must have a larger say, directly contradicts the nature of the ECB, an institution that serves the whole Euro area, not its individual members, certainly not because they are large. It also contradicts the brief of Executive Committee members who should never see themselves as representing their own countries. We noted that one weakness of the Euro area is the excessive weight of national central bank governors; the de facto large-country seats arrangement worsens the problem.

For such important positions, one would expect a wide search for the best talents, for functions discussed below. In fact, the European Council announces its decision without appropriate consultations.[16] The nominee must then be approved by the European Parliament, on which more below. For the large countries, the choice is left to each respective government; the other countries do not wish to interfere. For the two remaining small-country seats, some countries put up candidates but the choice usually reflects horse trading for other important European positions.

The question of defining what talent is needed is not innocuous either. The Executive Board members are not just making monetary policy decisions. They have multiple responsibilities, both policy-making and management. This has several undesirable implications. EB members use a significant amount of their time to exercise their management responsibilities. It also dilutes the job description: do we need monetary policy experts or good managers? As a result, the scope for political meddling is widened.

The vetting of nominees by the European Parliament is also troublesome. For awhile, the European Parliament was merely endorsing the Council decisions. The latest appointment led to a negative vote by the Parliament because it violated 'gender balance', defined as at least one female on the EB. The Council simply ignored the Parliament's negative vote and went ahead with the appointment of its preferred (male) candidate. Besides leaning against the wind of increasing female participation at the highest levels of power, this episode further increased the democratic deficit of the EU.

Concluding Remarks

We referred abundantly to the first issue in CEPR's monitoring the ECB series because it was published before the launch of the Euro and because it aimed at offering an exhaustive assessment of the experiment about to start. The series eventually included six issues and two updates before its somewhat untimely end in 2008. Each issue covered topics that mattered importantly at the time, often already touched upon in the first issue. Taken together, this series and many other contributions by CEPR researchers show that the Euro area crisis did not come as a surprise, at least to the academic community. To be sure, the precise way events unfolded was not foreseen, but the key weaknesses that provoked the crisis had been identified long beforehand.

Another aspect of these contributions is the increasing interactions between central banking and academic research. Central banks have innovated a lot over the last two decades or so with inflation targeting, improved communication strategies, new and unorthodox instruments, etc. These innovations were made by central banks on their own, but they relied in many ways on academic contributions and, in turn, they generated much new research. Research departments at central banks, at the BIS, and at the IMF are increasingly producing works that are published in the best academic journals, not to mention central bank reviews with academic content, in particular the *International Journal of Central Banking*. Most governors and top officials of major central banks are now card carrying economists with either a PhD, or distinguished academic work, often both.

The Euro system has, for some time, been rather slow in following this trend. This may explain that the warnings issued in the Monitoring the ECB series have long fallen on what seemed like deaf ears. The Euro system is now catching up, both at the ECB and in NCBs.

We believe that much has to be gained when academics learn from central bankers and when central bankers learn from academics, sometimes through migration. We feel privileged to have witnessed a clear evolution in that direction, including at the ECB.

Acknowledgement

This article builds on a paper originally presented at CEPR's 30th Anniversary Conference in November 2013, and issued as a CEPR electronic book.

Disclosure statement

No potential conflict of interest was reported by the authors.

Notes

1. See Begg et al. 1998.
2. Other monetary unions differ in several respects from the European one. The closest precedent, perhaps, is the adoption of the dollar in the highly decentralized USA in 1790 and of the Federal Reserve System more than a century later. Several lessons from this experiment have been ignored, more below.

3. Similar concerns had been expressed a few years earlier in a forward-looking paper by Folkerts-Landau and Garber (1992). See also Begg *et al.* (1991).
4. The argument was laid out in Eichengreen and Wyplosz (1998).
5. The underlying common pool externality is developed in von Hagen and Harden (1995).
6. As anticipated in Begg et al. (1998), the Pact was considered by European central bankers as a key element of stability, helping to ensure discipline in normal times but at the onset of a crisis it could turn into a stumbling block, implying that the whole burden of getting things back to track would rest on the shoulders of the ECB.
7. Policy coordination inside EMU was discussed in MECB 3 authored by A. Alesina, O. Blanchard, J. Galì, F. Giavazzi and H. Uhlig.
8. Here, we admit that we wrote that 'Germany is no longer likely to play the role of enforcer of fiscal restraint'.
9. This national bias is reinforced by the appointment process of the Executive Board members by the European Council, which has been clouded by political maneuvering around national pressure. We return to the problems this raises in the next Section.
10. With one exception, Vermont. For an overview of this evolution, see Henning and Kessler (2012). See also Gaspar (2015).
11. Interview with Jean-Claude Trichet, Federal Reserve Bank of Minneapolis, 2004, http://www.minneapolisfed.org/publications_papers/pub_display.cfm?id=3304.
12. Jean Claude Trichet. 'Communication, Transparency and the ECB's Monetary Policy', *BIS Review* 5/2005, 3.
13. Other central banks typically provide an inflation target and a margin of flexibility around the target. Svensson (2003) has argued that the ECB's definition hurts transparency.
14. The increase of the policy rate in June 2008, when the crisis was already building up, remains a mystery unless one accepts the primacy of a price stability objective defined not in terms of an inflation forecast but of current-month inflation only.
15. See e.g., 'Selection of the central bank Council is a fait accompli', by F. Giavazzi and C. Wyplosz, *Financial Times*, 10 February 2006.
16. A treaty requirement is that the ECB and the European Commission be consulted, but this is a formality designed to weed out egregious cases of incompetence.

References

Begg, David, Pierre-André Chiappori, Francesco Giavazzi, Colin Mayer, David Neven, Luigi Spaventa, Xavier Vives, and Charles Wyplosz. 1991. *The making of monetary union, monitoring European integration* No. 2. London: CEPR.

Begg, David, Paul de Grauwe, Francesco Giavazzi, Harald Uhlig, Charles Wyplosz. 1998. *The ECB: safe at any speed?* Monitoring the European Central Bank No. 2. London: CEPR.

Bini Smaghi, Lorenzo. 2015. Governance and Conditionality: Toward a Sustainable Framework? *Journal of European Integration* 37, no. 7: 755–68.

Blinder, Alan S. 1998. *Central banking in theory and practice*. Cambridge: MIT Press.

Blinder, Alan, Jordan J Thomas, Donald Kohn, and Frederic S Mishkin. 2013. *Exit strategy*. Geneva reports on the World Economy No. 15. London: CEPR.

Burda, Michael. 2013. *Redesigning the ECB with regional rather than national central banks*. Vox-EU, 15 July, London.

Cukierman, Alex, and Alan Meltzer. 1986. A theory of ambiguity, credibility, and inflation under discretion and asymmetric information. *Econometrica* 54, no. 5: 1099–128.

Dornbusch, Rudiger, Carlo Favero, and Francesco Giavazzi. 1998. Immediate challenges for the European Central Bank. *Economic Policy* 13, no. 26: 15–64.

De Grauwe, Paul, and Yuemei Ji. 2015. Correcting for the Eurozone Design Failures: The Role of the ECB. *Journal of European Integration* 37, no. 7: 739–54.

Eichengreen, Barry, and Charles Wyplosz. 1998. The stability pact: minor nuisance, major diversion? *Economic Policy* 26: 67–113.

Feldstein, Martin. 1997. The political economy of the European economic and monetary union: political sources of an economic liability. *Journal of Economic Perspectives* 11, no. 4: 23–42.

Folkerts-Landau, David, and Peter M. Garber. 1992. *The European Central Bank: a bank or a monetary policy rule*. NBER working paper No. 4016, March.

Gaspar, Vitor. 2015. The Making of a Continental Financial System: Lessons for Europe from Early American History. *Journal of European Integration* 37, no. 7: 847–59.

Gerats, Petra, Francesco Giavazzi and Charles Wyplosz. 2008. *Transparency and governance*. Monitoring the ECB No. 6. CEPR.

Hallerberg, Mark, Rolf Rainer Strauch, and Jürgen von Hagen. 2009. *Fiscal governance in Europe*. Cambridge: Cambridge University Press.

Henning, C. Randall, and Martin Kessler. 2012. *Fiscal federalism: US history for architects of Europe's fiscal union*. Working Paper 12-2. Washington, DC: Peterson Institute for International Economics.

Jones, Erik. 2015. Getting the Story Right: How You Should Choose between Different Interpretations of the European Crisis (And Why You Should Care). *Journal of European Integration* 37, no. 7: 817–31.

Leeper, Edward. 1991. Equilibria under 'active' and 'passive' monetary and fiscal policies. *Journal of Monetary Economics* 27, no. 1: 129–47.

Padoa Schioppa, Tommaso. 1999. *EMU and banking supervision*. Lecture delivered at the London School of Economics on 24 February, available at the ECB site.

Svensson, Lars E.O. 2003. *How should the Eurosystem reform its monetary strategy?* Briefing Paper for ECON of the European Parliament, February, Brussels.

von Hagen, Jurgen, and Ian Harden. 1995. Budget processes and commitment to fiscal discipline. *European Economic Review* 39, no. 3–4: 771–9.

Vines, David. 2015. Impossible Macroeconomic Trinity: The Challenge to Economic Governance in the Eurozone. *Journal of European Integration* 37, no. 7: 861–74.

Woodford, Michael. 2005. Central-Bank communication and policy effectiveness. In *The Greenspan era: lessons for the future*, 399–474. Kansanas: Federal Reserve Bank of Kansas.

Wyplosz, Charles. 2013. *Europe's quest for fiscal discipline*. European Economy Economic Papers 498, April 2013.

Correcting for the Eurozone Design Failures: The Role of the ECB

PAUL DE GRAUWE* & YUEMEI JI**

*School of European Studies, European Institute, London School of Economics and Political Science, London, UK;
** University College London, UK

ABSTRACT Macroeconomic policies in the Eurozone have been dysfunctional since the eruption of the financial crisis. The failure of these policies to guide the Eurozone out of the crisis has everything to do with the design failures in the Eurozone. In this article, we first remind the reader of the nature of these design failures. We then analyze how these have led to ill-designed macroeconomic policies. We then focus on the role of the ECB on correcting for these design failures. We conclude with some thoughts about monetary and political unification.

Introduction

Macroeconomic policies in the Eurozone have been dysfunctional since the eruption of the financial crisis. The failure of these policies to guide the Eurozone out of the crisis has everything to do with the design failures in the Eurozone. In this article, we first remind the reader of the nature of these design failures.[1] We then analyze how these have led to ill-designed macroeconomic policies. Finally, we discuss how these policies can be improved. Inevitably, this leads to a discussion of how the design failures of the Eurozone should be corrected.

The Eurozone's Design Failures

The design failures of the Eurozone find their origin in two factors. The first one arises from the endogenous dynamics of booms and busts that is endemic in capitalism. The second one finds its origin in the stabilizers that existed at the national level prior to the start of the union and that were fundamentally transformed when countries joined the monetary union. Let us expand on these two points.

Booms and Busts Dynamics

In the Eurozone money and monetary policy are fully centralized. However, the rest of macroeconomic policies (government spending and taxation, social policies, wage policies) has remained firmly in the hands of national governments. In addition, many institutional features in labor and goods markets have a strong national character. All these differences can lead to idiosyncratic movements that are unconstrained by the existence of a common currency. As a result, there is very little in the monetary union that can make the booms and busts converge at the Eurozone level. The effect of all this is that booms and busts originate at the national level and have a life of their own at the national level without becoming a common boom-and-bust dynamics at the Eurozone level.

In fact, it is even worse. The existence of the monetary union can exacerbate booms and busts at the national level. The reason is that the single interest rate that the ECB imposes on all the member countries is too low for the booming countries and too high for the countries in recession. Thus, when in Spain, Ireland, Greece the economy started to boom, inflation also picked up in these countries. As a result, the single nominal interest rate led to a low real interest rate in the booming countries, thereby aggravating the boom. The opposite occurred in the countries experiencing low growth or a recession.

Thus, the fact that only one interest rate exists for the union exacerbates these differences, i.e., it leads to a stronger boom in the booming countries and a stronger recession in the recession countries than if there had been no monetary union.

No Stabilizers Left in Place

When the Eurozone was started a fundamental stabilizing force that existed at the level of the member states was taken away from these countries. This is the lender of last resort function of the central bank. Suddenly, member countries of the monetary union had to issue debt in a currency they had no control over. As a result, the governments of these countries could no longer guarantee that the cash would always be available to roll over the government debt. Prior to entry in the monetary union, these countries could, like all stand-alone countries, issue debt in their own currencies thereby giving an implicit guarantee that the cash would always be there to pay out bondholders at maturity. The reason is that as stand-alone countries they had the power to force the central bank to provide liquidity in times of crisis.

What was not understood when the Eurozone was designed is that this lack of guarantee provided by Eurozone governments in turn could trigger self-fulfilling liquidity crises (a sudden stop) that would degenerate into solvency problems. This is exactly what happened in countries such as Ireland, Spain and Portugal.[7] When investors lost confidence in these countries, they massively sold the government bonds of these countries, pushing interest rates to unsustainably high levels. In addition, the euros obtained from these sales were invested in 'safe countries' like Germany. As a result, there was a massive outflow of liquidity from the problem countries, making it impossible for the governments of these countries to fund the rollover of their debt at reasonable interest rate.

This liquidity crisis in turn triggered another important phenomenon. It forced countries to switch off the automatic stabilizers in the budget. The governments of the problem countries had to scramble for cash and were forced into instantaneous austerity programs, by cutting spending and raising taxes. A deep recession was the result. We show some evidence for this in Figure 1. This relates a measure of austerity (the change in the structural primary balance) and the cumulative growth in GDP from 2009 to 2012. Note that as the austerity measure takes out the cyclical component in the government budget, it can be considered as an exogenous variable. We observe that austerity is strongly related to the decline in GDP. Similar evidence has been found by Blanchard and Leigh (2013). These authors show that the severity in the recession was due to the fact that the fiscal multiplier was larger than 1, which is much larger than traditional (DSGE) models predicted.

Thus, it appears that austerity contributed to deep recessions in the countries of the periphery; it also did not help in reducing the government debt burden as is shown in Figure 2. We show the same austerity measure (on

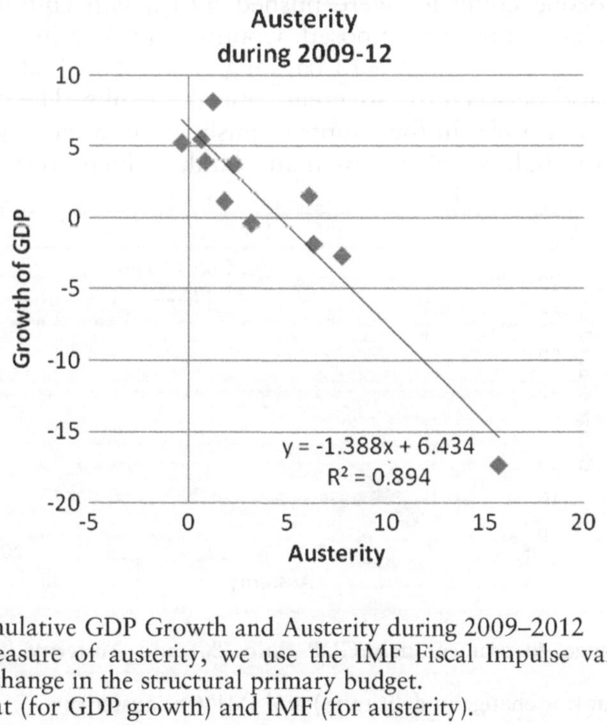

Figure 1. Cumulative GDP Growth and Austerity during 2009–2012
Note: As a measure of austerity, we use the IMF Fiscal Impulse variable which is defined as the change in the structural primary budget.
Source: Eurostat (for GDP growth) and IMF (for austerity).

the horizontal axis) and the change in the government debt ratio (on the vertical axis). We observe a strong and significant positive correlation. Countries that engaged in the strongest austerity measures also experienced the largest increase in their debt ratios. Thus, austerity does not seem to have increased the capacity of governments to service their debt, on the contrary. In that sense, austerity left these countries with a large debt overhang that leaves them with a legacy they will have to deal with in the future.

The Eurozone crisis that erupted in 2010 was the result of a combination of the two design failures identified here. On the one hand, booms and busts continued to occur at the national level. In fact, these were probably intensified by the very existence of a monetary union. On the other hand, the stripping away of the lender of last resort support of the member state countries allowed liquidity crises to emerge when the booms turned into busts. These liquidity crises then forced countries to eliminate another stabilizing feature that had emerged after the great depression, i.e., the automatic stabilizers in the government budgets. As a result, some countries were forced into bad equilibria. De Grauwe (2011) provides a theoretical model that generates multiple equilibria. See also Gros (2011).

It is interesting to note that member countries of the Eurozone face the same problem as emerging countries that because of underdeveloped domestic financial markets are forced to issue their debt in a foreign currency see Eichengreen, Hausmann, and Panizza (2005). In the words of Eichengreen, Hausmann, and Panizza (2005), this works as the 'original sin' that leads these countries into a bad equilibrium full of pain and misery.

When Eurozone countries were pushed into a bad equilibrium a third important design failure was exposed. Countries pushed into bad equilibria were immediately confronted with banking crises. This had to do with the 'deadly embrace' between the sovereign and the banks. The collapse of the government bond prices in the countries pushed into a bad equilibrium also deteriorated the balance sheets of many banks which were holding these

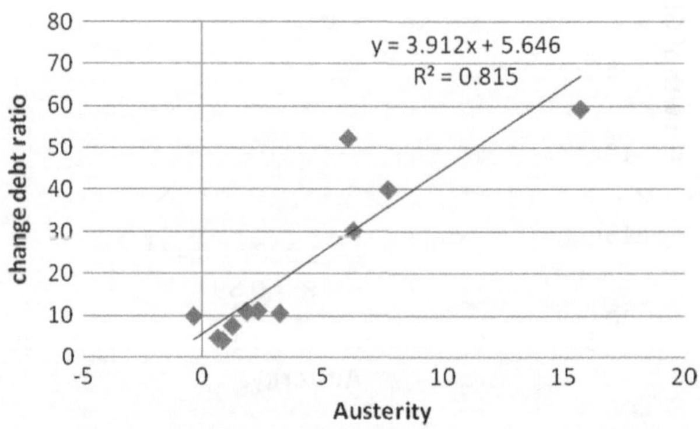

Figure 2. Change government debt/GDP ratio (%) and Austerity (% GDP) during 2009–2012
Source: Eurostat (for change in debt ratio) and IMF (for austerity).

bonds. They were threatened by insolvency. Remarkably, only when the banks were at risk (not when the sovereigns were), did the ECB start acting and provided massive liquidity support to the banking systems of the troubled countries (see Giavazzi and Wyplosz, 2015).

In fact, on 6 September 2012, the ECB announced its 'Outright Monetary Transactions' (OMT) program, which promises to buy unlimited amounts of sovereign bonds during crises. The ECB made the right decision to become a lender of last resort, not only for banks but also for sovereigns, thereby re-establishing a stabilizing force needed to protect the system from the booms and bust dynamics. By taking away the intense existential fears that the collapse of the Eurozone was imminent the ECB's lender of last resort commitment pacified government bond markets and led to a strong decline in the spreads of the Eurozone countries. It is no exaggeration to state the ECB saved the Eurozone in 2012. The remarkable thing about this success is that the ECB did not have to buy one euro of government bonds. The announcement that it would be willing to buy unlimited amounts of government bonds in times of crisis was sufficient to take out the fear from the government bond markets. This then led private agents who had become sufficiently confident about the future of the Eurozone to buy the bonds of the distressed governments.

However, the credibility of the program suffers because of continuing vehement criticism. This criticism reached its climax in early 2014 when the German Constitutional Court declared OMT illegal and referred the case to the European Court of Justice with the demand that conditions be imposed on the OMT program that would make it ineffective and useless. The main argument made by the German judges is that the spreads reflect underlying economic fundamentals. Attempts by the ECB to reduce these spreads are attempts to counter the view of market participants. In doing so, the ECB is in fact pursuing economic policy, which is outside its mandate.

Implicit in this argument is the view that markets are efficient (see De Grauwe 2014; Winkler 2014). The surging spreads observed from 2010 to the middle of 2012 were the result of deteriorating fundamentals (e.g., domestic government debt, external debt, and competitiveness). Thus, the market was just a messenger of bad news. Its judgment should then be respected, also by the ECB. The implication of the efficient market theory is that the only way these spreads can go down is by improving the fundamentals, mainly by austerity programs aimed at reducing government budget deficits and debts. With its OMT program, the ECB is in fact reducing the need to improve these fundamentals.

Another theory, while accepting that fundamentals matter, recognizes that collective movements of fear and panic can have dramatic effects on spreads. These movements can drive the spreads away from underlying fundamentals, very much like in the stock markets prices can be gripped by a bubble pushing them far away from underlying fundamentals. The implication of that theory is that while fundamentals cannot be ignored, there is a special role for the central bank that has to provide liquidity in times of market panic. This is the view we have defended in the previous sections.

This decision of the ECB provides us with an interesting experiment to test these two theories about how spreads are formed. In De Grauwe and Ji (2013), such a test was performed. The data sample, however, ended just before the OMT announcement. More data have become available allowing us to also test for the impact of OMT. We do this in the next section.

Testing Two Theories of the Spreads

The spreads in the government bond rates (10 year) have been subjected to wild fluctuations since the start of the financial crisis in 2008. While prior to the crisis these spreads had been close to zero, they started to increase spectacularly from 2010 on. In De Grauwe and Ji (2013), we showed that this spectacular increase can only in a very limited extent be associated with deteriorating fundamentals and that most of the surge is due to strongly negative market sentiments. Since 2012 (Q3), the spreads start to decline spectacularly. Our econometric analysis aims at determining how much of the decline is due to improving fundamentals and how much to positive market sentiments triggered by the announcement of OMT in the third quarter of 2012.

We specify an econometric model of the spreads. We rely on the existing literature to do so.[3] The most common fundamental variables found in this literature are as follows: variables measuring the sustainability of government debt. We will use the debt to GDP ratio as a measure of sustainability. In addition, we use the current account position, the real effective exchange rate and the rate of economic growth as fundamental variables affecting the spreads. The effects of these fundamental variables on the spreads can be described as follows.

- When the *government debt to GDP ratio* increases, the burden of the debt service increases leading to an increasing probability of default. This then in turn leads to an increase in the spread, which is a risk premium investors demand to compensate them for the increased default risk.[4]
- The accumulated *current account deficits* measure the net foreign debt of the country as a whole (private and official residents). It is computed as the current account deficits accumulated since 2000Q1 divided by its GDP level. If the increase in net foreign debt arises from the private sector's overspending, it will lead to default risk of the private sector. However, the government is likely to be affected because such defaults lead to a negative effect on economic activity, inducing a decline in government revenues and an increase in government budget deficits. If the increase in net foreign indebtedness arises from government overspending, it directly increases the government's debt service, and thus the default risk.
- The *real effective exchange rate* as a measure of competitiveness can be considered as an early warning variable indicating that a country that experiences a real appreciation will run into problems of

competitiveness which in turn will lead to future current account deficits, and future debt problems. Investors may then demand an additional risk premium.

- *Economic growth* affects the ease with which a government is capable of servicing its debt. The lower the growth rate the more difficult it is to raise tax revenues. As a result, a decline of economic growth will increase the incentive of the government to default, raising the default risk and the spread.

We specify the econometric equation in a nonlinear form in the debt ratio. The reason comes from the fact that every decision to default is a discontinuous one and leads to high potential losses. Thus, as the debt to GDP ratio increases, investors realize that they come closer to the default decision, making them more sensitive to a given increase in the debt to GDP ratio (Giavazzi and Pagano 1990).

$$I_{it} = \alpha + z \times CA_{it} + \gamma_1 \times Debt_{it} + \mu \times REE_{it} + \delta \times Growth_{it} + \gamma_2 \times (Debt_{it})^2 + \alpha_i + \beta_t + \varepsilon_{it} \quad (1)$$

where

- I_{it} is the interest rate spread of country i in period t,
- CA_{it} is the accumulated current account to GDP ratio of country i in period t,
- $Debt_{it}$ is either the government debt to GDP ratio or the fiscal space of country i in period t,
- REE_{it} is the real effective exchange rate,
- α is the constant term
- α_i is country is fixed effect. This variable measures the idiosyncrasies of a country that affect its spread and that are not time dependent. For example, the efficiency of the tax system, the quality of the governance, and many other variables that are country-specific are captured by the fixed effect.
- β_t is the time dummy variable. This measures the time effects that are unrelated to the fundamentals of the model or (by definition) to the fixed effects. If significant, it shows that the spreads move in time unrelated to the fundamentals forces driving the yields. We interpret this time dummy as reflecting market sentiments that exist at a point in time.

Note that we have not included an external risk factor in the econometric equation as is often done in the literature. We did this because the external risk factor turns out to be highly correlated with the spreads. As the latter increase, this increases perceived risk everywhere. As a result, the external risk factor is not an exogenous variable in Equation (1).

We performed a Hausman test suggesting that the fixed effect model is the right one compared to the random effects model. We also performed unit root tests and found that we cannot reject that the debt to GDP ratio has a unit roots. A co-integration test including the time dummy revealed that the variables are co-integrated.

The results of estimating this equation are shown in Table 1. We observe that the debt to GDP ratio has the expected sign and is significant. The same can be said about growth. The accumulated current account and the real effective exchange rate have the expected sign but are not significant. The time dummies have a jointly significant effect on the spreads.

We plot the time effects obtained from the estimated Equation (1) in Figure 3. We have split the countries into the core and periphery. We find very strong time dummies for the countries in the periphery. This suggests that especially in the periphery 'departures' occurred in the spreads, i.e., during 2010–2012, an increase in the spreads that cannot be accounted for by fundamental developments, in particular by the changes in the debt to GDP ratios. Similarly from 2012 (Q3), the spreads declined significantly. This decline cannot be associated with changes in fundamentals. They are again due to changing market sentiments, this time positive sentiments. This change in market sentiments coincides exactly with the announcement of OMT by the ECB.

These results suggest that since 2010, the markets were first gripped by negative sentiments and tended to exaggerate the default risks of individual countries, i.e., they pushed the spreads way above the fundamental risks. Since the announcement of OMT, the reverse has happened. The spreads went down spectacularly mostly driven by positive market sentiments unrelated to the improvements (if any) in the fundamentals.

In order to find out the relative importance of the fundamental variables and the market sentiments (as measured by the time dummies) in influencing the spreads, we computed the quantitative importance of these two factors in explaining the predicted spreads in the model. We analyze two periods. The first one goes from 2008Q1 to 2012Q2. This is the period of the buildup of the sovereign debt crisis. The second period goes from

Table 1. Estimation results equation (1)

Debt/GDP ratio (%)	−0.1202*** (0.0304)
Debt/GDP ratio squared	0.0009*** (0.0002)
Accumulated current account/GDP ratio (%)	−0.0048 (0.0034)
Real effective exchange rate	0.0554 (0.0332)
Growth rate (%)	−0.1851** (0.0659)
Country fixed effects	Controlled
Time fixed effects (quarterly)	Controlled
Number of observations	560
Number of countries	10
R-squared	0.8601

Note: Cluster at country level and robust standard error is shown in brackets.
Sample period: (2000Q1–2013Q4).
*$p < 0.1$.
**$p < 0.05$.
***$p < 0.01$.

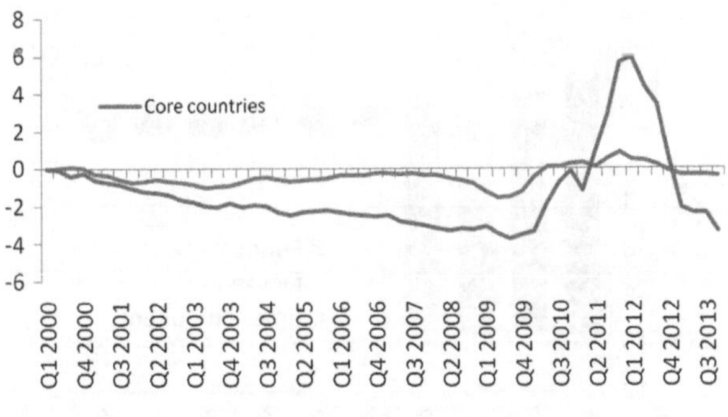

Figure 3. Time components of spreads in Eurozone
Source: Calculations based on regression equation (1).

2012III to 2013IV. It is the period following the OMT announcement that triggered the decline in the spreads. We show the results in Figures 4 (first period) and 5 (second period).

Concentrating on Figure 2, we find that the largest part of the surge in the spreads during 2008–2012 is due to negative market sentiments that were unrelated to the fundamentals (the time dummies). Nevertheless, the fundamentals play some role in explaining the surge in the spreads in the case of Greece and to a lesser extent in Portugal.

Things are very different during the second, post-OMT period. We find that the sharp decline of the spreads since OMT is totally dissociated from changes in fundamentals. The latter play no role at all in explaining this decline in the spreads. This result strongly suggests that the ECB's OMT announcement was quite effective in turning around market sentiments. These became very positive and corrected for the excessive pessimism that

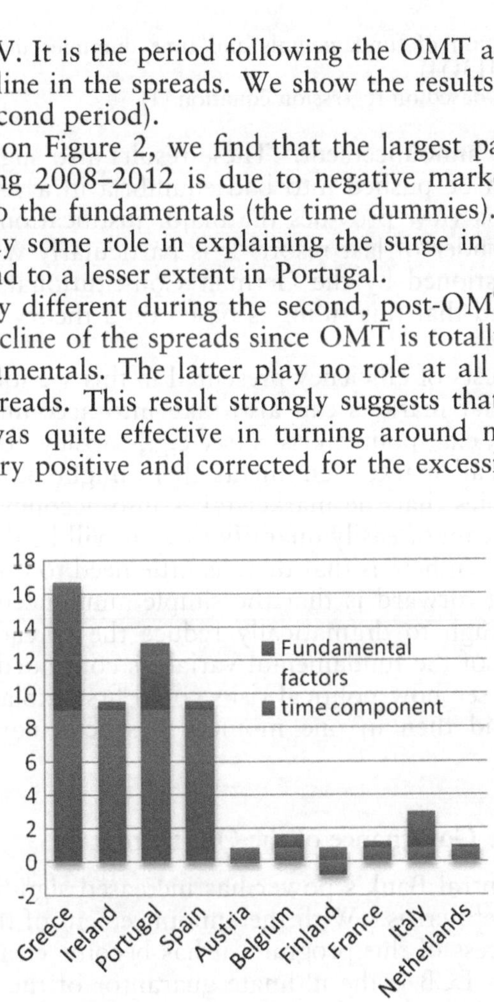

Figure 4. Contribution of fundamentals and time dummies in predicted change in spreads (2008Q1–2012Q2)
Source: Calculations based on regression equation (1).

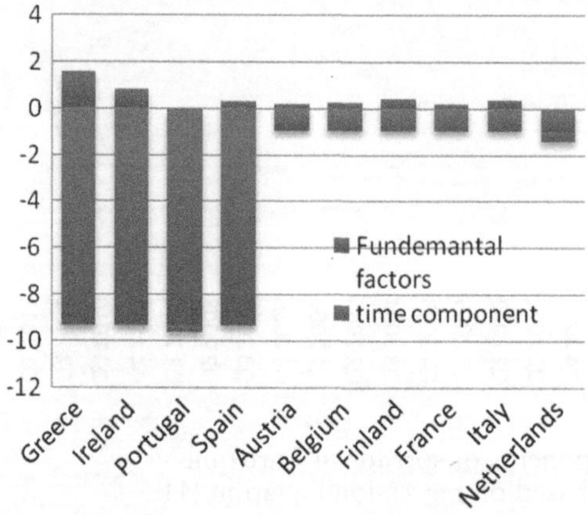

Figure 5. Contribution of fundamentals and time dummies in predicted change in spreads (2012Q1–2013Q4)
Source: Calculations based on regression equation (1).

existed before the announcement.[5] These results also suggest that the view that countries can be pushed into bad equilibria in a self-fulfilling way is the right one. This view provides the major justification for a role of the central bank as lender of last resort. It is particularly worrisome that this role is being questioned by the German Constitutional Court's ruling of February 2014 and that this ruling is based on a theory that is rejected by the data.

The empirical tests of efficiency presented in this section can be criticized on the grounds that markets can also take into account a broader set of risks into account, e.g., political risks (see e.g., Mosley 2015). Thus, hidden behind what we call market sentiments there might be other not directly measurable variables that the market takes into account. This may be so, but as long as we cannot easily quantify these it will be difficult to test this. What we have shown here is that there is little need to do so. The strongest evidence we bring forward is that the simple announcement of the OMT program was enough to dramatically reduce the spreads. And this happened while most of the fundamental variables continued to deteriorate. It is also difficult to see how political risks could first explain a sudden surge of the spreads and then in one moment a spectacular decline in these spreads.

The Unsustainable Governance of the OMT Program

The European Central Bank's power has increased significantly as a result of the sovereign debt crisis.[6] With the announcement of the OMT program and given the success of this program, it has become clear (at least outside Germany) that the ECB is the ultimate guarantor of the sovereign debt in the Eurozone. In this sense, the ECB has become a central bank like the Federal Reserve and the Bank of England. There is one important difference though. In the US and the UK, there is a primacy of the government over the central bank, i.e., in times of crisis, it is the government that will force the central bank to provide liquidity. When the sovereign in these countries is threatened, it will prevail over the central bank. This is not the case in the Eurozone. In the latter, the governments depend on the goodwill of the ECB to provide liquidity. They have no power over the ECB and cannot force that institution, even in times of crisis, to provide liquidity. Thus, in the Eurozone today there is a primacy of the central bank over the sovereigns.

Thus, we arrive at the following conundrum. The role of the ECB as a lender of last resort is essential to keep the Eurozone afloat. Yet at the same time, the present governance of this crucial lender of last resort function is unsustainable because its use depends on the goodwill of the ECB, thereby making democratically legitimate governments' fate depend on the judgment of unelected officials. In order to sustain this role of the central bank as a lender of last resort, it has to be made subordinate to the political power of elected officials, as it is in modern democracies such as the US, Sweden, and the UK. This can only be achieved by creating a Eurozone government that is backed by a European parliament and that has primacy over the central bank.

The Failure of Macroeconomic Policies in the Eurozone

Since the financial crisis of 2007–2008, most developed countries have been unable to return to their pre-crisis growth path. Nowhere in the developed world is this more visible than in the Eurozone. The difference is striking when comparing the evolution of real GDP in the Eurozone with real GDP in the US and in the EU countries not belonging to the Eurozone (EU10). We chose this latter group as it contains all the EU countries that do not belong to the Eurozone.

Prior to the financial crisis, the Eurozone real GDP was on a slower growth path than in the US and in EU10. Since the financial crisis of 2008, the divergence has increased even further. Real GDP in the Eurozone stagnated and in 2014 was even lower than in 2008. In the US and EU-10, one observes (after the dip of 2009) a relatively strong recovery. Admittedly, this recovery is below the potential growth path of these countries (see Summers 2014) and Baldwin and Teugels 2014), but surely this recovery has been much more pronounced than in the Eurozone where stagnation prevailed. Note also that there was a recovery in the Eurozone from 2009 to 2011 and that from 2012 to 2013, the Eurozone experienced a double-dip recession.

A comparison of the trends in unemployment in these three groups of countries leads to the conclusion. It appears that after 2010, the US and the EU-10 saw their unemployment rates decline, while in the Eurozone continues to increase so that in 2014 it was almost twice as high as in the EU-10, the group of EU countries that chose not to be in the Eurozone.

Why has the Eurozone been an island of stagnation in the developed world? We identify two causes. The first one is the asymmetry in the adjustment mechanism to redress external imbalances in the Eurozone; the second one has to do with misdiagnosis of the sovereign debt crisis.

Asymmetry in the Adjustment

As a result of divergences in booms and bust cycles southern European countries (including Ireland) experienced booms and bubbles financed by debt accumulation. The northern European countries made all this possible by massive credit provision to the southern countries. Thus, the responsibilities for the ensuing current account imbalances were shared between the creditor and debtor nations. One could have expected that the adjustment to the imbalances would have been symmetric, i.e., debtor nations reducing and creditor nations increasing their spending. This symmetric view, however, did not prevailed in the relations between the creditor and debtor nations of the Eurozone. The former were viewed as having followed virtuous policies and the latter as having followed foolish ones. As a result, the debtor nations were forced to bear the full brunt of the adjustment.

This has led to an asymmetric process where most of the adjustment has been done by the debtor nations. The latter countries have been forced to reduce wages and prices relative to the creditor countries (an 'internal devaluation') without compensating wage and price increases in the creditor countries ('internal revaluations'). This has been achieved by intense austerity programs in the south, while in the north, no compensating stimulus was imposed (see De Grauwe 2014).

The burden of the adjustments to the imbalances in the Eurozone was borne almost exclusively by the debtor countries in the periphery. This created a deflationary bias that explains why the Eurozone was pulled into a double-dip recession in 2011–2012, and why it continues to be subject to deflationary forces and as is also testified by the sharp decline in inflation, which in the first half of 2014 dropped to less than 1 per cent.

Misdiagnosis of the Crisis

Since 2010, macroeconomic policies in the Eurozone have been dominated by two ideas. First, Eurozone policymakers took the view that the sovereign debt crisis should be fought by restoring budget balance as quickly as possible so as to stop the government debt accumulations. Second, in order to stimulate economic activity, structural reforms should be implemented, i.e., a series of institutional changes should be introduced aiming at making the supply side of the economy more flexible.

It is now increasingly recognized that these two ideas are based on a misdiagnosis of the debt crisis and the second idea on an economic fallacy.

The *misdiagnosis* has consisted in thinking that the origin of the sovereign debt crisis was fiscal profligacy while it was private sector profligacy (with a possible exception of Greece where it was both). Private profligacy led to excess private debt accumulation. After the bust, the private sector had to deleverage. The failure to recognize the nature of the recession, i.e., that it was a 'balance sheet recession' led the European policy makers to push national governments into austerity (see Koo 2011; Krugman 2012; Wolf 2014). As a result, both the private and the public sector tried to deleverage at the same time. This introduced a deflationary bias in the

Eurozone that led to a new recession during 2012–2013, the second one since the start of the financial crisis in 2007–2008. The non-Euro EU members were spared this second recession in five years time.

The *structural reform* programs that were forced onto many Eurozone countries were based on an economic fallacy. This fallacy arose from the application of Say's Law. As will be remembered, this says that supply creates its own demand. This led the European policymakers to believe that structural reforms that lead to an increase in the capacity to produce (the supply) would automatically increase production.[7] The latter did not happen. The main reason is that these structural reform programs were enforced while the same policymakers, through their austerity programs, did everything they could to reduce aggregate demand. No wonder that output declined.

One (but not the only one) manifestation of these austerity programs was the decline in public investment in the Eurozone.

The correct policy mix should have been to institute structural reforms that increase the long-term growth potential together with policies that stimulate aggregate demand.[8] Unfortunately, policymakers were led astray by an economic fallacy (Say's Law) that promised them that raising growth potentials would automatically raise production. At the same time, austerity programs, by forcing deleveraging on both the private and the public sectors, actually reduced production.

All this leads to the question of what to do today, in 2015? Governments of the Eurozone, in particular, in the northern member countries now face historically low long-term interest rates. The German government, for example, can borrow at less than 1 percent at a maturity of 10 years. These historically low interest rates create a window of opportunities for these governments to start a major investment program. Money can be borrowed almost for free while in all these countries there are great needs to invest in the energy sector, the public transportation systems and the environment.

This is therefore the time to reverse the ill-advised decisions made since 2010 to reduce public investments. This can be done at very little cost. The country that should lead this public investment program is Germany. There are two reasons for this. First, as we have argued earlier the asymmetric nature of the macroeconomic adjustment programs within the Eurozone unnecessarily magnified the cost of these programs in the debtor nations, leading to historically high levels of unemployment, and much suffering for millions of people. Second, public investments as a percent of GDP in Germany are among the lowest of all Eurozone countries. In 2013, public investment in German amounted to a bare 1.6 percent of GDP vs. 2.3 percent in the rest of the Eurozone (see Fratzscher [2014], who argues that Germany's lack of investments reduces long-term growth in that country).

Such a public investment program would do two things. First, it would stimulate aggregate demand in the short run and help to pull the Eurozone out of its deflationary bias that continues to keep economic growth below potential. Second, in the long run, it would help to lift the long-term growth potential in the Eurozone.

The prevailing view in many countries is that governments should not increase their debt levels lest they put a burden on future generations. The truth is that future generations inherit not only the liabilities but also the assets that have been created by the government. Future generations will not understand why these governments did not invest in productive assets that improve these generations' welfare, while present day governments could do so at historically low financing costs.

Conclusion

The decision made by the ECB in 2012 to act a lender of last resort (the OMT program) was a major regime change for the Eurozone. It significantly reduced the existential fears that slowly but inexorably were destroying the Eurozone's foundations. It is clear that while necessary the OMT program is insufficient to guarantee the survival of the monetary union.

First, the credibility of the OMT program has been undermined by the incessant 'guerilla warfare' conducted from Germany against this program. This culminated in the decision of the German Constitutional Court that the program is illegal. The European Court of Justice has issued its own ruling in 2015 and contradicted the German Court when it ruled that the OMT program is legal. This may lead to a future clash between the two courts. If that happens, the credibility of the OMT program will be put into doubt.

Second, in order to guarantee the survival of the Eurozone macroeconomic policies will have to be made more symmetric. The asymmetric nature of the macroeconomic adjustments that puts most of the adjustment burden on the deficit countries has created a deflationary bias in the Eurozone. More symmetric macroeconomic adjustment mechanisms are key to avoid a long and protracted deflation that will not be accepted by large parts of the Eurozone population. Indeed, the greatest risk for the survival of the Eurozone today is the risk emanating from social and political upheavals in countries that are forced into a deflationary spiral. Thus, while the ECB's decision to act as a lender of last resort has reduced the risk of a financial implosion, this risk has been substituted by a new risk, i.e., the risk of implosion due to uncontrollable social and political disturbances in the south of Europe.

We also analyzed the governance problems of the OMT program. We argued the present governance of this lender of last resort function is unsustainable because its use depends on the goodwill of the ECB, thereby making democratically legitimate governments' fate depend on the judgment of unelected officials. In order to sustain this role of the central bank as a lender of last resort, it has to be made subordinate to the political power of elected officials, as it is in modern democracies such as the US, Sweden, the UK, etc. This can only be achieved by creating a Eurozone government that is backed by a European parliament and that has primacy over the central bank.

Acknowledgements

The research reported in this article has been made possible by a grant of the Seventh Framework Programme 'Finmap'. We are grateful for comments made by Marco Buti, Francisco Torres, Shanin Vallee, Frank Vandenbroucke and members of seminars given at the University of Leuven, and the University of Oxford.

Disclosure statement

No potential conflict of interest was reported by the authors.

Notes

1. See Jones (2015) for a very complementary analysis.
2. Greece does not fit this diagnosis. It was clearly insolvent way before the crisis started, but this was hidden to the outside world by a fraudulent policy of the Greek government of hiding the true nature of the Greek economic situation (see De Grauwe 2011).
3. Attinasi, Checherita, and Nickel (2009), Arghyrou and Kontonikas (2010), Gerlach, Schulz, and Wolff (2010), Schularick, (2012), Caceres, Guzzo, and Segoviano (2010), Gibson, Hall, and Tavlas (2011), Aizenman and Hutchinson (2012), Beirne and Fratzscher (2012). There is of course a vast literature on the spreads in the government bond markets in general. See, for example, the classic Eichengreen and Mody (2000). Much of this literature has been influenced by the debt problems of emerging economies. See for example, Edwards (1984), Edwards (1986) and Min (1999).
4. We also experimented with the government deficit to GDP ratio. But this variable does not have a significant effect in any of the regressions we estimated.
5. Given the fact that the time dummies have reached negative territory in 2013, one may raise the question of whether the market has become too optimistic about the periphery, in a similar way as it was prior to the start of the crisis. During that period, the time dummies were negative suggesting that the according to the fundamentals the spreads of the periphery countries should have been higher. Optimism (euphoria), however, prevailed then and prevented the markets from seeing the risks. Our results suggest that the same may be happening since 2013.
6. See Giavazzi and Wyplosz (2015) for other aspects of the governance of the ECB.
7. This belief is well represented by De Mello and Padoan (2010) and European Central Bank (2015).
8. Begg et al. (2015) argue the case for structural reforms as a basis for sustainable growth.

References

Aizenman, J., and M. Hutchison. 2012. *What is the risk of European sovereign debt defaults? Fiscal space, CDS spreads and market pricing of risk*. Paper Presented at the Conference on "The European sovereign debt crisis: background and perspectives", Organized by the Danmarks Nationalbank/JIMF, Copenhagen. April 13–14.

Arghyrou, M., and A. Kontonikas. 2010. *The EMU sovereign-debt crisis: fundamentals, expectations and contagion*. Cardiff Economics Working Papers, E2010/9.

Attinasi, M., C. Checherita, C. Nickel. 2009. *What explains the surge in euro area sovereign spreads during the financial crisis of 2007–09?* ECB Working Paper, No 1131. December.

Baldwin, R., and Teulings, C.. 2014. *Secular stagnation. Facts, causes and cures. A new vox ebook*. October, http://www.voxeu.org/article/secular-stagnation-facts-causes-and-cures-new-vox-ebook.

Begg, Iain, Annette Bongardt, Kalypso Nicolaïdis, and Francisco Torres. 2015. EMU and Sustainable Integration. *Journal of European Integration* 37, no. 7: 803–16.

Beirne, J., and M. Fratzscher. 2012. *Pricing and mispricing of sovereign debt in the Euro area during the crisis*. Paper Presented at the Conference on "The European sovereign debt crisis: background and perspectives", Organized by the Danmarks Nationalbank/JIMF. April 13–14.

Blanchard, Olivier, and Daniel Leigh. 2013. *Growth forecast errors and fiscal multipliers*. IMF Working Paper. January.

Caceres, C., V. Guzzo, and M. Segoviano. 2010. *Sovereign spreads: global risk aversion, contagion or fundamentals?* IMF Working Paper. May.

De Grauwe, P. 2011. *The governance of a fragile Eurozone*. CEPS Working Documents, Economic Policy. May, http://www.ceps.eu/book/governance-fragile-eurozone.

De Grauwe, P. 2014. *Economic theories that influenced the judges of Karlsruhe*. VoxEU, http://www.voxeu.org/article/economic-flaws-german-court-decision.

De Grauwe, P., and Y. Ji. 2013. *Panic-driven austerity and its implication for the Eurozone*. VoxEU. 21 February, http://www.voxeu.org/article/panic-driven-austerity-eurozone-and-its-implications.

De Grauwe, P., and Y. Ji. 2014. *The future of the eurozone*. The Manchester School. 82: 15–34.

De Mello, P., and Padoan, P. 2010. *Promoting potential growth: the role of structural reform*. Economics Department Working Paper, No. 793. OECD.

Edwards, S. 1984. LDC foreign borrowing and default risk: an empirical investigation 1976–1980. *American Economic Review* 74, September: 726–34.

Edwards, S. 1986. The pricing of bonds and bank loans in international markets: an empirical analysis of developing countries' foreign borrowing. *European Economiv Review* 30: 565–89.

Eichengreen, B., R. Hausmann, and U. Panizza. 2005. The pain of original sin. In *Other people's money: debt denomination and financial instability in emerging market economies*, eds. B. Eichengreen and R. Hausmann. Chicago, IL: Chicago University Press.

Eichengreen, B., and A. Mody. 2000. Lending booms, reserves and the sustainability of short-term debt: inferences from the pricing of syndicated bank loans. *Journal of Development Economics* 63: 5–44.

European Central Bank. 2015. Progress with structural reforms across the euro area and their possible impacts. *Economic Bulletin*, no. 2.

Fratzscher, M. 2014. *Die Deutschland-Illusion: Warum wir unsere Wirtschaft überschätzen und Europa brauchen*. Berlin: Hanser Verlag.

Gerlach, S., G. Schulz, and W. Wolff. 2010. *Banking and sovereign risk in the euro area*. Frankfurt: mimeo. Deutsche Bundesbank.

Giavazzi, F., and M. Pagano. 1990. Can Fiscal Contractions be Contractionary: Tales of Two Small European Countries. In *Annual 1990*, Vol. 5, ed. N.B.E.R. Macroeconomics. Cambridge, MA: MIT Press.

Giavazzi, Francesco, and Charles Wyplosz. 2015. EMU: Old Flaws Revisited. *Journal of European Integration* 37, no. 7: 723–37.

Gibson, H.G., G. Hall, and G. Tavlas. 2011. *The Greek financial crisis: growing imbalances and sovereign spreads*. Working Paper. March. Bank of Greece.

Jones, Erik. 2015. Getting the Story Right: How You Should Choose between Different Interpretations of the European Crisis (And Why You Should Care). *Journal of European Integration* 37, no. 7: 817–31.

Gros, D. 2011. *A simple model of multiple equilibria and default*. mimeo. Brussels: CEPS.

Koo, R. 2011. The world in balance sheet recession: causes, cure, and politics. *Real-world Economics Review*, no. 58. Tokyo: Nomura Research Institute.

Krugman, P. 2012. *End this depression now!* 272 p. Norton & Company.

Min, H. 1999. *Determinants of emerging market bond spread: do economic fundamentals matter?* World Bank, http://elibrary.worldbank.org/content/workingpaper/10.1596/1813-9450-1899.

Mosley, L. 2015. 9 (De) fault lines? The EU, national governments, and private capital markets in the postcrisis era. In *Crises in Europe in the transatlantic context: economic and political appraisals*. CRS Press.

Schularick, M. 2012. *Public debt and financial crises in the twentieth century*. Paper presented at the ECB conference on sovereign debt. 22–23 June. European Central Bank, Frankfurt.

Summers, L. 2014. *Reflections on the new "Secular Stagnation Hypothesis"*. VoxEU. October, http://www.voxeu.org/article/larry-summers-secular-stagnation.

Winkler, A. 2014. *The Federal German constitutional court decides which theory of finance is correct*. Frankfurt: mimeo. European Central Bank.

Wolf, M. 2014. *The shifts and the shocks. What we have learned – and have still to learn – from the financial crisis*. London: Penguin.

Governance and Conditionality: Toward a Sustainable Framework?

LORENZO BINI SMAGHI*,**

*WCIA, Harvard University, Cambridge, USA;
**School of European Political Economy, LUISS, Rome, Italy

ABSTRACT The article examines how conditionality has evolved in the Eurozone during the debt crisis. Four main aspects are examined. The first is the trade-off between adjustment and financing, and in particular the possible resort to debt restructuring in advanced economies. The second is the decision-making process, which is particularly cumbersome in the Eurozone, as it relies largely on intergovernmental agreements and procedures, which proved to be inefficient and slow. The third issue concerns the financing conditions, which have initially been inspired on IMF programs, but proved excessively restrictive for a monetary union where countries cannot devalue in order to regain competitiveness. Finally, the article examines the contents of conditionality, and in particular the recent emphasis on structural reforms as a way to strengthen the supply side. A more sustainable framework requires greater political integration, in particular in the fiscal sphere, which is not easy to achieve in particular in the midst of a crisis.

Introduction

The Eurozone governance reflects its complex institutional framework which combines a centralization of competences in certain policy area — such as monetary, competition, state aid, external trade, now banking supervision — with a form of 'constrained' decentralization in other areas — such as fiscal, structural policies. The number of centralized competences has evolved over time, as a result of the Union having to tackle the new challenges resulting from the incompleteness of the institutional framework. On the other hand, it is an illusion to think that the Eurozone governance could have been perfect from the very start — if there is anything as perfect governance. It is also illusory to assume that the Eurozone governance could simply be copied from other existing systems, like the US, because Europe is different and the historical and political contexts are different.

This article focuses on conditionality within the European policy framework. Conditionality — which implies setting conditions in order for certain decisions to be implemented, typically by other institutions or countries, in a form of quid pro quo — is a way to coordinate or bind the behavior of institutions which are independent from each other or respond to different layers of government. For instance, budgetary transfers or financial assistance from the Eurozone to the member states are conditional on the latter meeting some parameters or abiding to specific behavior. Within a fully fledged fiscal union, conditionality would not be as relevant because fiscal transfers are decided within an integrated political system in a quasi-automatic way, for instance, through the progressive tax system or the nation-wide unemployment compensation scheme. Another example is the intervention by the central bank in the financial market, which in Europe is conditional on specific actions taken by the Union or the member states' authorities, which derives from the fact that the latter have retained several competencies. In sum, conditionality derives from the need to bind the behavior of separate authorities into agreements that improve the overall policy result.

This is the way in which several European institutions, like the European Stability Mechanism (ESM) and the Outright Monetary Transaction (OMT) have been designed. The ESM defines the conditions that countries experiencing difficulties in accessing capital markets must satisfy in order to receive financial assistance, in particular concerning the policy measures that the country commits to implement within a program agreed with the European Union and/or the IMF. The OMT specifies that the ECB can intervene, even for unlimited amounts, to counter destabilizing forces in financial markets which may put at risk the ability of a country to stay in the euro. But this can happen only if that country adheres to an adjustment program with the ESM.

Conditionality is needed because the implementation of the 'federal' policy — monetary or financial assistance — requires an assessment about the appropriateness of the actions undertaken by the non-federal level of government (fiscal, structural policies). Given that these policies are still in the hands of national institutions, and likely to remain so long as the Union makes a more decisive move toward political integration, conditionality will remain an important component of the European policy framework.

This concept of conditionality is different from the one which is used in other contexts, to characterize relations between independent countries, or with institutions. It is different, for instance, from the conditionality which is used in the EU when assessing the possible entry of a new country, which characterizes the Maastricht criteria or the Copenhagen criteria that precede the transfer of economic or political sovereignty, and represents a fundamental step in the change in governance (Schimmelfenning and Sedelmeier 2004). It is also different from the conditionality used by international institutions, such as the IMF, to induce member states to implement specific adjustment policies. In the latter, the conditions are attached to the adjustment program implemented by a country in exchange for receiving financial support. In the Eurozone, conditionality is a broader concept, as it embraces not only specific measures but also the acceptance of the rules governing the monetary union as a whole. Just to give an example, when the negotiations between Greece and 'the Institutions' (which replaced the so-called Troika, composed of the IMF, European Commission in liaison with the ECB) broke up at the end of June 2015, other policies, which were not directly under the control of the country, such as the access of Greek banks to the refinancing window of the Eurosystem were also impacted. When the Greek government called for a referendum, which implicitly questioned Greece's permanence in the euro, the whole conditionality was affected. In summary, conditionality in the Eurozone is an over-encompassing concept, which applies not only to specific policies but to the whole membership of the Union.

On the other hand, conditionality is not a unique feature of monetary union and does not apply only in case of financial crises. It also applies within political unions and when monetary policy adopts specific policy actions. In Chapter 1, Giavazzi and Wyplosz celebrate the ECB's decision to act as lender of last resort, in particular through the OMT, but the OMT is not unconditional, as mentioned above. More generally, the lender of last resort function is always conditional on the solvency of the financial institutions that receive emergency lending assistance (ELA), independently of who is responsible for assessing solvency, and on the country's determination to be a member of the union. The separation between the supervisory authority and monetary policy prevailing in several countries before the crisis proved to be quite problematic, for instance, in the UK. When the ECB granted ELA to banks in countries under program, the solvency of the banks could be assessed only by the national supervisor. Only by joining the Troika could the ECB make its own direct assessment of banks' solvency. Since November 2014, with the creation of banking union, the ECB has become directly in charge of supervision, and is therefore able to assess banks' eligibility to ELA, which does not mean — however — that ELA is without conditions.

This article assesses the evolving nature of conditionality in the Eurozone since the start of the crisis.

It has been suggested (see for instance, De Grauwe and Ji, Chapter 2) that even with conditionality, a decentralized policy framework is not sustainable. Unless the European Union moves rapidly to political integration, it risks imploding. For instance, a system of financial assistance to countries that have lost market access — similar to the one created with the ESM — while being a step forward compared to the pre-crisis situation is still inefficient. In a fully fledged fiscal union, in particular, the difficulties experienced by local authorities do not create widespread contagion to the whole union. In the EU, instead, as long as the fiscal responsibility remains with the member states, the risk of contagion from a local crisis will remain high. Furthermore, the risk of not meeting the requirements for being eligible to the ECB's OMT remains, which can thus not exclude that a country can exit from the euro, thus producing highly disruptive contagion effects.

In the current political environment, it is utopian to imagine a quick move to full fiscal union. This is the reason why over the coming years policy makers should concentrate on improving the current model of conditionality, making it more sustainable, rather than assuming unrealistic steps forward toward full political integration.

The issue of conditionality has been discussed in the past mainly in the context of IMF financial assistance (see Dreher 2009). Conditionality is constantly discussed and revised by the IMF (2012). After the Asian crisis, in particular, the Washington consensus moved toward a streamlining of conditionality, reducing the emphasis on micro-policies and focusing more on macroeconomic adjustment, in particular with respect to monetary and fiscal policies. The need to strengthen surveillance also emerged as a main priority, although it turned out to be much more difficult to implement in practice.

This framework has inspired the actions of the Troika in program countries during the euro crisis and the creation of the ESM. The experience has been assessed ex post, in particular with respect to the Greek program (IMF 2013). Based on this experience, and these assessments, one might ask what should be changed in the structure and management of conditionality within the Eurozone. This is particularly relevant in the context of the 2015 discussions about a possible extension or a new Greek adjustment program, and the margins for maneuver for changing conditionality, or even eliminating it as requested by the Greek government.

I will address four issues which characterize a conditionality framework, in particular in a European context: (a) Adjustment vs. financing; (b) decision-making process; (c) financing conditions; (d) contents of conditionality.

Before concluding, I would also raise a fundamental issue which underlines any conditionality framework, which relates to the asymmetry of adjustment in a monetary union.

Adjustment vs. Financing

The trade-off between adjustment and financing is the key issue that policy makers need to address when facing balance of payments problems. The optimal combination largely depends on how quickly the country can regain access to financial markets and thus how quickly imbalances can be adjusted to ensure debt sustainability. The longer is the adjustment period, however, the greater is the need for official financing and, as a consequence, the more debt sustainability is at risk. If the financing cannot be provided by capital markets at sustainable interest rates, some form of official assistance at preferential rates will be needed. On the other hand, the greater is the external financing received by a country, the higher is the amount of cumulated debt, which may ultimately not be sustainable. In extreme cases of debt overhang, some form of restructuring has to be considered to alleviate the debt burden and make the adjustment possible.

Given that official financing generally has to be considered 'senior', the burden of the restructuring will fall mainly on private creditors.

In a monetary union, without exchange rate flexibility, the adjustment of external imbalances requires more time and thus more financing (Tressel *et al.* 2014). The debt sustainability constraint becomes more binding. If the adjustment is too abrupt, and excessively front-loaded, the short-term debt dynamics may lead to perverse effects, increasing the debt level instead of reducing it. This may delay country's return to market financing and require additional funding by the international institutions. This is very much what happened to Greece in 2010, where the size of the adjustment was so large that it needed much more time to be implemented in a gradual way to avoid a vicious circle. However, the longer the adjustment period, the larger the external funds needed and ultimately the higher the risk to make the debt rise further and become unsustainable.

Debt restructuring seems like a nice way to solve the dilemma and reduce upfront the overall level of the debt (Bolton and Jeanne 2007). However, as the Greek experience shows — again — this is not a panacea. First, it is not easy to engineer a market-friendly restructuring, involving a large majority of bondholders. Second, in advanced economies, residents hold a large share of the public debt. The restructuring of the debt thus leads to huge capital losses for households and especially for financial institutions (banks, pension funds, insurance companies). This is likely to produce repercussions on domestic consumption and investment and on the solidity of the financial system. If not quickly recapitalized, banks facing losses will sharply cut their lending to the private sector. The combination of a credit crunch and fiscal adjustment produces even stronger recessionary effects, further endangering debt sustainability. Additional foreign aid will be needed. The Greek experience has shown that nearly half of the savings achieved through debt restructuring had to be compensated by additional borrowing from official creditors in order to recapitalize the banking system.

Overall, the optimal combination of financing vs. adjustment is much more complex in advanced economies that are members of monetary unions, compared to the traditional cases considered by the IMF in the past, which mainly concerned developing economies with flexible exchange rates. There are no simple solutions. Even the concept of debt sustainability cannot be easily applied, because it involves not only making assumptions about economic growth and the impact of the fiscal measures but also assessing the political will and capacity of the government to deliver. The debt sustainability analysis has to be based on assumptions regarding not only the effects of the policies contained in the adjustment program but also their political feasibility (IMF 2011). The Greek experience showed that structural reforms, which are key to enhance growth potential in countries that cannot rely on exchange rate devaluation, are politically difficult to implement — sometimes even more difficult than budgetary measures. Internal devaluation, through wage cuts, and price liberalizations are also controversial and tend to be opposed by interest groups. Furthermore, privatization and the sale of state property look easy on paper but are much more complicated to implement if the country does not have appropriate administrative capacity or if they face strong internal opposition by interest groups. Sometimes even the measures which have been adopted by the Government and approved by Parliament end up being considered unconstitutional by the local courts, as it happened, for instance, in Portugal or in Italy. It is thus not sufficient for Government, and even the political opposition, to make commitments for conditionality to be adequate.

To sum up, while on paper it looks easy to design an adjustment program which may ensure that a country is capable of accessing financial markets again, it is in practice very difficult to identify an optimal combination of financing and adjustment, especially in a monetary union. Although other experiences in Europe have been more successful than the Greek one, the lack of exchange rate flexibility and the difficulty to implement reforms in a recession suggest that adjustment tends to be longer and thus requires more financing.

The Decision-making Process

The decision to implement an adjustment program in the Eurozone is still sub-optimal, and filled with negative incentives. The first is the stigma for the country requiring a program. Experience shows that governments that apply for a program are not likely to survive politically. They tend to be accused by their own voters of having surrendered to external pressure and having imposed excessive pain on their citizens. For this reason, governments tend to postpone the request for financial assistance until it becomes inevitable, when they suggest that they have no alternative because the country lost market access and interest rates have skyrocketed.

This is very inefficient because in such a late situation, the dimension of the financial package increases significantly, as it incorporates the assumption that the country might not be able to finance itself in the markets for a long time. When market credibility is lost, it takes a long time to regain it. Furthermore, if the request for financial assistance occurs late, when market confidence has been lost, the policies required to regain confidence need to be much tougher, and potentially more damaging for the economy. Had Greece decided to tackle decisively the deterioration of the budget already in the Fall 2009, instead of waiting for the markets to lose confidence, the adjustment program could have been less restrictive than the one finally adopted in Spring 2010. The impact on the economy would have been milder, and the prospects for debt sustainability much improved.

There is also the incentive to exit prematurely from a program, to try leveraging politically with the domestic audience. A government that is capable to access again capital markets can claim to have definitively cured the country. The Greek announcement in the Fall of 2014 that it would not renew the program in 2015 was largely based on a favorable market environment, which unfortunately did not last for very long.

A more extreme position was held by the main opposition parties, Syriza in particular, which denounced the previous program and the role of the Troika in the design and management of conditionality. This strong position was largely supported by Greek voters, who evidently wanted a change after several years of hardship. The new government, led by Alexis Tsipras, tried to carry that position with the other Eurozone partners, but with little success. It would have been very difficult for the 18 other Eurozone partners to give in and accept to eliminate conditionality, as this would have encouraged similar behavior in all other countries and lead to the disaggregation of the union.

To sum up, as long as adjustment programs are tainted with stigma, due to the fear of losing sovereignty, the natural tendency for governments will be to delay the request until it becomes inevitable. This destabilizes the system and increases contagion. The adjustment programs will thus tend to be harsher and the financing needs even bigger.

An alternative would be to make the request for adjustment program semiautomatic, subject to the country's interest rate on the public debt reaching a preset threshold. For instance, the convergence criterion for the monetary union foresees a maximum interest rate spread on long-term government bonds of 200 basis points with respect to the best performer. A similar spread could trigger the application for an adjustment program. This would reduce the stigma for countries, and possibly create positive incentives for governments to adopt policies at an early stage without waiting to lose market access.

Another problem deriving from the current system whereby countries apply very late for the adjustment program is that the representatives of the Eurozone and the IMF — the so-called Troika — are portrayed in a very negative way within the country. The pain endured during the adjustment is blamed on the Troika, rather than on previous governments (Committeri and Spadafora 2013). This fuels anti-European sentiment, as European institutions are perceived as inflicting austerity and discouraging growth.

The design of the current system is inefficient in other ways. In particular, the decision-making process foresees that national parliaments of creditor countries can express themselves on whether the ESM should provide financing to an applicant country. Furthermore, the ESM provides countries with the right to veto a decision. This system differs from the IMF where decisions are taken by simple majority.

The explicit involvement of national parliaments, especially in Germany, gives the impression that it is ultimately up to the latter to agree on whether another Eurozone country can access the ESM and receive financial assistance. This creates a direct opposition between countries, and their own people and media, which is very detrimental to the process of political integration. The ESM decision-making process should be made more similar to that of the IMF. This does not prevent national parliaments from being involved, but this should be at an early stage, in giving mandate to the respective national representatives in the institution rather as appearing to be the ultimate decision-maker and judge.

Financing Conditions

The experience of the first adjustment programs, which were based largely on the IMF model, has shown how the latter are not suitable for the Eurozone context (Pisany-Ferry, Sapir, and Wolf 2013). In particular, the interest rate surcharge proved to be too high and the maturity of the loans too short for an area where the exchange rate adjustment is not available and the underlying rate of economic growth much lower compared to emerging economies. These conditions had to be changed over time, as they proved not to be realistic. However, it took time before the need for change was understood and the change agreed and implemented, which led to a loss of credibility of the European institutions in the eyes of the markets.

The maturity of the loans, in particular, need to be much longer than the standard IMF standby arrangements, because the main problem in the European case comes from the need to refinance the public debt, whose size is larger and maturity longer than standard balance of payment financing. Ultimately, if a country experiences debt sustainability problems, the maturity of the financial assistance needs to be stretched over several decades.

Another aspect, already mentioned above, is the size of the package. Given the lack of exchange rate flexibility, the amount of the financing has to much larger in a monetary union, to such an extent that the IMF alone cannot meet the requirements. The access requirements of the IMF, which are based on countries' quotas, have been stretched to the limit in order to provide official financing to Greece. This shows that the IMF alone cannot address the adjustment problems of the Eurozone. The ESM is necessary to ensure adequate financing to EMU countries in difficulty.

Overall, the current size of the ESM is insufficient to meet the potential needs of the Eurozone, especially in case of a major shock. This creates a problem of credibility in the eyes of the markets. Eurozone countries have implicitly committed to increase the size of the ESM if needed, but this is not sufficient to calm the markets, given the complexity of the decision-making process required for such a decision. This has become evident when the ECB announced the OMT, which has no limits, even though it can be used only if countries apply for an adjustment program. Markets became convinced that there would be no problem of size only when it was clear that the ECB's instrument was not quantitatively constrained. This in turn stopped the panic. A specific limit to the size of the safety net is the best way to encourage panic selling as market participants tend to be afraid that they may be the last out of the door if all the others start disinvesting. This typical market behavior has not been fully understood by the public authorities, especially the German Constitutional court.

Contents of Conditionality

The final issue concerns the contents of the adjustment program. In a monetary union, conditionality needs to take into account the lack of exchange rate flexibility and the fact that the debt held by households, companies, and the public sector is de facto denominated in foreign currency. Monetary policy is not part of the conditionality. Indeed, monetary policy cannot engineer a devaluation nor increase inflation to reduce the debt burden. The interest rate is set by the ECB with a view to the whole union, not the crisis countries alone. Furthermore, the lender of last resort for the banking system is determined on the basis of common Eurozone rules. The same applies to state aid rules for bank bailouts.

Fiscal policy is also constrained by the need to ensure a proper adjustment of the budgetary imbalance. The experience has shown, however, that within a monetary union, the fiscal multiplier might be higher than expected. The speed and composition of the fiscal adjustment over time needs therefore to be carefully calibrated. In particular, a country that needs to restore competitiveness should use tax policy in a way as to penalize consumption while reducing the burden on labor, so as to cut labor costs.

In this context, structural policies become more relevant. This suggests that, differently from other regions, policy adjustment in the Eurozone should not rely only on macro-policies but rather on structural reforms, with a view to improve growth potential (see Begg et al., Chapter 6, who discuss the importance of structural reform within a sustainable growth strategy for EMU's long-term viability).

An essential aspect of the policy adjustment resides in the financial sector. When a country loses access to capital markets, the domestic financial system tends to be seriously affected. The natural reaction of bank managers and shareholders is to reduce leverage as quickly as possible, mainly by cutting exposures, in particular to firms. This incentive creates the basis for a credit crunch, which reinforces the recessionary effects of the fiscal adjustment and increases the likelihood of a vicious cycle. This has been the experience in Greece, Ireland, and Portugal.

The adjustment program thus needs to focus on the recapitalization of the banking system, to absorb potential losses in the balance sheet and avoid a credit crunch. This may require a swift action by the policy authorities, also through direct intervention with state funding. This type of intervention encounters several obstacles. The first is the opposition of the public opinion, which in times of austerity does not like that taxpayers' money is used to bail out banks and bankers. This is one of the reasons why politicians rarely try to use public money to intervene in the financial system, even when this would avoid worse results. The European regulation on state aid is another limit to the use of public money. The recent decisions by the European Community on the bail-in of private creditors make the latter quasi-automatic when banks are bailed out with public funds. This principle, while understandable on the basis of equality of treatment and social justice, if applied in a mechanical way may lead creditor to flee as soon as they see the first signs of a crisis emerge, which may actually precipitate a crisis.

The experience in Ireland, in particular, has shown that avoiding the bailing-in of senior bank bondholders, although more painful for taxpayers, can prevent contagion and encourage a quick turnaround in market sentiment.

Structural reforms are key to restore competitiveness. Most often those countries that need adjustment programs are also the laggards in reforming their economies (Bongardt and Torres 2013): With the exception of Ireland, those member states that have failed to achieve progress on the Lisbon goals are the countries that have started or continued to diverge.

The request for external aid can be seen as a way to accelerate the catching up. Structural reforms are a way to increase the credibility of the program and thus to achieve a more gradual fiscal adjustment.

One of the criticisms which is often made of structural reforms as the central pillar of adjustment programs is that these reforms take time before they produce their effects. This view does not take into account the impact that these reforms can produce on market expectations and thus on the ability of the country to regain market access and be able to finance deficits for longer. The experience in countries like Spain or Portugal has shown that the implementation of reforms accelerates the improvement in market sentiment and makes the exit from the program credible (Draghi 2015).

Furthermore, the implementation of structural reforms is a way to achieve a more gradual approach to budgetary adjustment in the context of adjustment programs. The European Commission produced in January 2015 a communication on how to make the best use of flexibility in the Stability and Growth Pact, which establishes an explicit trade-off between the reforms implemented by the member states and the speed of fiscal adjustment (European Commission 2015).

One of the key elements of conditionality is the participation to the euro. Given that the adjustment program is one of the conditions for the implementation of the OMT by the ECB, the latter can act only under the assumption that the country will remain in the euro area. Otherwise the intervention in the financial markets would give rise to losses for the ECB which would have to be borne by all the Eurozone taxpayers.

A related issue is the potential conflict of interests for the ECB entailed by conditionality (Darvas and Merler 2013). The first conflict derives from being part of the Troika, which contributes to the design and monitor the adjustment program and is also an indirect lender to the Greek economy, through its refinancing operations with the Greek banks. In fact, the ECB participated to the Troika mainly with a view to assess the stability of program countries' banking system, to which it would be lending. With the creation of the banking union, such a competence has de facto been transferred to the ECB, not only for program countries. The participation to the Troika by the ECB becomes now less relevant. The second potential conflict concerns the conditionality of the monetary policy, in particular in the context of the OMT, which has been also objected by the German Constitutional Court. In theory, the single monetary policy should apply throughout the monetary union, which is defined by the political authorities. It is not the task of the ECB to decide whether a country is part or not of the Eurozone. However, given that it cannot be excluded that a country wants to exit the Eurozone, producing losses for the ECB and its shareholders, it is not inappropriate for the ECB to ask a reassessment of the commitment to membership, through an adjustment program.

Symmetry vs. Asymmetry of Adjustment

The conditionality of IMF programs concerns primarily the countries that undertake financial adjustment. The rest of the constituency is not affected and their policies are taken as given, within the regular surveillance process. The reason is that countries requesting programs are considered to be small compared to the rest of the world, and the burden of adjustment has to be borne by them. This is consistent with the way in which the international monetary system has been built as a result of the Bretton Woods conference in 1944. Keynes' ideas about symmetry of adjustment at the global level whereby both debtors and borrowers need to adjust were not accepted.

Within a monetary union which comprises a subset of the world economy, however, the issue of symmetry is not irrelevant. The deficit of some countries becomes the surplus of others. If the deficit countries have problems in accessing financial markets, the problem affects also the surplus countries which finance these deficits. It is thus essential to understand what are the causes of the excessive deficits and what should be the adjustment policies in both parts which should minimize costs.

One element of symmetry derives from the single monetary policy, but operates in the wrong way. Given that the ECB can set only one level of interest rate, that level with unavoidably be too high for the countries implementing the adjustment, and which experience a recession, and too low for the countries that have a surplus ad have a favorable cycle. In other words, monetary policy operates in a pro-cyclical way during the adjustment.

The experience of the euro crisis shows that this asymmetry can get even worse when the financial system impairs the transmission mechanism of monetary policy, for instance, as a result of the correlation between bank and sovereign risk. Banks in deficit countries tend to experience a deterioration of their access to financial markets, which results in higher interest rates, which penalize domestic borrowers and slow down their de-leveraging process. Without a monetary union, monetary policy would be more accommodative and favor a faster and less costly adjustment.

The question is whether the ECB or the surplus countries could implement measures which would relieve the burden of adjustment of deficit countries and make the adjustment more symmetric. The ancillary question is how to induce the surplus country to implement such a measure given that the latter does not have an adjustment program.

Considering first the nature of the adjustment policy, it is often claimed that surplus countries should reflate their economies, to boost aggregate demand and thus compensate partly for the reduction in the deficit countries. For instance, Germany, the Netherlands, Finland, and Austria should expand their budget to compensate for the contraction of Italy, Spain, Portugal, and Greece. However, this depends on the spillover effects of these measures. On the one side, the fiscal expansion in surplus countries would increase imports, including from the deficit countries. On the other side, it would raise inflation and thus interest rates and the euro exchange rate, which would produce negative effects on deficit countries. The positive spillovers are likely to be relatively small if the surplus countries are in a situation of full employment, as the impact of any stimulus would be short lived. If instead the surplus countries also experience an economic slowdown, there might be scope for stimulating aggregate demand and thus benefitting their own economies and those of the deficit countries.

In sum, the case for symmetry depends not only on the external balance — i.e., surplus vs. deficit — but mainly on internal balance of both sides. The more the surplus country departs from internal balance, and experiences growth below potential, the more a symmetric approach is justified.

Coming to the procedure, there is currently no mechanism to condition policy adjustment in deficit countries to a symmetric adjustment in the surplus ones (Moschella 2014). There is nevertheless a macroeconomic surveillance procedure which assesses the sustainability of balance of payments surpluses and deficits. This procedure sets different benchmarks for the deficit (3 percent of GDP) and the surplus (6 percent). It is not clear why. Furthermore, it is not clear why these benchmarks are disconnected from countries' internal conditions. In particular, a 6 percent current account surplus has a very different meaning for a country which experiences a boom than for one which is in recession. Indeed, countries with growth above potential should normally record a deficit in their current balance, as they are expected to invest and consume more than in the long run. Inversely, countries in recession should be in surplus as they have to adjust their external balance to a previous overheating.

A country experiencing a 6 percent current account surplus and is in full employment is not in steady state and can be sustainable only if there is a symmetric deficit elsewhere. If the latter deficit is not sustainable, then the surplus is not sustainable either, and need to be corrected. If only the deficit country makes the correction, the adjustment in the external imbalances will lead to a misallocation of resources and a departure from internal balance both in the deficit and in the surplus country. In other words, if the surplus country aims at maintaining a surplus while the deficit in the deficit country needs to be corrected, the whole area will end up in an overall excess savings and lower growth.

In the specific case, the excess of savings over investment in the surplus country is the result of policies which discourage consumption and investment, in particular in the areas of taxation and investment incentives, including public investments as a catalyzer for private ones. Surplus countries should aim in particular at reducing taxes on consumption and discourage savings. If this is not done explicitly, through active measures, it will end up being the case as a result of the saving glut, in particular through low — or negative — interest rates on savings (Bini Smaghi 2014).

The problem is how to induce surplus countries to implement less restrictive policies, given that they do not need the money as they do not have an adjustment program. As long as the EU institutions try to lever on adjustment programs to induce countries to change their policies, conditionality is bound to be asymmetric. Greater symmetry requires a change in the institutional framework underlying policy cooperation within the union. This requires, however, that countries accept to give up more sovereignty in a broader range of policies. The Stability and Growth Pact, for instance, would have to move from a system of rules aimed at avoiding excessive deficits to a mechanism which aims at inducing countries to adopt budgetary and structural policies designed at improving the performance of the euro area as a whole.

Conclusions

To sum up, a sustainable governance of the Eurozone would require the transfer of more powers to the Union, in particular with respect to budgetary policy. However, this is unlikely to be politically feasible over the near term. On the other hand, the Eurozone needs a stronger mechanism for financial solidarity, to address asymmetric shocks and to counter destabilizing contagion. This entails transfers, of a temporary or permanent nature, across countries, which may lead to moral hazard unless they are bound by explicit conditions. Conditionality is thus likely to remain central in the governance of the Eurozone. Such conditionality needs, however, to be better designed. It cannot be based only on rules or on mechanisms like the IMF, which are designed for countries that have a flexible exchange rate system.

Furthermore, prevention is more important than the correction of imbalances. The Union has adopted a series of new procedures aimed at monitoring and correcting excessive imbalances. However, the experience of the past suggests that these instruments are not very effective in curbing policy behavior within the member states. They tend to fuel resentment toward the European institutions that are considered too intrusive in the member states' own decisions.

Overall, the IMF experience shows that it is not easy to design better conditionality while making the perception of adjustment programs less intrusive. Crises do take place and cannot simply be assumed away, as the Union did at the euro. The Union has to improve its resilience, in particular by moving forward toward greater political integration. This would mean in particular creating a more efficient adjustment to exogenous asymmetric shocks, including through a broader sharing of budgetary powers. This is not a politically easy solution, as many in Europe today oppose a move toward devolving more powers to the federal level. One should not forget, however, that the United States adopted a federal tax and welfare system only after the Great depression and WWII, i.e., when the need for such a change became a matter of survival. Europe has shown not to be that different, after all.

Disclosure statement

No potential conflict of interest was reported by the author.

References

Begg, Iain, Annette Bongardt, Kalypso Nicolaïdis, and Francisco Torres. 2015. EMU and Sustainable Integration. *Journal of European Integration* 37, no. 7: 803–16.

Bini Smaghi, Lorenzo. 2014. Here's why Germany needs to start spending. *Ft.com.* 28 October.

Bolton, Patrick, and Olivier Jeanne. 2007. *Structuring and restructuring sovereign debt: the role of bankruptcy regime.* IMF Working Paper WP/07/192. August.

Bongardt, Annette, and Francisco Torres. 2013. Forging sustainable growth: the issue of convergence of preferences and institutions. *Intereconomics* 48, no. 2: 72–7.

Committeri, Marco, and Francesco Spadafora. 2013. *You never give me your money? Sovereign debt crises, collective action problems and IMF lending.* IMF Working paper WP/13/20. January.

Darvas, Szolt, and Silvia Merler. 2013. *The European Central Bank in the age of banking union.* Bruegel. 3 October.

Draghi, Mario. 2015. *Structural reforms, inflation and monetary policy.* ECB Forum on Central Banking, Sintra. 22 May.

Dreher, Axel. 2009. IMF conditionality: theory and evidence. *Public Choice* 141: 233–67.

European Commission. 2015. *Making the best use of flexibility within the existing rules of the stability and growth pact.* Com 12, 13 January. Brussels: European Commission.

IMF. 2011. *Modernizing the framework for fiscal policy and debt sustainability analysis.* Paper Prepared by the Fiscal Affairs Department and the Strategy, Policy, and Review Department, IMF. 5 August.

IMF. 2012. *2011 review of conditionality.* Overview Paper. 19 June.

IMF. 2013. *Greece, ex post evaluation of exceptional access under 2010 stand-by agreement.* Country Report 13/56. 5 June. Washington, DC: International Monetary Fund.

Moschella, Manuela. 2014. Monitoring macroeconomic imbalances: is EU surveillance more effective than IMF surveillance? *JCMS: Journal of Common Market Studies* 52, no. 6: 1273–89.

Pisany-Ferry, Jean, André Sapir, and Guntram Wolf. 2013. *Financial assistance in the euro area.* Peterson Institute. April.

Schimmelfenning, Frank, and Ulrich Sedelmeier. 2004. Governance by conditionality. *Journal of European Public Policy* 11, no. 4: 669–87.

Tressel, Thierry, Shengzu Wang, Joong Shik Kang, and Jay Shambaugh, directed by Jörg Decressin and Petya Koeva Brooks. 2014. *Adjustment in Euro area deficit countries: progress, challenges and policies.* Staff discussion notes 14/7, July.

Responses to the Euro Area Crisis: Measuring the Path of European Institutional Integration

FRANCESCO PAOLO MONGELLI*,**, ETTORE DORRUCCI**, DEMOSTHENES IOANNOU** & ALESSIO TERZI***,****

*Goethe University, Frankfurt am Main, Germany;
**European Central Bank, Frankfurt am Main, Germany;
***Bruegel, Brussels, Belgium;
****Hertie School of Governance, Berlin, Germany

ABSTRACT The euro area crisis has exposed flaws in the institutional framework of the European Economic and Monetary Union (EMU). The immediate causes of the crisis have been widely debated — including weak governance, persistent erosion of competitiveness in some countries and easy financing by banks. However, there is little discussion about a fundamental shift in the nature of European integration, which took place in mid-1990s when plans for launching the euro became credible and binding. It was not understood that Europe had shifted from a Common Market Era, during which EMU's foundations were laid, to a 'Union Era' which in retrospect exhibited an incomplete institutional framework. This article reviews the leap in governance now taking place, whilst taking stock of what has worked and proved resilient over the previous 60 years. This is done by means of an index — the European Index of Regional Institutional Integration (EURII) — providing a tool to synthesise and monitor European institutional integration since 1958, and track all institutional reforms since 2010. EURII has both backward as well as forward-looking components anchored on the project put forward in the 2012 Four Presidents' Report.

Introduction

Over the last eight years, the euro area has endured a seemingly unending financial crisis, which has unravelled through various phases punctuated by short-lived recoveries. The crisis has exposed and exacerbated several flaws and gaps in the architecture of Europe's Economic and Monetary Union (EMU). EMU's governance could not impede — and in part, it has been argued, endogenously fuelled — the accumulation of substantial private and public debt in several euro area countries.[1] Diverse interpretations of the crisis are also in Jones' contribution in Chapter 7. Nor could it prevent significant losses in competitiveness and overleveraging by banks. Moreover, when the sovereign crisis erupted in 2010, there were no financial backstops for stressed sovereigns or strained banks to counter sudden stops in financial flows.[2]

Several financial market segments collapsed or fragmented (Durre, Maddaloni, and Mongelli 2014). Adverse feedback loops built up between weak sovereigns, weak banks and weak economies (Shambaugh 2012). Strong trade and financial links among euro area countries became a vehicle of contagion. This brought a risk of financial implosion in some countries, with Greece, Ireland and others experiencing a sudden stop, and then needing adjustment programmes. Break-up risks soared in 2011 and 2012. Growth plunged, unemployment soared and inflation tumbled in some countries. Confidence and trust in European institutions fell dramatically, and remain low.

In response to the crisis, exceptional fiscal and monetary policy responses, various financial adjustments and selected structural reforms were deployed. Moreover, the cumulative impact of the mutating crisis also spurred a rethinking of institutional integration in Europe. Since 2010, some of the most important institutional reforms in nearly 60 years of European integration have emerged, including enhanced fiscal governance, procedures to address macroeconomic imbalances, a crisis management and resolution framework, and financial backstops for sovereigns and banks. In other words, the crisis was both an abrupt wake-up call and a catalyst for change and reforms that implied significant steps towards further EU integration.

A framework to kick-start anew the process of integration was outlined in the *Four Presidents' Report* delivered in December 2012 (Van Rompuy 2012). The report embeds the elements of a 'genuine union' characterised by a 'financial market union' often referred to as simply a 'banking union,' a 'fiscal union,' an 'economic union,' and a 'political union'. The advice of the report is to progress with the four unions in parallel, although they are advancing at different speeds and are defined to different degrees (as we examine below). Still the four unions provide an anchor for various reform efforts. In Chapter 6, Begg et al., centring on the 'economic union', argue for the need of structural reforms at the national level in order to promote sustainable growth as a credible crisis exit strategy and for a durable economic recovery.

The aim of this article is to review in particular the reforms in governance that took place during the crisis and the ensuing leap in EU/EA integration. It should not be forgotten that some of the first significant steps towards economic integration took place already with the 1957 Treaty of Rome that entered into force a year later. We are referring to the customs union, the free trade zone, the single market, the shared institutions and so on. Other steps followed which the index presented herein charts, reaching the age of EMU in the 1990s and the most recent developments during the crisis in the 2010s.

Specifically, analysis is conducted utilising the European Index of Regional Institutional Integration (EURII). EURII maps developments in European integration from 1958 to 2014 on the basis of a monthly data-set. It captures what we call: (i) the 'Common Market Era' which lasted from 1958 until 1993; and (ii) the first twenty years of the 'Union Era' which began in 1994, but gained new impetus in response to the euro area crisis.[3] Hence, EURII provides a tool to articulate, synthesise and monitor the process of European institutional integration since the start of the Common Market.

The rest of the article is organised as follows. In Section 2, we outline the index. In Section 3, we explain EURII's structure. In Section 4, we remeasure the Common Market Era, whereas in Section 5 we measure the Union Era. In Section 6, we present the main findings of the index. Then, in Section 7 we conduct a different exercise and subdivide most institutional steps into four types of integration: economic, financial, political and fiscal. Some final remarks are provided in Section 8. Diverse caveats apply. EURII is to some extent subjective and relies on our judgement in various components. Moreover, it may take variable lags for the elements of the new governance to be transposed into national law and display their effects.

A New Institutional Integration Index

Our previous index of institutional integration was backward looking and cumulative. Instead, EURII has a backward-looking component that we call 'Common Market Era', but also a forward-looking component that we call 'Union Era'. Together they allow us to map developments in European integration from 1958 to 2014, while taking the four unions as a point of reference.

As regards the methodological approach of the index, it aims to measure European integration defined index being normative is that it measures integration defined as the pooling of national sovereignty. In the public policy sphere, this refers to the pooling of national decision-making and competence. In the market sense, this pooling refers to the extent to which restrictions (for example in product, capital and labour markets) are removed; it thus n terms of the OCA principles. Although in general we perceive this integration as a positive development, the positive scoring of the index. A negative score indicates that the integration agreed and entered into force is not kept to. For example, the index falls with the dismantling of the currency-board 'Snake' arrangement in the 1970s.

A Shift Between Two Eras

The 'Common Market Era' of the index displayed most of its effects between 1958 and end-1993 along 'five stages' of integration identified by Balassa (1961): the gradual realisation of a free trade area (FTA); a customs union (CU); a common market (CM); an economic union (EUN), with increasing coordination and even unification of several policies; and, finally, total economic integration, with shared European institutions and laws (see Dorrucci *et al.* 2005; Mongelli, Dorrucci, and Agur 2007). These components have proven resilient throughout the crisis. In fact, euro area countries still remain highly integrated and interdependent. The crisis has shown that events in any euro area member can rapidly spill over to the others through diverse channels of transmission.

The 'Union Era' started, in our view, in 1994 with Stage Two of EMU and continued in 1999 with Stage Three. We argue that the launch of EMU in the 1990s brought about a transformation of European integration, whose consequences and implications were not fully understood at the time. Thus, a major discontinuity materialised when Europe shifted from the Common Market Era to the Union Era in 1994. That is, the moment when the preparatory work for the launch of the euro started becoming more credible and binding. The nature of European integration changed. Developments in each country could affect the others as the crisis has shown. Our index brings a change in perspective: it takes stock of the pillars of European integration but also anchors its scoring to the elements of the four unions that are within reach.

Setting Right Incentives

Crisis management and resolution frameworks brought a fundamental change to EMU's political economy. The economic adjustment programmes for Greece, Ireland, Portugal, Spain and Cyprus were supported financially by the European Financial Stability Facility (EFSF), and later also by the permanent European Stability Mechanism (ESM). This framework also drew on the crisis management expertise of the IMF. *The funding of the ESM* comes from paid-in capital plus joint and mutual guarantees pledged in proportion to the share of ECB capital.

The governance of the euro area was then strengthened to counter the moral hazard inherent in such an insurance scheme by restoring fiscal sustainability and preventing or correcting macroeconomic imbalances. For example, the Stability and Growth Pact has been tightened up by the so-called 'six-pack' of economic governance measures, including the Macroeconomic Imbalance Procedure (MIP). They in turn have been complemented by the 'two-pack'.

Structure of EURII

EURII follows a balanced quantitative structure between the 'Common Market Era' and the new 'Union Era' (Table 1). A maximum score of 50 is assigned to each era. Thus, the maximum score for EURII is 100. Each era

Table 1. The building blocks of the EURII index

	'Common Market Era' (1957)					'Union Era' (1994–today)				
Components	FTA Free trade area	CU Custom union	IM Intern. market	CME Coordination of monetary & exchange rate policies	SID Supranat. institutions & decision-making	MU Monetary union	EU Economic union	FIU Fiscal union	FMU Financial market union	DLA Democratic legitimacy & accountability
Max. score	12.5		20	5	12.5	12	10	10	12	6
Aggreg. max. score				50				50		
Total					100					

is in turn partitioned in various components illustrated below and explained in the next two sections.

We apply a mix between equal weighting and judgement as regards the extent of pooling of national sovereignty and importance of the decision-making and institutional development observed. While the Common Market Era and the Union Era are given equal weights, judgement is applied for diverse components.[4] Moreover, we do not apply an 'equal weighting' policy as utilised for example in the Human Development Index.[5] When constructing EURII, we apply the relative merits of both the equal weighting and the judgemental approach on a case-by-case basis.

After careful reflection, this seems indeed to be the least arbitrary solution. For example, it would not be meaningful to give the same weight to the European Monetary System and to EMU given that the degree of competence surrender to the European level of governance is significantly greater in the latter case. However, we are also conscious of the fact that without some of the first steps of integration, ensuing ones may not have been possible (at least to some extent). It therefore does not seem reasonable to assign the same weight to each institutional steps and decisions in the index (see Dorrucci *et al.* [2015] and index available online).

Re-measuring the Common Market Era

This section reviews the construction of the Common Market Era (CME). This is when the foundations for EMU were laid. In fact, all CME components are either wholly completed or close to being completed. We argue that the current push towards the four unions may have positive reverberations also on the CME components. For example, the banking union will also ease financial flows.

Free Trade Area (FTA) and Customs Union (CU)

Changes over time of tariffs and quotas on trade within the area (FTA) and vis-à-vis third countries (CU) are used to measure the progress made in establishing the FTA/CU. This process evolved between January 1958 and July 1968, when it was completed by the EU6, the six founders of the EU. This acts as an upper bound for the subsequent integration of the 22 other EU Member States in the following decades. The euro area obtains a score of 12.5 as shown in Figure 1. The final step towards a FTA/CU in 1968 is assigned a higher weight to mark the completion of this Balassa-stage. The same approach applies to other dimensions of the EURII index described hereafter.

The Internal Market (IM) and the Uneven 'Four Freedoms'

The internal market has four elements. It is about integrating product and service markets, including financial services,[6] as well as lifting restrictions to the movement of capital, people and workers i.e. promoting financial and labour market integration. The internal market has advanced through

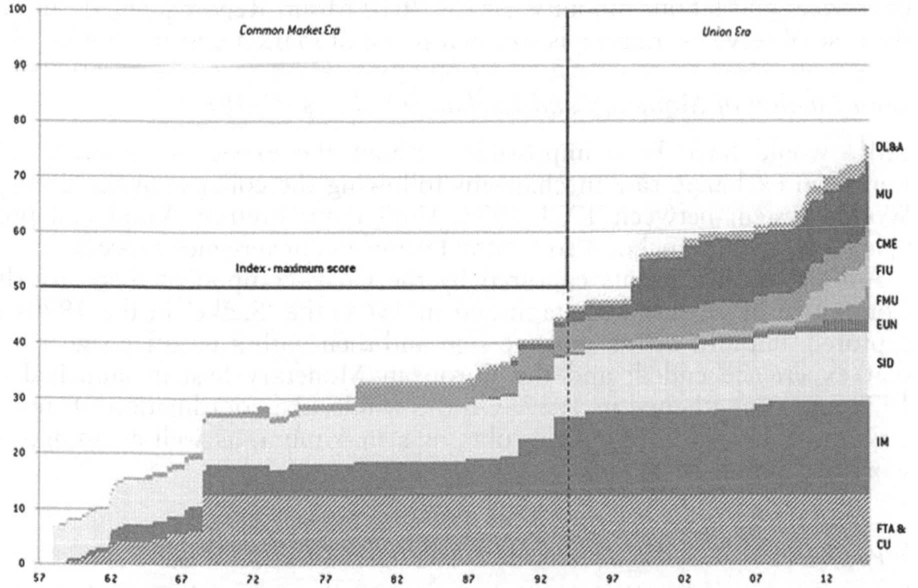

Figure 1. European Index of Regional Institutional Integration (EURII)

various steps including the abolition of all residual trade barriers inside the EU, the attribution of strong powers to the Commission for competition policy (1962) and the harmonisation of VAT on trade of goods (1967). The 1985 *White Paper*, abolishing residual non-tariff barriers with the *European Single Act* of 1986, was estimated to have been 95 per cent completed by the end of 1992. Concerning capital movement, in the 1960s and 1970s, restrictions were tolerated. Later on, starting in the 1980s the liberalisation of capital movements became one of the key drivers of monetary union. It also became a key disciplining factor forcing policy-makers to pursue economic convergence.

Six key steps stand out for the compilation of the EURII index: (1) the attribution of strong powers to the European Commission in the area of competition policy (1962); (2) harmonisation of VAT on services trade (1967); (3) Council Directive on the abolition of restrictions on the freedom of establishment and freedom to provide services in respect of self-employed activities of banks and other institutions (1973); (4) official launch of a single market for services in 1993, as part of the European Single Market; (5) the Payment Services Directive (2007); and (6) the 2009 'Bolkestein Directive' on services.

Concerning the movement of people and workers, the relevant measures are far from being fully implemented. Less than 3 per cent of the working age population of the EU consists of people from one Member State working in another. This explains why the maximum score possible for this indicator cannot be given to EU countries in this field (a score of 3.25 is reached).On the whole, the internal market attains 16.85 point out of a maximum score of 20 points. More remains to be done to free movement of services and labour mobility. As the 2010 Monti Report pointed out, 'in the case of services, Europe is still in a phase of market construction'.

Coordination of Monetary and Exchange Policies (CME)

EMU would have been impossible without the experience gained with European exchange rate mechanisms following the collapse of the Bretton Woods System between 1971–1973. Until then, Bretton Wood had provided a monetary anchor also for the European convergence process.

Among the key events captured by the CME component there are the Committee of Governors established in 1964; the 'Snake' in the 1970s is captured, initially with a positive sign and then with a negative sign when that experience ended; and the European Monetary System launched in 1979 and strengthened in 1987. On the whole, the coordination of monetary and exchange rate policies obtains a maximum, as well as an actual, score of 5 points.

Supranational Institutions and Decision-making Bodies (SID)

Supranational institutions — such as the Parliament and Commission — and laws were set up at the very outset of European integration and have been strengthened over time. Thus, a basic supranational framework was already envisaged in the Treaty of Rome (1957). This implies the assignment of 7 points back in 1958, when the Treaty came into force. Out of several subsequent developments, the following stand out: (i) the establishment in 1974 of the European Council as a permanent forum providing political impulses; (ii) the introduction of Qualified Majority Voting (QMV) on Single Market issues with the Single European Act (1987); (iii) the extension of QMV with the Maastricht Treaty (1993); (iv)–(v) the subsequent Treaties of Nice (2003) and Lisbon (2009), with further extension of QMV.

We include in the SID component of the index also the start of structural policies such as the launch of the Common Agricultural Policy (1962) and its strengthening in 1966, as well as the establishment of the European Regional Development Fund, which in 1975 started the provision of structural and cohesion funds. On the whole, this component of the index obtains a maximum, as well as an actual, score of 12.5 points.

Measuring the Union Era

The launch of the euro in January 1999 brought to a completion a process of monetary integration, which had started after the collapse of the Bretton Woods system. Yet the main lesson from the crisis is that an Economic and Monetary Union like EMU needs several components — several unions — and a coherent constitutional framework — to function well. The opportunity to complement the monetary union presented itself with the *Four Presidents' Report*. The aim of the report, as well as the EU Commission Blueprint of 2012, is to formulate a 'shared European vision for a coherent and viable architecture of EMU'.

The vision should embed the following elements of a 'Genuine Union' that integrate the monetary union:

- an 'economic union' comprising an integrated economic policy framework;
- a 'financial market union' with a 'banking union' at its core, comprising an integrated financial framework with: the Single Supervisory Mechanism (SSM), a common deposit insurance scheme and a shared resolution framework;
- a 'fiscal union' comprising an integrated budgetary framework that will go beyond the fiscal compact; and
- a 'political union' enhancing the democratic legitimacy and accountability of EU decision-making bodies. The goal is to engage citizens more deeply in European decision-making.

The Monetary Union (MU)

We start our discussion with the 'monetary union', the most advanced and established union so far, before turning to the above four new unions. In January 1999, the ECB and the Euro system started managing a single monetary and exchange rate policy for the whole euro area. The Euro system was set up with fully federalised decision-making and with the Governing Council granted independence concerning the definition of its objective (s) and monetary policy framework. This implied a significant step in terms of sovereignty transferred to the euro area level and European integration.

The euro was then officially launched in January 1999, when also the TARGET system (later replaced by TARGET2) began operating. At the same time, the European Exchange Rate Mechanism (ERM II) replaced its predecessor, as a full part of the overall EMU framework and a requirement for euro accession. In January 2002, euro notes and coins entered into circulation replacing the legal tender in each country. The Four Presidents' Report does not identify any further steps to be taken under Monetary Union, which seems to fully justify the maximum score of 12 out of 12 which we are assigning to it (Durre, Maddaloni, and Mongelli 2014).

The EUN

In 1988, Heads of States and Governments decided to recalibrate and increase the financial firepower of the EU's Structural Funds. Then, in 1997 the *Luxembourg Process*, reinforced by the Amsterdam Treaty, established a European Employment Strategy. The year after, in 1998, at a European Council meeting in Cardiff, the 'Cardiff process' for product market reform was introduced as a way to improve peer review of economic reforms. One year later, when the European Council met in Cologne, these processes were complemented by a Macroeconomic Dialogue of social partners at European level. The aim was to improve cooperation on wage formation among all stakeholders.

All these processes were based largely on existing Treaties — essentially the so-called *Broad Economic Policy Guidelines* and the Employment Guidelines of today's TFEU Articles 121 and 148) which later converged into the so-called Integrated Guidelines — and in essence relied on an open method of policy coordination. They had limited effectiveness and we assign very small scores of 0.10 to each of them.

The *Lisbon Strategy* of 2000, and its revamped version in 2005, also enters our index as an attempt to a strategic and comprehensive approach to policy coordination. Both had limited results and entered the index with a small score. An arrangement which had the potential to prove significant, but with practically no elements of additional shared sovereignty and enforcement methods, was the *Euro Plus Pact* adopted in the early stages of the crisis. As a consequence, it had limited results and also receives a very small score in the index.

The latest, and most substantial, attempt at putting in place a shared mechanism that would monitor and foster policies aimed at boosting macroeconomic stability and competitiveness is the *Macroeconomic Imbalances Procedure (MIP)* embedded in the European Semester established by the so-called 'six-pack' in 2011. Its macroeconomic scoreboard and objective thresholds, allows for much less discretion than previous arrangements. The MIP also includes an Excessive Imbalances Procedure (EIP) that can ultimately also lead to pecuniary fines similar to those of the SGP; it marks a notable departure in the economic sphere from the peer support, pressure and OMC-type of surveillance and thus deserves a higher score than its predecessors.

On the whole, we judge the overall level of EMU as being still distant from that required for a resilient and beneficial EMU. The EUN component is assigned an overall score of 2.2 out of a maximum of 10. In order to reach the maximum score, economic integration would have to be pursued along the lines of creating a stronger system that encourages structural reforms in low-productivity countries, thereby improving the overall stability of EMU to macroeconomic shocks. One possible form for this, as detailed in the report, would be a system of national reform contracts, to be signed with EU institutions, in exchange for financial support. The other crucial milestone would require passing strong economic reforms promoting competitiveness and economic convergence in order to be part of a European macroeconomic stabilisation mechanism.

The Financial Market Union (FMU) with Banking Union (BU)

Financial market integration has been an integral component of European integration since the early days of the Community. As early as 1973, directives were being passed abolishing restrictions on providing services with respect to self-employed activities of banks and other financial institutions. In an attempt to increase the degree of harmonisation of the market, various directives were also passed on banking supervision, own funds, solvency ratios, large exposures, just to mention a few. These were all small steps, which do not enter our index with a score. However, in 2000 the main pieces of legislation on banking were consolidated into the Single Banking Directive from Basel I — to which we assign a small positive score.

In the following years, several technical fora were established, including the Committee of European Securities Regulators (CESR) in 2001, followed by the Committee of European Banking Supervisors (CEBS) and the Committee of European Insurance and Occupational Pensions Supervisors (CEIOPS) in 2003. These fora represented the predecessors of the three European Supervisory Authorities, i.e. respectively, the European Banking Authority (EBA), the European Securities Markets Authority (ESMA) and the European Insurance and Occupational Pensions Authority (EIOPA). Together with the European Systemic Risk Board (ESRB), which was set up in 2011 to provide analysis, warnings and recommendations on macroprudential policy, these authorities form the European System of Financial Supervisors (ESFS). The last substantive step was the entry into force, in July 2013, of the Capital Requirements Directive (CRD) IV and Capital Requirements Regulation (CRR), implementing the Basel III agreement.

In June 2012, the European Council agreed to advance with centralised European banking supervision. After the necessary preparatory work, stress tests and comprehensive assessments, the ECB took up supervision of euro area banks under the *Single Supervisory Mechanism (SSM)* on 4 November 2014. An EU Regulation, co-decided by the EU Council and European Parliament, has set up a *Single Resolution Mechanism (SRM)*, with a Single Resolution Board (SRB) and a bank-levy funded Single Resolution Fund (SRF) that became operational on 1 January 2015, while the SRF will be built up gradually. In the meantime, it will be buttressed by national financial backstop arrangements. The Bank Recovery and Resolution Directive (BRRD), with the senior bail-in provisions that will enter into force on 1 January 2016, also have been adopted. Moreover, in August 2013, the Commission updated its rules concerning state aid for the assessment of public support of banks. A Deposit Guarantee Schemes Directive (DGSD) has been adopted, ensuring the protection of deposits across Europe for up to 100,000.

Finally, Direct Bank Recapitalisation (DBR) by the ESM, establishing the direct recapitalisation of banks through European public funds as an *ultima ratio* and in line with the bail-in provisions of the BRRD, SRM and ESM conditions, also has been agreed. It is set to enter into force on 1 January 2016 (together with the bail-in of senior creditors). A more integrated solution could envisage the harmonisation of bankruptcy law, improving the markets for high-quality securitisation, harmonising the rules pertaining to market infrastructures and so on. On the whole, the FMU component is roughly only 30 per cent complete, with a total score of 3.55 out of a maximum of 12.

The Fiscal Union (FU)

The need for euro area fiscal discipline and coordination was already recognised in the Treaty of Maastricht with the Excessive Deficit Procedure

(EDP). The EDP was later operationalised by the Stability and Growth Pact under the purview of the EU Commission. We recognise both steps in our index. However, the SGP has been breached on a number of occasions. It was subsequently weakened in 2005, signalling a greater tolerance for profligate public finances that contributed to the sovereign debt crisis in some euro area countries that erupted in May 2010 following Greece's exclusion from the international capital markets (Durre, Maddaloni, and Mongelli 2014). The reform of the SGP in the mid-2000s thus enters our EURII index with a negative sign, illustrating a setback for the integration of fiscal policies.

A large part of the initial crisis response in 2010 focused on the fiscal side. It is captured quite visibly in EURII. In December 2011, the SGP was once again strengthened as part of the so-called 'Six-Pack' legislation containing two regulations updating the SGP Regulations of 1997, as well as a Directive on national fiscal frameworks. Furthermore, with the so-called 'Fiscal Compact', a new Treaty on Stability, Convergence and Governance (TSCG) was ratified, leading most notably to the embedding of a balanced-budget rule of constitutional status at national level.

Last, the fiscal framework has been strengthened through the 'Two-Pack' permitting the Commission to subject draft budgets to European surveillance vis-a-vis the SGP. This entails faster decision-making once the Commission has decided to apply the preventive and corrective arms of the SGP to correct high public deficits and debts. These steps receive a significant weight in EURII.

Important steps were also taken on the burden-sharing side. The first such step was the creation of the Greek Loan Facility in May 2010 that channelled bilateral loans to the Greek government. Then, in May 2010, the decision was taken for setting up the EU-wide *European Financial Stabilisation Mechanism (EFSM)*, allowing the Commission to borrow in financial markets up to 60 billion under the implicit guarantee of the EU budget, in order to provide financial assistance to EU Member States in need. Notwithstanding its relatively limited financial envelope, this is considered to be a significant step in terms of integration, as a decision regarding the activation of the EFSM facility can be taken by a qualified majority of the Council, and implies a fairly far-reaching form of pooling of fiscal resources.

The other milestone was the European Financial Stability Fund (EFSF), which was a euro area special purpose vehicle that came into operation soon after the inception of the first Greek Economic Adjustment Programme. Notwithstanding its temporary nature, its strict unanimity rules, and the fact that liabilities continued to be allocated to individual countries, the EFSF takes on an important role in the EURII given its strong firepower allowing for an effective containment of the sovereign debt crisis and acting as the precursor to the European Stability Mechanism (ESM). The EFSF was later replaced by the ESM, a permanent international organisation with a high lending capacity (700 billion) with 80 billion in paid-in capital and some 620 billion of callable capital. The ESM, based on an inter-governmental Treaty, has a large toolkit of lending options and market support facilities to assist euro area countries under the stress of financial markets.

Decisions in the ESM are taken with a very high majority threshold (with lower thresholds under emergency situations). It is assigned a high score in EURII that might be higher if the ESM were to acquire a more supranational dimension. On the whole, these steps bring the overall score of the Fiscal Union heading to 6.25 out of 10. This is remarkable, given the short time in which most of these steps were agreed and implemented. There are however still a number of elements missing in order to reach a genuine EMU. These would include the creation of a euro area fiscal capacity, the possibility for some sort of shared issuance of euro area debt, enhanced tax coordination and a fiscal backstop to both the SRM and a Deposit Guarantee Scheme.

The Political Union (PU)

This component is at the moment the least well defined. It is also at the epicentre of the most sensitive debate concerning the future of European integration and the democratic deficit (Siedentop 2000; Scharpf 2011). For the purposes of the EURII index, we concentrate on accountability and legitimacy steps related to EMU matters. Due to its limitations, this EURII component is identified only as DLA rather than 'Political Union' and is assigned a maximum score of six points.

The first notable steps involved the European Parliamentary Assembly that held its first meeting as early as 1958 and evolved into the European Parliament (EP) in 1962. More recently, in the run up to the May 2014 EP elections, a public debate was held among the *Spitzenkandidaten* of the EU political groups; at the same time, turnout has been falling from the original very high percentage of 1979.

In recent years, accountability requirements vis-à-vis the European Parliament has gradually increased. With the *Nice Treaty*, the nomination for Commission President had to receive the consent of Parliament, while Parliament could reject the Commission President's proposal for the 'College' of Commissioners. Thus, in 2009, the EP effectively 'brought down' the Santer Commission, and in 2009 and 2014 rejected some of the proposed Commissioners. With the *Lisbon Treaty of 2009*, the Heads of State have to 'take into account' of the result of the European elections when proposing to Parliament the Commission President (as with the appointment of Juncker as Commission President).

Moreover, under the Maastricht Treaty, the ECB is accountable to the European Parliament, while the Council Regulation establishing the Single Supervisory Mechanism (SSM) under Article 127(6) of the Treaty provides for the accountability of the ECB's supervisory tasks towards the European Parliament and the Council via the ECB's Chair of the Supervisory Board.

A number of other provisions have over the years strengthened the legitimacy of EU decisions. During the crisis, the *European Council*, composed of the Heads of State or Government, turned into a full-fledged European institution in the last EU Treaty revision in Lisbon. It has a permanent

President for two and one half years and also meets in euro area composition as necessary. The role of the Eurogroup was formally recognised in a Protocol of the Treaty. The Eurogroup's President is appointed for a fixed term also of two and one half years (unlike the six-month rotation of the Council Presidency).

Yet, despite the progress in raising the democratic legitimacy and accountability of the Union, the Four Presidents' Report recognises the need for still further steps. However, these are identified only in general terms, such as the need for deep, institutionalised cooperation between the EP and national parliaments for law-making and accountability purposes, full SRM (including SRF) accountability, deeper if not full involvement of the EP in the European Semester (and also possible involvement in the scrutiny of national budgets), still-to-be-determined accountability of the fiscal capacity. In light of these steps still to be taken, our aggregate score for the completion of the Democratic Legitimacy and Accountability pillar comes to 44 per cent.

Findings of the EURII Index

When we sum up all the components of the Common Market Era and of the Union Era, the path of the EURII index is illustrated in Figure 1 and Table 2. The index records each step of European integration from the 1958. It shows how the nature of European integration changed following the Maastricht Treaty, ushering in a new phase of European integration: the Union Era. This era was initially focused on monetary union, plus of course the common market. The launch of the euro brought instead a discontinuity in the EURII index, which jumped from 48/100 to 58/100 in 1999–2002 in Figure 1. Jumps in the index had also occurred previously

Table 2. Components of common market and union era: degree of completion and needs for future steps

	Stage of completion (%)	Expected (%)	Future steps (%)	Total (%)
FTA & CU — Free trade area & custom union	100	0%	0	100
IM — Internal market	84	0	16	100
CME — Coordin. monetary & exch. rate policies	100	0	0	100
SID — Supranat. institut. & decision-making	100	0	0	100
EUN — Economic union	22	0	78	100
FMU — Financial market union	55	17	28	100
FIU — Fiscal union	63	3	35	100
MUN — Monetary union	96	4	0	100
DL&A — Democratic legitimacy & accountability	44	0	56	100
Total	76	3	21	100

(e.g. with the completion in 1968 of the free trade and customs union, which led to a rise in the index from 20/100 to 28/100). However, these increases did not lead to a fundamental discontinuity in the nature of institutional integration. The index then shows a steady rise from 2010 to early 2015 from 62/100 to 78/100 largely to address the flaws in the EMU's institutional framework.

At the same time, the European process of institutional integration is not yet complete (see Table 2). Diverse elements identified in the Four Presidents' Report are incomplete. With the most recent advances in the banking union having added significantly to what is considered a well-integrated financial markets union. The areas where further progress is indispensable include the EUN, fiscal union and political union. Sadly, Democratic Legitimacy and Accountability, a subset of a Political Union, is the least well-defined union: a deficit that is urgent to tackle due to the plunge in EU confidence and trust.

Advances can also be expected in other spheres. Some parts of the Single Market have yet to be completed, while the banking union does not exhibit further steps in the financial sphere. Moreover, the third pillar of the banking union is a common deposit insurance system, which still has to be implemented. Finally, capital markets are arguably not integrated enough to provide deep and evenly distributed funding across the European economy as a stable complement, to bank funding (Cœuré (2014)).

A Change in Perspective: Four Sub-indices

As it stands, the EURII classifies fundamental steps according to nine components divided between the Common Market and Union eras. However, alternative classifications can be envisioned. Several steps in the history of European integration might have directly contributed to multiple goals. We therefore divide the fundamental steps used to construct the standard EURII along the lines of financial, economic, fiscal and political integration. These new sub-indices, as we call them, no longer have a requirement of excludability, which was somewhat arbitrary in the initial EURII composition, and allows monitoring how integration has evolved along different headlines. What this means is that, for example, the introduction of the euro will have contributed both to financial integration and to economic integration, through enhanced trade. Whereas this figures only under Monetary Union in the standard EURII setting, in order to set the ceiling to 100, it is allowed to appear in both the financial and economic integration sub-indices (Figure 2).

Comparisons among the sub-indices are simply indicative, yet these series carry important information. Economic integration was the key policy focus in the late 60s, at a time when progress in other policy areas was stagnant. Furthermore, after a generalised period of little or no integration in the early 80s, we see how financial integration took the lead, as the foundations of the euro were being put in place. Economic integration followed hand in hand. Interestingly, that is the time in which fiscal integration started moving its first steps, albeit at very low rate. The largest

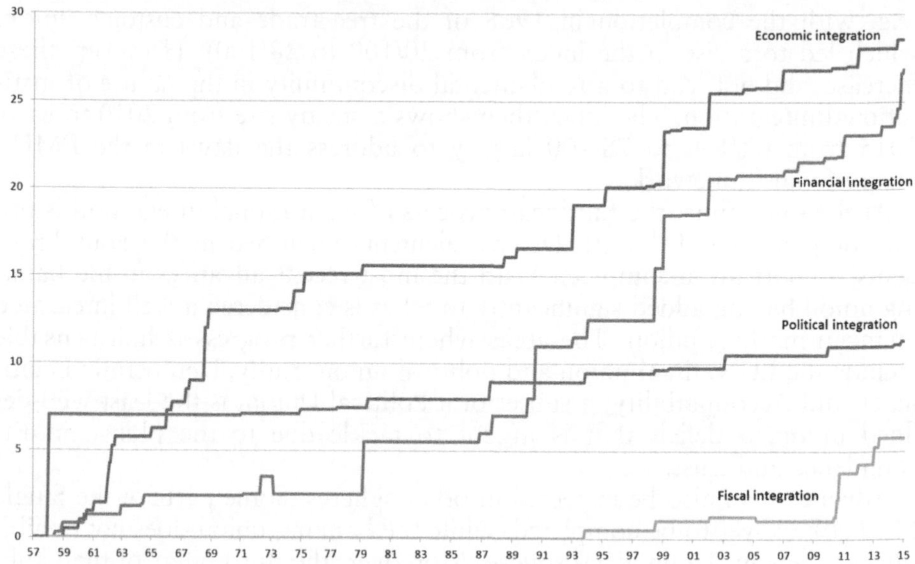

Figure 2. Four indices of integration

progress under this heading was to be sparked by the euro area crisis. Finally, it is worth reflecting on how, conversely from all other components, political integration is the only one to have proceeded only in very small steps.

Final Remarks

Some steps towards a 'Genuine EMU' might undergo a trial and error process, not always in a consistent and coherent manner (Niemann and Ioannou 2015). An example, is the financial markets union itself, which began with the setting up of committees (e.g. CEBS), then of authorities (e.g. ESAs, ESRB) and is now being complemented with centralised European banking supervision (SSM).

Various caveats apply. Institutional integration remains a dynamic process that will likely go beyond what is envisaged in today's Four Presidents' Report. Therefore, the EURII index is anchored by a new governance framework, whose contours are slowly taking shape but which might still shift. Plus the various unions are advancing in parallel but at different speeds. Last, we are not yet out of the crisis and its impact may last a bit longer. Yet, strengthening EMU's constitutional framework is indispensable to lay the ground for a genuine EMU with the right incentive structures and mechanisms for countries to benefit from each other.

Acknowledgements

The authors would like to thank for helpful comments Francisco Torres, Max Watson and participants to a Seminar on 'The Governance of EMU:

Recasting Political, Fiscal and Financial Integration' that took place at Oxford's St. Anthony College in March 2014. The views expressed in this paper do not necessarily reflect those of the ECB, and we remain responsible for any errors or omissions.

Disclosure statement

No potential conflict of interest was reported by the authors.

Notes

1. See Fernandez-Villaverde, Garicano, and Santos (2013) and De Grauwe (2013). For a 'fiscal narrative' of the crisis see Schuknecht *et al.* (2011), for the 'banking narrative' see Constâncio (2013) and for the 'competitiveness narrative' see Sinn and Valentinyi (2013).
2. See Dorrucci *et al.* (2015) and Mongelli (2013) for an analysis of the crisis.
3. The construction of the index, and the underlying list of events, is available as an annexe to the ECB Occasional Paper nr. 160 (Dorrucci *et al.* 2015).
4. Being an institutional index, methodologies such as the Principal Components Analysis (PCA) cannot be implemented, as our weights cannot be determined statistically. The same applies to factor analysis and Unobserved Component Models (UCM).
5. The United Nations (UNDP) has produced a Human Development Index (HDI) which is a composite statistic of life expectancy, education, and per capita income indicators.
6. A functioning internal market for services is especially vital, as today services account on average for over 70 per cent of EU GDP. For a discussion on the differentiated implementation of the Single Market across countries as well as sectors see Howarth and Sadeh (2010). Moreover, in Dorrucci *et al.* (2015) we point to a differentiation between *de jure* and de facto implementation of EU legislation.

References

Balassa, B. 1961. *The theory of economic integration*. Homewood, IL: Richard Irwin.

Begg, Iain, Annette Bongardt, Kalypso Nicolaïdis, and Francisco Torres. 2015. EMU and Sustainable Integration. *Journal of European Integration* 37, no. 7: 803–16.

Cœuré, B. 2014. *Ein Binnenmarkt für Kapital*[An Internal Capital Market]. FAZ, 30 June 2014.

Constâncio, V. 2013. Establishing the Single Supervisory Mechanism speech at the BAFT-IFSA 2013 Europe Bank-to-Bank Forum, 29 January 2013, see ECB website.

De Grauwe, P. 2013. *Design failures in the euro zone: can they be fixed?* European Commission, European economy economic papers No: 491.

Dorrucci, E., D. Ioannou, F.P. Mongelli, and A. Terzi. 2015. *The four unions "pie" on the monetary union "cherry": a new index of European institutional integration*. ECB occasional paper nr. 160.

Dorrucci, E., S. Firpo, M. Fratzscher, and F.P. Mongelli, 2005. The path of institutional and financial integration. *Journal of Economic Integration* 20, no. 2.

Durre, A., A. Maddaloni, and F. Mongelli. 2014. Financial fragmentation and ECB monetary policy. *Comparative Economic Studies* 56, no. 3: 396–423.

Fernandez-Villaverde, J., L. Garicano, and T. Santos. 2013. *Political credit cycles: the case of the euro zone*. NBER Working Paper No. 18899.

Howarth, D., and T. Sadeh. 2010. The ever incomplete single market: differentiation and the evolving frontier of integration. *Journal of European Public Policy* 17, no. 7: 922–35.

Ioannou, D., and L. Stracca. 2014. Have euro area and EU economic governance worked? Just the facts. *European Journal of Political Economy* 34: 1–17.

Mongelli, F.P. 2013. *The mutating euro area crisis — is the balance between 'sceptics' and 'advocates' shifting?* ECB occasional paper series, No: 144.

Mongelli, F.P., E. Dorrucci, and I. Agur. 2007. What does European institutional integration tell us about trade integration? *Integration & Trade* 26, no. 11: 151–200.

Monti, M. 2010. *A new strategy for the single market* (Monti report on the single market). Brussels, Belgium: EU Commission.

Niemann, A., and D. Ioannou. 2015. European economic integration in times of crisis: a case of neo-functionalism? *Journal of European Public Policy* 22, no. 3: 105–24. Special Issue.

Scharpf, F. 2011. *Monetary union, fiscal crisis and the preemption of democracy*. MPIfG discussion paper. Max-Planck-Institut für Gesellschaftsforschung.

Schuknecht, L. P. Moutot, P. Rother and J. Stark 2011. The Stability and Growth Pact: crisis and reform. *ECB Occasional Paper series nr. 129*.

Shambaugh, J.C. 2012. The euro's three crises. *Brookings Papers on Economic Activity*. spring, 2012: 176–212.

Siedentop, L. 2000. *Democracy in Europe*. London: Penguin.

Sinn, H.W., and A. Valentinyi. 2013 *European imbalances*, VoxEU, http://www.voxeu.org/article/european-imbalances.

Van Rompuy, H. 2012. *Towards a genuine Economic and Monetary Union* (Four Presidents' report), Report by the Presidents of the European Council, European Commission, Eurogroup and the ECB, European Council (2012).

Avoiding Another Crisis in the Euro Area: Public and Private Imbalances and National Policy Responses

RUSSELL KINCAID & MAX WATSON

European Study Centre, St Antony's College, University of Oxford, Oxford, UK

ABSTRACT Early critics of the euro's design pointed to the disruptive potential — both political and economic — of country-specific shocks in a monetary union that is a far cry from an optimal currency area. The euro crisis has confirmed the risks associated with a 'one-size-fits-all' monetary policy, decentralized financial supervision, and inadequate fiscal backstops. This article examines how the active use of national fiscal policies and macroprudential policies can mitigate these risks. Cross-border coordination of macroprudential policies is essential to ensure their effectiveness. In addition, area-wide reforms are necessary including a more complete banking union with a well-funded common backstop.

Introduction

Euro-sceptics have long pointed to the disruptive potential — both political and economic — of country-specific shocks in a monetary union that was not an optimal currency area. The euro crisis has confirmed the risks associated with a 'one-size fits all' monetary policy, decentralized financial supervision, and inadequate fiscal backstops. When the euro was designed, significant concerns were expressed about its implications for fiscal discipline in individual members and the possible spillover to other members. Some designers feared that expectations of a 'bailout' would give rise to moral hazard (and insufficient market discipline), triggering larger public deficits, and government debt levels. This preoccupation affected the constraints placed on fiscal policy, which were addressed by treaty provisions — no monetary financing of government deficits and no required 'bail-outs' — and by the stability and growth pact (SGP).

The issue of private sector (corporate and household) deficits and debts and the risks that those imbalances can pose were, in contrast, largely ignored in part because the 'Lawson Doctrine' held sway. According to this view, current account deficits were only bad if they stemmed from government deficits because in the absence of distortions, private sector imbalances were rationally determined and welfare improving — the 'efficient market hypothesis'. Possible pressures on macro-imbalances and supervision flowing from larger funding, in particular from banks, to private borrowers (from a bigger euro-area financial market), were not a central part of the euro-design debate.

The institutional framework for banking supervision under the euro relied consequently upon two principles: (1) national competence enshrined in 'home country control'; and (2) cooperation among the competent national authorities. The ECB's role in banking supervision was to contribute 'to the smooth conduct of policies pursued by the competent authorities' by promoting cooperation. This setup was considered to have two main advantages at the time. One, it minimized any potential conflict between the conduct of policies by the ECB to achieve price stability and to financial stability (e.g., lender of last resort function). Two, national responsibility for national banking systems would preserve continuity, would benefit from their greater knowledge and expertise, and would properly align incentives, avoiding mutualization (e.g., national deposit insurance schemes).

The cost of any bank/supervisory failure would be borne by the relevant national fiscal authority, which thanks to the SGP would be able to absorb these costs without endangering fiscal solvency. However, this national approach also risked having different national supervisory practices creating an uneven playing field that could help maintain 'national champions' in the banking sector by limiting competition, allow national banks to support domestic industrial policies, and help assure government access to bank credit. In effect, home country bias would be reinforced.

Some critics focused on the possibility that asymmetric economic shocks could lead to strong country-specific booms/downswings against the background of the common monetary policy. As a booming economy expanded, its inflation rate would rise, and real interest rates at the national level would fall, intensifying 'perversely' the national boom. Higher national inflation would also result in loss of competitiveness vis-a-vis the currency union. Both factors would contribute to deterioration in the current account balance driven. These dynamics were central to the 'Walters Critique' developed in the late 1980s. Economic modeling work in the 2000s — notably in Brussels and Oxford — explored whether these national booms/downswings could reach destabilizing levels, and whether 'active' national fiscal policies had a role to play in dampening such country-specific cycles.

The financing implications of persistent national current account deficits were under appreciated at that time. With a bank dominated financial system, intra-euro imbalances would be overwhelmingly intermediated by commercial banks using debt instruments. In addition, national banking systems possessed an inherent advantage in providing retail financing to their domestic corporations and households. With lower real interest rates in periphery countries, loan demand boomed and periphery banks were able to supply that heightened demand, owing to their expanded access to wholesale euro funding. Banks' risk management practices bolstered by official prudential supervision were supposed to preserve the financial health of individual banks and the national banking system as a whole.

This article reconsiders these issues in light of the euro-area crisis. It argues that the euro-area experience with wide swings in competitiveness, and the persistence of large current account deficits, supports the case for focusing national fiscal policies on dampening country-specific cycles and therefore, although the SGP is necessary, it is not sufficient to ensure macrofinancial stability. The new Macroeconomic Imbalance Procedure (MIP) is thus welcomed as it fills a previous void by helping to identify worrisome imbalances in the private sector and proposing remedial policy actions, although MIP improvements are needed. In addition, macroprudential policies can help dampen financial sector booms and busts at the national level, contributing to better-suited monetary conditions at the national level as well as enhanced financial stability. Within the single financial market, prudential policies are, however, unlikely to prove effective unless they are coordinated across the euro area. The European Systemic Risk Board (ESRB), and the ECB's new single supervisory role, both offer scope for such coordination. Finally, even considering the positive steps toward banking union, individual euro-member financial systems are still too exposed to country-specific shocks compared to the more geographically diversified exposure of the US financial market.

Pre-crisis Concerns about Private Sector Imbalances

The pre-crisis EMU architecture was criticized by those economists who were concerned potentially problematic adjustment dynamics within the monetary union. Specifically, when a euro member was hit by a country-specific shock, the common monetary policy and constrained national counter-cyclical fiscal policy would not be sufficiently stabilizing — the Walters Critique:

- One euro-area member might enter a country-specific boom, causing higher-than-average inflation. With no national monetary policy to react, the key market mechanism that could eventually slow the economy would be a loss of competitiveness. This mechanism would also need to counteract the 'perverse' fall in the national real interest rate associated with rising national inflation.
- This boom could extend over a long period. The current account balance would deteriorate, and wage costs would rise: subsequently, a slowdown induced by a lack of competitiveness (and higher

unemployment) would improve the current account balance and put downward pressure on real wages. However, this process could be protracted and difficult — socially and individually costly.

- Some economists using models thought that such swings in competitiveness/wages would be stable. Others feared overshooting, and perhaps a destabilizing oscillation and advised the active use of national fiscal policy to dampen country-specific cycles. Among the sceptics were Allsopp and Vines (2008), while the European Commission (EC 2006) considered internal euro dynamics to be stable.

These serious flaws in euro economic governance, as described in greater length in this volume by *Giavazzi and Wyplosz*, and *de Grauwe and Ji*, were the architectural cracks that widened into the euro crisis, although they focus heavily on the design flaws related to the European Central Bank. The near fatal nature of these design flaws coupled with enforcement and data shortcomings particularly related to the SGP have become increasing recognized even by EU officials (see Trichet's 2015 speech). While agreeing with these flaws, *Vines* stresses the important stabilizing role that should be placed by national fiscal policies; a point we also make while noting some real-time technical and political constraints.

Financial Market Lessons from Intra-euro Imbalances

But the euro-area crisis also pointed to financial issues — risk premia, capital flows, credit, and asset prices — which economic analysts tended to ignore previously:

- Financial booms can flatter the budget with very strong temporary revenues from banking, real estate, and private consumption, leading to a false sense of fiscal security and well-being.
- Risk premia should have risen earlier as the riskiness of private and sovereign imbalances became evident, but this mechanism occurred too late and abruptly.
- Weak risk management by private financial institutions coupled with inadequate official oversight was contributing factors.
- In addition, the official may have sent signals — from zero risk weights on sovereigns by supervisors and common collateral treatment by the ECB — that the private participants (incorrectly (?)) interpreted as blessing the compression in credit risk spreads for sovereigns within the euro area.
- In the downswing, very severe feedback — 'doom loops' — emerged between the deteriorating balance sheets of the private and public sectors, which had not been identified or analyzed before the crisis.

The euro-area crisis provides evidence of how quickly and severely financial integration can go awry. During the crisis, the single financial market became fragmented, dividing along national lines. This fragmentation was seen in higher interest rates on bank loans in core countries than in periphery countries and reduced net private cross-border exposures to periphery countries. Fragmentation derived in part from the dominant role, played by national banks in retail lending, while bank funding was considerably more integrated. Periphery banks had assets concentrated in their households (and sovereign — correlated risk), which were funded in euros on shorter terms — maturity transformation — and priced at near zero credit risk. As periphery banks' assets were perceived to be impaired, cross-border euro funding disappeared for these banks (and was largely, but not wholly, replaced by official funding). Had loans to the periphery's private sector been distributed widely among euro-area banks (rather than just funded by them), such diversified risk sharing would have made dealing with an idiosyncratic (housing) bust more manageable. Put another way, the euro financial market was insufficiently integrated at the retail lending level.

In some cases, national authorities had to bail out their national banks, worsening their public debt positions. This deterioration in public finances caused their sovereign interest rates to soar and with that the funding costs for their national banks, which pushed up their lending rates. In yet other cases, the prospect of a bank bailout caused sovereign interest rates to rise. With banks holding large amounts of their government's debt, a vicious circle resulted, which was reinforced by the depressing demand effects of higher bank lending rates and deleveraging (for an in-depth discussion in the Irish context, which has wider applicability, see Regling and Watson 2010). Market-driven interest rates were seen by some overshoot perversely. The ECB and EC took steps to help resolve these problems including notably by adapting its refinance facilities and creating new asset purchase programs, and by establishing the Single Resolution Mechanism and the Deposit Guarantee Scheme. A comprehensive analysis of these resolution efforts goes beyond the scope of this article. Nonetheless, the risk-sharing properties of these two pillars of the banking union are still far from complete, leaving national banking systems and their sovereigns still exposed to country-specific shocks; indeed, the euro banking union is still only 'half a banking union' (see Posen and Vernon 2014).

In short, the behavior of risk premia, credit, asset prices, and capital flows — both prior to and after the crisis — has added a further dimension to earlier concerns about unstable country-specific boom/bust cycles. Questions need to be answered about the proper roles for national macroprudential and fiscal policies, and the adequacy of euro-area policy coordination.

New Roles for National Fiscal and Macroprudential Policies

Nominal interest rate convergence, owing to the elimination of exchange rate risk, was an expected outcome of euro adoption. However, financial markets also priced sovereign credit risks at near zero, which was unproductive. As a consequence, financing constraints were eased excessively for some countries — Spain and Greece notably — and some sectors — real estate. The prominence of financial factors in explaining the euro-area crisis suggests a need for national measures targeted at dampening swings in credit and in asset markets and responding to perverse real interest rate movements.

The euro area and global financial crises demonstrated that financial stability cannot be assured only by the efficient operation of private financial markets. More intrusive financial supervision is needed. In addition, both crises spotlighted a conundrum for monetary policy; it was too blunt a tool to cope with sectoral — real estate — booms when inflation was well contained. Higher policy interest rates dampen activity in the entire economy and not just the housing sector. Within the euro area, the common monetary policy has similar limits; ECB policy interest rates were too low for some national economies — Ireland and Spain, for example — that were experiencing rapid economic expansion — real estate booms. Raising area-wide policy interest rates to slow activity in these booming economies would dampen unnecessarily activity in the entire euro area. The common — 'one size' — monetary policy therefore did not fit all economies equally well.

In principle, national fiscal policy was available to address country-specific cycles that were not in sync with the euro-area average. But this proved to be too challenging. Why?

- Economic expansions yielded sizable fiscal revenues which created political pressure to increase spending; this pressure was redoubled in cases where lower interest rates on sovereign debt created room to expand non-interest public expenditures.
- Economists underestimated the temporary component of fiscal revenues, making the structural budget appears stronger than it really was. This undermined the economic rationale for strengthening the fiscal position.
- Real-time statistical estimates of potential output — an unobserved variable — tend to be correlated with the business cycle — rising during a boom and falling during the bust. Thus, spare capacity can appear larger during the boom, imparting an unintended procyclical bias to fiscal policy.
- Moreover, consensus did not exist that for employing actively fiscal policy to mitigate swings in competitiveness and current account balances.

Overall, national fiscal policies failed to dampen the upswing sufficiently and, therefore, the subsequent bust was larger. So how can national economies within the euro area cope better with booms and thus mitigate the busts, assuring more securely future financial stability?

An initial answer begins by rethinking the measurement of the underlying fiscal position. Measurement of the fiscal stance needs to incorporate full information about the cyclical position and the durability of budget revenues. While harmonized statistical techniques provide a useful cross-country analytical benchmark, such techniques do not adequately utilize country-specific information, potentially mis-measuring the fiscal stance.

EC analysis of Spain, published before the crisis broke, illustrates that a careful country-level review can correctly identify measure countries' underlying fiscal position during booms; these EC analysts rightly assessed

Spain's structural fiscal deficit, while standard techniques — used by the EC for official purposes — produced higher fiscal revenues, owing to the asset price boom. In particular, standard techniques were estimated to have overestimated structural revenues in 2006 by 2¼–3.0 percentage points of GDP (Martinez-Mongay, Maza-Lasierra, and Igal 2007). Recent International Monetary Fund (IMF) estimates of Spain's structural fiscal position in 2006 were downgraded by 3.0 percentage points of GDP compared with earlier IMF estimates and now correspond with the Martinez-Mongay results. (Contemporaneous mis-estimation of the underlying fiscal position in Ireland — 6.7 percentage points of GDP — was even greater than in Spain!)

Even if the underlying fiscal stance had been properly measured, the focus of national fiscal policy under the SGP was, and still is, on fiscal sustainability and not on national competitiveness or private sector imbalances. Thus, national fiscal policies were not, and have not been, assigned the task of moderating swings in competitiveness and private imbalances. Indeed, the changes to the SGP/EDP — the two and six packs — have made those procedures more technically complicated and thereby less understandable to the general public, risking their support. Indeed, those SGP/EDP changes did not alter the fiscal sustainability orientation, but gave the Commission more power to influence national fiscal policies toward meeting the needs of the euro area as a whole. Fiscal deficit policy, however, can be, like monetary policy, too blunt at tool to deal with asset/sector booms, while tax and spending policies, which are more precise, are often too political to be implemented in a timely and sufficient manner.

Macroprudential policies conducted at the national level can complement national fiscal policies or, if need be, substitute for inactive national fiscal policies. This concept has been termed 'intellectually radical and potentially transformative' (Baker 2013), although owing to countervailing political and practical challenges, he expected a gradual transformation. Therefore, it is useful first to describe these policies, and how they are different from microprudential supervision.

- Macroprudential policy aims to promote 'financial stability' at the systemic level. This contrasts with the focus of microprudential supervision, which is on the financial health of individual financial institutions. Macroprudential policy takes a top-down perspective, while microprudential policy has a bottom-up perspective. These tools can be structural — working across business cycles — or time varying — working during the business cycle. Time-varying macroprudential tools are our chief interest.
- Macroprudential tools are varied, overlapping at times with microprudential tools. Counter-cyclical capital buffers (CCCB), loan-to-value ratios (LTV), debt-to-income ratios (DTI), and capital flow measures (CFM) are examples of macroprudential tools; the first three tools are also in the hands of microprudential supervisors. One instrument with two hands on the lever creates a coordination issue.

- How do macroprudential tools operate? Essentially, they make it more expensive to borrow, reduce the availability of credit, and/or build up buffers to protect against losses. LTV and DTI ratios can target segments of the economy, such as housing. Raising these ratios makes it harder to qualify for loans, reducing spending pressures in the targeted sector. On the other hand, capital buffers and CFMs can act to limit national credit expansions; particularly those fuelled by foreign inflows in the case of CFMs.
- The effectiveness/calibration of various macroprudential tools has received considerable recent attention (e.g., from the BIS, FSB, IMF, and central banks). Empirical evidence suggests that macroprudential instruments can effectively address systemic risk if employed appropriately, timely, and properly targeted. For example, for countercyclical macroprudential measures, quantity-based measures (e.g., LTV) seem to be more effective than price-based measures (e.g., risk weights) in dampening housing price booms. These measures also take time (2–3 years) for their full impact to be realized. Evidence also suggests that macroprudential tools may be more effective when implemented jointly rather than individually. Macroprudential measures can have little, or no, 'bite' on nonbank flows.
- CFMs can be deployed to cope with surges and sudden stops that can threaten both macroeconomic and financial stability. Their use, however, has its own separate and controversial history. Recently, the IMF has taken a new 'institutional view' finding in certain circumstances that CFMs can be useful and appropriate to support macroeconomic policy adjustment, particularly to cope with inflow surges. Such measures can also be imposed after a crisis breaks to help the adjustment process as has happened in Iceland and Cyprus. However, introducing CFMs can risk triggering a rush to the exit, exacerbating outflows rather than controlling them. Official actions that fragment the currency union may be necessary, however, in order to preempt fragmentation caused by the private sector. Macroprudential measures to dampen financial cycles within a monetary union should be seen in the same light: they bear resemblance to CFMs, but their intent is to prevent market-driven fragmentation of the single financial market and not to undermine the single financial market.
- Political obstacles may emerge to the use of some macroprudential tools because of their distributional consequences, or quasi-taxation properties. These obstacles, uncertainties in identifying emerging vulnerabilities, and calibration concerns are among the reasons for 'inaction bias'. Finally, macroprudential tools impose costs on the economy via the financial sector that must be evaluated against their benefits

Time-varying macroprudential measures can do a degree substitute for a national monetary policy within a currency union. Such macroprudential policy can make monetary conditions at the national level better suited to a member's economic circumstances, while structural macroprudential policies can remain targeted on financial stability. Thus, a 'one-size-fits-all' interest rate policy can be tailored using macroprudential tools, to fit the needs of an individual economy within that currency union (Brzoza-Brzezina, Kolasa, and Makarski 2013; Quint and Rabanal 2013). But national macroprudential policy is a poor substitute for national interest rate policy, owing to leakages associated with an open financial system. These leakages can be plugged by national CFMs and by internationally coordinated macroprudential measures. While recognizing the advantages of more tailored national monetary conditions, the ECB has rightly pointed to possible abuses and risks (Dombret 2014).

In sum, dealing with country-specific booms and downswings entails recourse not just to national fiscal policies but also to national macroprudential policies; these latter policies may prove ineffective without cross-country coordination. The ECB, as the Single Supervisor, and the ESRB, as the EU-wide macroprudential agency, can contribute importantly to euro area and EU coordination efforts. The next section examines in greater depth these coordination issues, especially in a EU/euro context.

Coordination of Macroprudential Polices

The effective conduct of macroprudential polices requires cross-border coordination. Why is this? Financial institutions, including their branches, are supervised on a consolidated basis by their home supervisor. Host countries supervise their domestic financial institutions, which includes subsidiaries of foreign financial institutions. Thus, macroprudential tools applied by a host country would not apply to branches located in the host country. Moreover, corporations and even households could borrow directly from financial institutions domiciled abroad. The latter is especially true within a currency union (a fuller treatment can be found in Kincaid and Watson 2013).

The Basel Committee on Banking Supervision (BCBS) has recognized this coordination issue in the context of the international use of CCCBs. Specifically, their guidance to national supervisors (see BCBS 2010) established the principle of 'jurisdictional reciprocity'. Under this principle, foreign supervisors apply to their banks that lend to the host country additional capital buffers posed by the host supervisor on their banks. All banks would thus operate on a level playing field when lending to entities in the host country. Unfortunately, this reciprocity principle only applies to CCCBs and not to the entire range of macroprudential tools.

These BCBS principles also apply to members within a currency union unless bank supervision is conducted at the supranational level. In November 2014, the ECB became the Single Supervisor for the euro area, harmonizing supervisory standards, and promoting their consistent application.[1] The ECB cooperates with other EU financial regulatory bodies, notably the European Banking Authority, and the ESRB. It directly supervises 120 significant credit institutions, holding about 85 percent of the banking assets within the euro area, while the national competent authorities (NCAs), which are not in all cases the national central bank, supervise all other credit institutions. The NCAs together with the ECB form the SSM. By narrowing the scope for regulatory arbitrage and national enforcement bias, the SSM can significantly enhance the effectiveness and even-handedness of banking supervision. But the new SSM is largely staff by former national supervisors who may bring their national bias with them. The SSM also must utilize accounting and audit regulations and practices that are still national competencies. Finally, the unwinding of the home country bias in bank portfolios will likely be subject to both technical and political challenges.

Macroprudential tools within the SSM are shared between the ECB and NCAs. Capital and liquidity buffers are determined by the ECB and apply to all banks governed by SSM regulations. NCAs can impose, following a notification period, stricter national prudential requirements to address national systemic risks. On the other hand, the ECB may, if it deems necessary and after a notification period, apply higher capital buffers than established by NCAs, in order to address national systemic risks. The reciprocity principle pertaining to CCCBs would allow the ECB as the euro-area supervisor to request that supervisors of non-euro EU banks with exposure to the country apply the same CCCBs. A similar request could also be made to non-EU supervisors, such as those in Switzerland. However, the ECB does not have the mandate to require euro-area banks to implement macroprudential tools such as LTV, DTI, and leverage ratios. These macroprudential tools remain in the hands of the NCAs.

Banks face competition from capital markets and non-bank financial institutions. From a macroprudential perspective, this competition is a source of leakage, undermining the effectiveness of these tools. The ESRB monitors the entire EU financial system: it can issue warnings and recommendations to the relevant regulatory bodies should it deem that financial stability is at risk. It can therefore help national authorities to dampen financial market swings that may accompany the inter-country adjustment process under EMU. The ESRB intends to overcome possible inaction bias by employing 'guided discretion' — the use of judgment anchored firmly by a clear set of principles that are supported by indicators and thresholds. Conceptually, this guided discretion is similar to the BCBS approach for CCCBs.

Coordination issues between supranational and national authorities at the EU level are (unsurprisingly) similar to those at the euro level. Capital and liquidity buffers are determined at the supranational level. National authorities can impose stricter prudential buffers to address national systemic risks. The use of these measures is subject to prior notification if the measure is expected to have significant cross-border effects on other EU members or on the internal market. Advanced notification allows other EU members to express their opinions on the proposed measures.

EU members can also deploy macroprudential measures that are not covered by EU legislation (Capital Requirements Regulation and Directive — CRR/CRD IV); the most noteworthy are LTV, DTI, and leverage ratios. The ESRB must provide an opinion to the Council, EC, and the concerned member, regarding the proper use of macroprudential measures. This opinion would assess whether the measure is necessary, effective, and proportionate, or could be address by other instruments. The ESRB seeks to balance the financial stability needs of individual members against the adverse spillovers on other EU members and the potential negative impact on the internal market. Exact reciprocity is only possible if the other countries have the same instrument available, which may not always be the case. The ESRB may recommend reciprocal action on its own or following a request by the implementing member. Such a recommendation, as with all ESRB recommendations, is not legally binding; instead, a softer 'act or explain' mechanism applies to ESRB recommendations.

The ESRB has only limited initial experience with the national implementation of macroprudential policies within the EU. Reciprocal action was requested in only one case — by Estonia in 2014. EU members with large branches in Estonia were requested to reciprocate on a voluntary basis, applying a systemic risk buffer to all exposures and introduce a capital conservation buffer. Estonia has not as yet reported any experience.

The EU and euro area have developed impressive coordination structures for macroprudential policies. These structures are by necessity complex, owing to divisions between supranational and national responsibilities/competencies and between regulation of banks and nonbanks. Reciprocal action by other EU/euro members will in principle enhance the effectiveness of macroprudential policies. The degree of enhancement is uncertain, however, because several macroprudential tools need to be utilized jointly to achieve maximum effectiveness but these tools lie in different institutional hands (e.g., SSM, ESRB); institutional complexity may add to the well-known inaction bias. Size and impact asymmetries can make cross-border policy coordination more difficult. It remains to be seen whether the various governance arrangements (SSM, ESRB, EBA, etc.) will be sufficiently responsive to the policy requests from smaller members for assistance. For example, supervisors in large EU countries could come under pressure by their financial institutions not to apply the reciprocity principle because those institutions could fear losing market share to banks from non-participating EU countries and from banks outside the EU (remember that the excessive deficit procedure ran aground when it needed to be applied to France and Germany). Also, will the analysis and recommendations of the SSM and ESRB be sufficiently independent from those of the ECB to ensure proper coordination of euro-wide macroprudential and monetary policies? Finally, macroprudential policies may need to be deployed in conjunction with fiscal policies, adding to coordination burdens at the national and euro-wide levels.

New Warning Indicators and Procedures

As a crisis response, the MIP was created in late 2011 to identify emerging macroeconomic imbalances to remedy an omission in the euro economic governance. Private sector imbalances are now monitored via a set of (11) indicators and their thresholds. Excessive imbalances can be subjected to a corrective action plan (CAP) that should detail specific policy measures and set an implementation timetable. As regards content, the policy response should be tailored to the member's circumstances and should cover, as needed, fiscal and wage policies, labor markets, product and services markets and the financial sector. The MIP is a step in the right direction but additional steps are necessary.

MIP-indicators focus on both internal and external imbalances and their likely sources such as competitiveness and credit booms. Attention is thus directed on private sector imbalances, which were previously largely ignored by EU surveillance; government imbalances continue to receive attention under the SGP. MIP's thresholds, however, tend to be set asymmetrically; 9 of 11 thresholds only signal excessive deficits with no threshold for an emerging excessive surplus. Two thresholds — for the current account balance and changes in the real effective exchange rate — are designed to capture both types of imbalances, but their thresholds are set asymmetrically — tighter on the deficit side than on the surplus side. The EU defends this asymmetry on the (arguable) grounds that deficits are more problematic than surpluses. Corrective actions therefore likely fall on deficit countries, creating a possible deflationary bias within the euro area (*Bini-Smaghi* makes a similar point, focusing more on euro adjustment programs and conditionality). Such a deflationary bias repeats the asymmetric adjustment mechanism — with its deflationary bias — witnessed at the global level.[2]

The MIP has a backward monitoring orientation because its 11 indicators utilize data that are mainly a year old. It cannot therefore identify turning points, or cotemporaneous crossing of MIP thresholds. Meanwhile, recommended policy actions are implemented only in the coming year at the earliest and their main impact would be felt only even later. An adverse feedback loop could result from the combination of backward-identified macroeconomic imbalances and forward-leaning policy actions. Employing current-year estimates and developing agreed forecasts could rectify these problems.

As regards the substance of the in-depth reviews and the associated country-specific recommendations, these are tilted heavily toward structural reforms pertaining to labor and product markets. Fiscal policy is viewed narrowly through the SGP lens, while monetary policy is basically ignored. The focus on structural reforms is problematic because the impact of structural reforms on macroeconomic imbalances is typically harder to calibrate and takes longer to materialize than the annual MIP horizon. In addition, some national authorities have questioned the specificity of recommended structural reforms, arguing that the Commission is intruding too deeply into domestic affairs and is exceeding its mandate; the Council has made on occasion Commission recommendations less prescriptive and less precise.

Turning to fiscal and monetary policies, the EC has a rules-based approach to fiscal policy that ignores monetary policy or monetary conditions. The adequacy of fiscal policy is assessed against SGP metrics and the convergence programs under the Excessive Deficit Procedures, if relevant. In the EC's reports, no direct link is made between fiscal policy and correcting macroeconomic imbalances or managing aggregate demand, or the implications for real growth and imbalances of the fiscal-monetary mix.[3] Differentiated monetary conditions are also not cited as an influence on the recommended national fiscal stance. Indeed, in-depth reviews for three non-euro countries (Hungary, Sweden, and United Kingdom) do not make any mention of monetary policy, or the policy mix, and make no country-specific recommendation related to their monetary policies.

Macroprudential policy must contend with the 'fuzzy' concept of financial stability, although financial instability is obvious to all. This fuzziness contrasts with inflation, which is measured and reported frequently. Thus, a key question is what should trigger macroprudential intervention? It has long been recognized that multiple influences cause systemic financial vulnerability, making multiple indicators relevant for financial stability assessments. This multiplicity makes development of a transparent operational target for financial stability — comparable with projected inflation, or the fiscal deficit or public debt ceiling — a major challenge. Several researchers have stressed therefore that financial crises are associated with peaks in the financial cycle, in the tradition of Hayek, von Mises, and Minsky. Financial cycles can be parsimoniously characterized by credit growth and property prices. Empirical analysis supports the view that credit growth matters, but financial crises are also strongly associated with other factors, such as stable exchange rates.

Use of credit indicators as a trigger received a boost when the BCBS provided guidance to national supervisors (BCBS 2010) for employing a common methodology to calculate an internationally consistent credit/GDP gap to implement CCCBs. The appropriate threshold can, however, vary from country to country and as the BCBS stresses, country authorities should utilize other variables and qualitative information to assess risks. This methodology could also guide the use of other macroprudential instruments. Indeed, the June 2014 Financial Stability Report by the Bank of England utilized many BSBS indicators to make the analytical case to introduce a LTV limit on mortgage lending. The macroprudential research network of European System of Central Banks has made significant strides in developing early warning indicators and formulating macroprudential models and tools.

In sum, considerable progress has been made in a short time period in developing useful operational indicators that can identify emerging financial vulnerabilities and macroeconomic imbalances, particularly in the private sector, within the euro area and more broadly within the EU. But clearly, these efforts need to be refined further. In particular, the MIP-indicators need to become more forward looking and grounded in statistical analysis to better understand their strengths and weaknesses. National fiscal and macroprudential policies must also be utilized more actively to redress emerging macrofinancial imbalances; this will require a different mindset by supranational and national authorities. In this vein, signals given by MIP-indicators and financial stability indicators need to be interpreted coherently by the EC and ECB/ESRB; this will require new supranational coordination efforts as well as heightened coordination with national authorities. Developing greater confidence in these indicators and warning systems could also help lessen 'inaction bias' — too little, too late — by all policy makers. Nonetheless, coordinated policy responses are at least equally crucial.

Conclusions

The euro crisis has validated pre-crisis concerns about perverse movements in national real interest rate and destabilizing swings in competitiveness, following country-specific economic shocks. Moreover, these destabilizing swings can be amplified by intra-euro-area capital flows, which were not foreseen. National fiscal policies actively counter such perverse and destabilizing forces but such a role requires a different mindset by supranational and national policy makers. In particular, while the SGP remains necessary, it is not sufficient, guidance for fiscal policy.

National time-varying macroprudential policy can also help dampen destabilizing swings in national financial markets. Such macroprudential actions are unlikely to be successful unless coordinated across countries and relevant authorities. A real test will occur when a NCA from a small country implements macroprudential policies to address its national imbalances and asks NCAs from large countries to take reciprocal actions that run counter to the business interests of their financial institutions. (The excessive deficit procedure proven ineffective when it came time to be applied to France and Germany.)

Stronger national policy responses to country-specific economic shocks within the euro area are complementary to an area-wide banking union with a well-funded common backstop. Reliance cannot be placed solely on the timeliness and adequacy of national fiscal and macroprudential measures, even when coordinated across borders, to prevent financial stress arising under EMU. The political economy of such pre-emptive actions can be problematic, and the traction of fiscal and macroprudential measures in such a context remains unproven.

More diversified risk sharing — e.g., less home country bias in asset holdings — by the euro banking system would help buffer national idiosyncratic shocks within the euro area; such buffering would be similar to the private risk sharing that takes place via financial markets in the United States. It remains to be seen whether the new SMM will unwind the previous national supervisory bias. A meaningful euro-area banking union would increase cross-border risk sharing by both the private and official sectors. In particular, a larger and more mutualized single resolution fund and deposit guarantee system is necessary. Such changes are indispensable complements to rethinking the conduct of national policies. However, the banking union as it has been presently constituted is incomplete.

The economic and governance reforms undertaken and underway will transform the euro architecture moving it from a loosely coordinated system predicated on the no-bail-out principle, to a more tightly coordinated system that recognizes more collective responsibility. This new framework is untested. Untested as yet by adverse market pressures and by the political economy forces that were the undoing of the excessive deficit procedure, for example. Moreover, this new framework still falls short of the fiscal union that some have long viewed as necessary to underpin a successful euro project. But voters support for an 'ever closer union' and the further transfer of sovereignty to Brussels is far from assured. Thus, while the currency union has been strengthened by recent actions, the project may remain incomplete and therefore vulnerable.

Disclosure statement

No potential conflict of interest was reported by the authors.

Notes

1. SSM is the first pillar in the new Banking Union. The Single Resolution Mechanism with the Single Resolution Fund constitutes a second pillar, while the Deposit Insurance Scheme is the third pillar.
2. In comparing macroeconomic surveillance by the EU and IMF, Moschella (2014) also finds fault with the MIP's asymmetric treatment and single-country, rather than systemic, focus, offering factors that may help explain the limited learning from IMF experience.
3. Fiscal policy is considered by the EC to be too cumbersome to utilize effectively for short-term demand management because of the need to involve national parliaments, which complicates coordination issues. Moreover, national (EU) fiscal multipliers are generally considered by the EC to be very small under normal circumstances.

References

Allsopp, C., and D. Vines. 2008. *Fiscal policy, inter-country adjustment, and the real exchange rate.* DG-ECFIN, Economic Papers No. 344.

Baker, A. 2013. The gradual transformation? The incremental dynamics of macroprudential regulation. *Regulation and Governance* 7: 417–34.

Basel Committee on Banking Supervision. 2010. *Guidance for national authorities operating the counter cyclical capital buffers.* Basel: Bank for International Settlements.

Brzoza-Brzezina, M., M. Kolasa, and K. Makarski. 2013. *Macroprudential policy instruments and economic imbalances in the euro area.* European Central Bank Working Paper No. 1589.

Dombret, A. 2014. The impact of macroprudential policy on financial integration. *Banque de France Financial Stability Review* 8, no. 1: 61–7.

European Commission. 2006. *Adjustment dynamics in the euro area: the European Commission annual economic report*, eds. Mary McCarthy and Maxwell Watson. Brussels: Directorate-General for Economic and Financial Affairs.

Kincaid, G.R., and M. Watson. 2013. *The implications of macroprudential policies for international policy coordination.* Discussion Draft for Programme on the Political Economy of Financial Markets, Oxford.

Martinez-Mongay, C., L.A. Maza-Lasierra, and J.Y. Igal. 2007. *Asset booms and tax receipts: the case of Spain, 1995–2006.* European Commission Occasional Paper 293.

Moschella, M. 2014. Monitoring macroeconomic imbalances: is EU surveillance more effective than IMF surveillance? *JCMS: Journal of Common Market Studies* 52, no. 6: 1273–89.

Posen, A., and N. Vernon. 2014. *Europe's half a banking union*, http://www.iie.com/publications/oepds/oped.cfm?ResearchID=2627.

Quint, D., and P. Rabanal. 2013. *Monetary and macroprudential policy in an estimated DSGE model of the euro area.* International Monetary Fund Working Paper 13/209.

Regling, K., and M. Watson. 2010. *A preliminary report on the sources of Ireland's banking crisis.* Dublin: Irish Government Publications Office.

Trichet, J.-C. 2015. Speech entitled *Ireland and euro area governance: past, present and future*, given at the Institute of International and European Affairs.

EMU and Sustainable Integration

IAIN BEGG*, ANNETTE BONGARDT*,**, KALYPSO NICOLAÏDIS*** & FRANCISCO TORRES*,**

*European Institute, London School of Economics and Political Science, London, UK;
**European Studies Centre, St. Antony's College, University of Oxford, Oxford, UK;
***Department of Politics and International Relations, University of Oxford, Oxford, UK

ABSTRACT This paper considers what will be required to make Economic and Monetary Union (EMU) sustainable following the successive crises of recent years. It starts by laying out the policy benchmark, namely the successive 'President Reports' produced by EU institutions. It then suggests three dimensions of sustainable integration relevant to EMU, namely the pursuit of sustainable growth, the need to take into account what we call 'varieties of modernisation' and the 'ownership' of democratically sustainable reforms. It then evaluates the recasting of EMU governance against the benchmark of sustainable integration.

1. Introduction

Managing the crises affecting Europe's Economic and Monetary Union (EMU) has been top of the policy agenda for the last five years. EU member states have managed the fallout of the crisis and implemented reforms in emergency mode while at the same time laying the foundations for a more resilient system. Opinions differ on the effectiveness of these reforms in addressing short-term challenges, but, the increasingly urgent question is whether they offer a lasting solution to the well-known shortcomings of the single currency.

Here, we argue that EMU reform must result in a more effective form of integration, capable of assessing and reconciling short-term actions against long-term goals (Nicolaïdis 2010). This is very simply a new governing idea of integration calling for the reconfiguration of the integration process away from the old remedies of 'deeper and faster'. Instead, EU actors should embed in institutions and procedures a systemic commitment to *sustainable* integration, defined as something that is durable, resilient and politically acceptable. Such an approach entails both an ethos and practice, a state of mind and benchmarks for decisions by all actors involved in economic and policy action in the EU. It also means changing the way change occurs in the EU and recognizing that intergovernmental bargains need to be sustained by inter-societal and inter-generational bargains.

Such an attitude chimes with principles underpinning the internet revolution, with its emphasis on empowerment, resilience, robustness and adaptive learning. Concretely, the EU should foster a sustainable integration culture and take more account of long-term objectives in managing current problems, thereby creating the preconditions for later action. Sustainable integration is not about policy blueprints but about the negotiation of guidelines for action, linking multiple agenda and actors around a set of shared long-term goals.

To make EMU sustainable, the first imperative is to acknowledge that it had been left incomplete at Maastricht due to divergent Member State preferences (Torres 2009). Expectations that these preferences would converge over time across all member states have been dashed and the consequences exposed by the euro crisis. Before 2008, there was little felt urgency to address the known frailties in EMU's governance construct (see Giavazzi and Wyplosz, 2015), yet as the crisis unfolded EMU's very existence was threatened. Major advances in economic governance were subsequently adopted, mainly driven by the short-term imperatives of system survival. The question now is whether they also put EMU on the path to a long-term sustainable future, defined in terms not just of the basics of monetary economics, but also of the viability of the underlying economic model and public support.

EMU was set up as a political project in the knowledge that the EU was not an optimum currency area. Nevertheless, monetary union was achieved rapidly, with the smooth launch of the euro and the transition to the European Central Bank (ECB) for the conduct of monetary policy. By contrast, the economic union side — the 'E' in EMU, including provisions for coordination of budgetary and structural policies — was left incomplete. As a result, the many interdependencies between member states of a currency union and higher coordination needs were neglected, while the tentative attempts to enhance coordination processes for economic reform (i.e. the Lisbon Strategy) did little to curb the large negative spillovers from the unfinished economic into the monetary sphere.[1] Subsequent efforts to complete the economic union part of EMU have gone some way to strengthen EMU's resilience in the face of market pressures. However, institutional innovation was conditioned by the needs and constraints of the moment: sometimes within and sometimes outside the Community framework; sometimes through variations on intergovernmental cooperation, sometimes by reverting the Community method; sometimes restricted to the Euro area level, sometimes extending to the EU as a whole. The result has been the creation of new institutions and mechanisms, at an extraordinary pace but not necessarily always with a view to long-term sustainability.

This article goes beyond the proposals to counter the crisis by completing EMU through 'a coherent governance architecture' or a 'Genuine' EMU. The latter was adopted in various versions of the Presidents' Reports (European Commission 2012; Van Rompuy 2012; Juncker *et al.* 2015a, 2015b). Its building blocks are an integrated financial framework (mostly a banking union), an integrated budgetary framework (implicitly fiscal union), an integrated economic policy framework (economic union) and enhanced democratic legitimacy and accountability of EMU governance (closer political union).

Although some of the reform proposals under these headings can be criticized for going further than is needed, many are undeniably necessary and some are quite bold, but they will arguably not be sufficient to render EMU sustainable over the long term. In particular, despite the institutional resilience on display, they have largely failed to mobilize support from governments and citizens for sustainable European integration. The challenge now is to promote growth in a form compatible with fiscal consolidation and reduced indebtedness while at the same time ensuring long-term sustainability.

In the end, restoring public support for EMU will depend on the delivery of common goals that serve the broader purpose of sustainable integration. The ECB (2015) recognizes that public support for the EU, especially in its EMU incarnation, will rest on the prospects for sustainable growth as the sine qua non for the smooth functioning of EMU. For that to happen, the development of the integrated economic policy framework building block will have to be embedded in a sustainable growth strategy, which pursues structural reform in a logic of modernization of national economies with ownership of reforms at the national level.

The next section examines the concept of sustainable integration more closely, focusing on sustainable growth, approaches to modernizing national economies and the issue of ownership of reforms. Section 3 evaluates the progress made to date and the reform initiatives needed to render it sustainable. Section 4 analyses EMU governance in the light of sustainable integration, with reference to the above discussed properties. Section 5 concludes.

2. The Mainstream: EMU Reform and the Presidents' Reports

The smooth functioning of a currency union, as compared to a less ambitious economic union, makes additional demands on labour, product and financial markets to become more flexible as a means of adjusting to shocks, given that monetary policy is no longer available for this purpose and fiscal policy has to be constrained. Coordination of national policies is, however, vital to prevent damaging spillovers from actions in one member state to others, weakening the overall coherence of the union's economic policy.

Efforts to create a 'genuine EMU' (see also Mongelli *et al.*, 2015), have only led to limited progress in creating what the Four Presidents' report (Van Rompuy 2012) calls an 'integrated economic policy framework'.

Dealing with the legacy costs of the crisis, restoring growth and reducing imbalances, although essential, is not enough. Underlying competitiveness problems also need to be addressed, but moving the Euro area closer to an optimal, or at least sustainable, currency area requires reforms in areas where competencies have remained at the member state level.

The various Presidents' reports on EMU governance provide orientations for a policy framework that would not only correct many of the known flaws in EMU, but also anticipate future problems. Actions in four areas were set out, with a distinction made between short- and long-term ambitions, providing for:

- An integrated financial framework to ensure a financially stable system; a common interpretation of this pillar is banking union, and a key objective is to break the so-called doom-loop (Gaspar, 2015) in which problems for banks become problems for national public finances and *vice versa*.
- An integrated budgetary framework with the dual aim of assuring fiscal discipline and developing new, common fiscal policy instruments, measures which would steer the Eurozone in the direction of fiscal union, albeit one which falls well short of the extensive cross-regional fiscal flows found in most other monetary unions.
- An integrated economic policy framework able to reconcile growth, employment and competitiveness with the sustainability of EMU, while avoiding negative spillovers across national borders.
- Enhancement of democratic legitimation and channels of accountability which is justified particularly by the loss of national autonomy in budgetary and other economic matters of greater top-down constraints on national autonomy in economic decision-making.

Proposals for developing each of these building blocks were presented in a 'blueprint' by the European Commission (2012), but progress has been mixed, with only banking union having been substantially advanced. Fiscal union has made scant progress since 2011 and there is, as yet, no strong sense of what will be done to improve legitimation, not least in relation to the enhanced powers of oversight conferred on the EU institutions (Schmidt 2013). The spread of political protests and institutional conflicts, both within and between Member States, highlights the challenges because the economic governance model is one based increasingly on executive rather than representative power.

In paving the way for further reforms, Juncker *et al.* (2015a) pose a series of questions about the future governance framework and, implicitly, the reform initiatives needed to render EMU sustainable. These questions fall into three main categories. The first can be summarized as asking whether the current rules and institutions are robust enough to prevent a recurrence of problems, and whether the mechanisms in place will ensure sufficient resilience against future shocks, including through structural reforms. A second theme is whether risk pooling, both through private and public interventions, can be enhanced and can forestall further episodes of financial instability. Third, the paper returns to one of the original four themes: the accountability and legitimacy of governance. Although many proposed solutions had been canvassed in the 2012 contributions, that they are still unresolved testifies to the difficulties of completing EMU's governance framework.

The follow-ups of the *Four Presidents' report* (Juncker *et al.* 2015a, 2015b) advocate the need for an immediate strengthened commitment to growth-enhancing structural reforms so as to create a virtuous triangle of structural reforms, investment and fiscal responsibility, and a deepened single market to improve adjustment capacity. While these are worthy aims, they fall short of defining an economic development model that can guide the long-term sustainability of EMU. While we do not pretend to provide such a model, we aim to suggest the principles that might sustain it under the broad heading of sustainable integration.

3. A Vision for EMU: The Three Pillars of Sustainable Integration

We believe that the notion of sustainable integration offers a more comprehensive perspective on what is needed. We suggest that in the field of EMU, it rests on three main pillars, namely the pursuit of sustainable growth, reform strategies adapted to the modernization paths of national economies and national ownership of reforms. Each of these pillars of sustainable integration, in turn, requires new approaches to overcome the shortcomings exposed by the crises.

3.1. Sustainable Growth

Sustainable growth is central to the EU's economic narrative and is enshrined in the treaties as a fundamental objective. Though most often connected with environmental objectives, sustainable growth in the EU lexicon encompasses social and economic dimensions, as set out, notably, in the Europe 2020 Strategy (Bongardt and Torres 2013). It can provide both a crisis exit strategy and a renewed long-term agenda for EU sustainable integration, and requires long-term commitments and necessary public investments (Lenschow 2010; Sachs 2012).

A sustainable polity is one that endures through time and changes in circumstances, including shocks. The EU is future friendly, which is, somewhat paradoxically, the silver lining of its so-called democratic deficit or lesser direct accountability since institutions are less susceptible to short-term electoral concerns and pressures than its Member States (Nicolaïdis 2010).

In this spirit, a durable economic recovery from the crisis starts with action today (ECB 2015). However, economic growth will be neither politically nor economically sustainable unless environmental damage, excessive resource depletion and long-term, inter-generational effects are internalized, while engendering greater resilience to natural hazards (Hallegatte *et al.* 2011). Combatting climate change by accelerating de-carbonization can, through well-designed policies, have positive growth effects in the short and long run — see for instance Fay *et al.* (2015), Nordhaus (2006), Spence (2014), Stern (2006, 2015). A call for 'whatever kind of growth' risks ignoring the economic case for environmentally and socially sustainable solutions.

Critically, the environment sector has managed to create employment since the outbreak of the crisis in 2009, notwithstanding the fact that in the approach towards sustainable growth, soft coordination has so far failed to realize the innovation, competitiveness and growth potential that it promises (EEA 2015).[2] A more systematic look at the transmission mechanism between the completion of the single market and Europe 2020 strategy is warranted (European Commission 2010).

Progress towards sustainable growth therefore hinges on decision-making for the long term and on an economy capable of flexible adjustment with an innovation-friendly business environment, given that it involves both structural change within the economy and in society and a long-term-oriented governance system (Pearce and Turner 1990, 24; Randers 2012). Policies and instruments that are consistent with long-term objectives need to provide the right incentives while minimizing possible short-term trade-offs between environmental protection and growth. However, the governance of sustainable growth relevant areas is piecemeal and methods and enforcement possibilities vary significantly and relies on soft coordination processes (typically, characterized by sweeping ambitions, but a dearth of disciplining tools). These included the Lisbon (2000–2010) and Sustainable Development strategies (2001, revised in 2006), before coming together in the Europe 2020 (2011–2020) strategy. Diverse governance methods are not intrinsically a problem, but the EU still lacks a coherent strategy for sustainable growth. As a result, and although the EU environmental sector expanded and created employment since 2008 in the midst of the crisis, its full potential remains to be exploited (EEA 2015).

3.2. *Varieties of Modernization*

Although monetary union enjoyed a benign first decade, the slow pace of national reforms in some member states and the incapacity of financial markets to distinguish between Eurozone sovereigns contributed to growing intra-EMU macroeconomic imbalances. EMU's governance institutions were unable to encompass increasing policy interdependence, let alone capable of dealing with the effects of the crises. Monetary union brought about a qualitative change in the economic context, resulting, on the economic side, in unsustainable tensions.

Different EU states have followed different paths to modernization in terms of their socio-economic make-up, the attributes of their states, their state-society relations, their social and institutional traditions as well as the distribution of costs and benefits and the obstacles stemming from modernization dynamics. These varieties in turn determine the fit between the requirements of EMU and the country or countries in question.

Since the publication of the 1993 'Delors' white paper on growth competitiveness and employment, the EU has launched a series of initiatives intended to bolster structural reforms within its member states. Their common objective has been to strengthen the EU's and individual countries' competitiveness in a world characterized by new realities and challenges, such as globalization, the information society, demographic ageing, climate change or enlargement. For example, the Lisbon Strategy highlighted the imperative of advancing the EU as a knowledge economy in tandem with building a socially more cohesive society. Despite having wide-ranging goals, the strategy lacked a specific EMU dimension and thus did not take enough account of how different progress on structural change affected other euro area members. Although the Europe 2020 strategy sought to be more comprehensive, it has faded from view during the crisis years and has been supplanted by the much more short-term semester process.

A possible explanation is that the instruments for policy coordination were not always differentiated enough to take into account the varieties of modernization faced across member states. On the fiscal side, the Stability and Growth Pact (SGP) was flouted (most notoriously, by France and Germany in 2002/2003), without a reckoning as to what its limitations were and how to accommodate the evident need for flexibility in the governance design itself. The resort to the open method of coordination (OMC) to engineer domestic reform had very differentiated success across states, suggesting that relying on tools such as benchmarking or best practice was insufficiently reinforced by public and peer pressure (Bongardt and Torres 2012). Analysts can disagree as to whether the culprit was the absence of binding and/or enforceable rules (in the Lisbon Strategy and in the SGP), only limited financial market pressure or, alternatively, the insufficient attention to the need for domestic institutions and habitus that would internalize externalities (Nicolaïdis and Watson 2015). What is clear however is that EMU was ill adapted to the kind of social, political and economic heterogeneity prevalent among Eurozone countries.

The sovereign debt crisis highlighted the large negative spillovers from economic divergences and the urgency of more systematic reform affecting policy domains with divisive political and distributional effects, in and between member states. The Euro Plus Pact (2011) subsequently introduced an EMU dimension to economic reforms, but had little impact due to its weak (intergovernmental, non-binding) method. Similarly, a Compact for Growth and Jobs was established in 2012, but has had few visible effects. Proposals to incentivize reforms in member states through contracts were abandoned when nearly all member states rejected them at the December 2013 European Council.

A new impetus has been given to reforms and their relevance has grown in a context where fiscal policy is also constrained due to the need for an enduring correction of budgetary imbalances (Bini-Smaghi, 2015). Taxation instruments –including environment related– can once again supplement tighter regulation as European countries slowly exit from crisis management. There has been an acceleration of structural reforms in laggard countries as a result of market and peer pressure and of formal and informal conditionality (Schmieding and Schulz 2014; OECD 2015). Yet, enforcing conditionality while at the same completing EMU's governance framework is a perilous exercise for political legitimacy (Nicolaïdis and Watson 2015).

3.3. Democratically Sustainable Reforms

The crisis has highlighted the need for citizens' political ownership of both reforms undertaken in their own countries and of the European integration project as a whole, in response to questions such as 'why (more) Europe?' or 'sacrifices in the name of what?' To the extent that institutional limits to integration come to constrain the capacity to resolve European common concerns, without a democratization of reforms, the long-term political sustainability of the European project is in doubt.

The choice of the OMC ostensibly reflected a perceived need for ownership of reforms (as a process of slow-moving and bottom-up convergence of preferences on institutions) and the notion of convergence as a gradual learning process. The approach was intended to foster reforms tailored to member states' heterogeneous situations and preferences, yet the EMU process largely failed to foster true ownership of reforms in line with the member states' own modernization goals. The fact that member states' political systems (governments, oppositions and even social partners) may have agreed to EMU-sustaining reforms in the 1990s and committed to them under the Lisbon Strategy (2000–2010) during EMU's first decade did not prevent many of them — to differing degrees — from backsliding and thus putting at risk their respective welfare states and the quality of life.

In the process, the question of the collective acceptance of EMU's redistributive implications has become more politicized.[3] This is in part due to the increased resort to executive decisions in economic governance, leading to significant divergences and political conflicts, both among and within Member States, as well as between them and supranational EU institutions, which have tended to be bypassed by intergovernmental or even bilateral bargaining. Many old conflicts about the ideal configuration of EMU, including within the European System of Central Banks and the ECB, have resurfaced. Clearly, EMU reforms cannot be sustainable if what they impose on individual member states is not democratically sustainable, both in terms of the electorate and in terms of the political leadership. Formerly vague references to European rules in national political debates have become more explicit constraints, better understood by citizens, thereby reducing the opacity of domestic political and policy processes and potentially raising policy effectiveness. But the visibility of constraints also leads to their contestation when they are perceived as sacrificing domestic democracy and autonomy (Rodrik 2011). Ideally, 'fiscal disciplines' enforced from Brussels will be progressively replaced by political 'commitments' in line with shared rules and expectations — admittedly, a tall order.

4. Progress and Pitfalls: Towards a Sustainable EMU?

The flaws in EMU's governance framework exposed by the sovereign debt crisis have been examined in a growing number of critical papers which exhibit a fair degree of consensus on the broad directions for reforms needed to render EMU sustainable (see for example: De Grauwe 2013; Eichengreen 2014, De Grauwe and Ji 2015, Giavazzi and Wyplosz, 2015; Juncker et al. 2015a). In parallel, rapid (by EU standards) agreement since

2010 on a range of measures to strengthen fiscal discipline and economic coordination has dealt with some of the acknowledged shortcomings. These responses, together with the creation of the European Stability Mechanism (ESM) as a permanent rescue fund, new arrangements for financial regulation and supervision and better tools for macro-prudential supervision, arguably reduce the risk of future crises and strengthen the capacity for crisis management. But how do these measures fare against the three pillars of sustainable integration for EMU suggested above?

First and most broadly, greater macroeconomic stability calls for the recasting of EMU governance and its embedding within a broader set of instruments meant to promote sustainable growth. Efforts to promote growth and jobs through the Europe 2020 strategy and the Compact for Growth and Jobs have had little obvious impact, while it remains to be seen how successful the Juncker Commission's flagship idea of a new European Fund for Strategic Investment (EFSI), with its headline target of 315 billion of new investment, will be (see Claeys 2015, for a sceptical view). Second, by disallowing either Euro-exit or a credible threat of default, and in the absence of a common fiscal stance, the functioning of EMU neglects the possible divergences resulting from distinctive national pathways to and progress on modernization.

Nor does the Five Presidents' report of June 2015 inspire confidence that what is in the pipeline will be sufficiently transformative to address these pitfalls. Although the report calls for a new 'fiscal stabilisation function', it has apparently jettisoned the idea of a euro area budget for stabilization purposes. Since 2012, little progress has been made on risk pooling as a form of fiscal union. Unsurprisingly, creditor countries resist calls for jointly and severally guaranteed Eurobonds; indeed, the very term Eurobond has become unmentionable in some Member States (Matthijs and McNamara 2015). There is still no easy means of arriving at an aggregate Eurozone-wide fiscal stance, despite extensive debate on the matter, which precludes agreeing an appropriate macroeconomic policy mix as a facet of economic sustainability. As various contributors to this issue also argued, it is necessary to tackle both the current need to stimulate domestic demand in surplus countries and the implementation of structural reforms to reduce built-up disequilibria in deficit countries. The link between fiscal policy and structural reforms is not irrelevant as the former is constrained by the need to ensure a proper adjustment of the budgetary imbalance and the latter can increase the credibility of the adjustment programme and thereby achieve a more gradual fiscal adjustment (Bini-Smaghi 2015).

Moreover, perhaps for reasons of institutional and constitutional propriety, the report fails to encompass developments in the governance of monetary policy, such as the de facto recognition that the ECB has to be a lender of last resort or intervene in sovereign bond market in ways that have fiscal policy impacts potentially affecting growth prospects by lowering debt servicing costs (De Grauwe and Ji 2015). While the establishment of the ESM fills a gap in emergency funding for Member States in (temporary) difficulty, it is less clear that there is adequate provision for the sort of comprehensive crisis management of an adjustment programme provided by the IMF.

More positively, banking union is the area that has made the most progress, and which can support all three of the pillars of sustainable integration. But common deposit insurance rapidly fell off the agenda (then restored by the Five Presidents), while the provisions on a single resolution mechanism may be too limited to break the 'doom-loop' between banks and sovereigns soon. It will take a decade for the new resolution fund to reach its intended level, so that a new 'bridging' facility advocated by the Five Presidents will be a useful reinforcement of banking union. Proposals for a capital markets union are ambitious (Véron 2014), but financial market fragmentation and difficult credit conditions, which are deterring recovery and growth prospects, are not adequately addressed as long run challenges. Some imbalances other than of public finances cannot easily be curbed. The macroeconomic imbalances procedure is, in principle, a means of doing so, but appears to be unable to deal with excessive external surpluses (Bini Smaghi 2015; De Grauwe and Ji 2015). The resulting asymmetry between deficit and surplus countries further deepens the challenge of political ownership of reform.

Although more extensive mechanisms for imposing discipline on member states have been introduced, potentially improving the economic sustainability of EMU, the strategic and political dimensions of sustainable integration are still in doubt. More broadly, while there has been a heated debate around austerity (Blyth 2012; Bini Smaghi 2013) and whether a disciplining approach is misguided (Nicolaïdis and Watson 2015), too little attention has been paid to the longer run determinants of growth and its quality (sustainable growth) or the appropriateness of EU approaches.

While the Presidents are persuasive in their reports in arguing that excessive debts constrain growth, EMU sustainability cannot be restricted to budget responsibility but requires more, particularly through sustainable growth. The question then is how to promote sustainable growth given budgetary constraints and a one-fits-all monetary policy. A fiscal stimulus is a crude instrument that does not necessarily result in 'quality' growth, unless it deals with the causes of competitiveness problems. Incentives for growth can be provided not only through the level, but also (perhaps more importantly) the composition of expenditure and incentives on the revenue side, notably taxation (Giavazzi and Wyplosz 2015). Monetary policy can dampen cyclical shocks but cannot solve structural problems. Structural reforms are therefore important not only for EMU resilience but also for higher potential growth (Draghi 2015) and hence for dealing with the legacy costs of the crisis, so that for EMU to be a sustainable form of integration, new approaches to coordination will be needed. This is recognized in general terms in the Five Presidents' report, but its prescriptions are disappointingly tame.

The dilemma is that growth-enhancing structural reforms are slow to act, even if they are desirable in the long run (IMF 2015),and often impose immediate budgetary costs, while causing frictions with a high political cost when they collide with entrenched interest groups or affect vulnerable social groups. Hence, sequencing matters in assessing the political sustainability of structural reforms: those that are growth enhancing in the short run should be prioritized, and private investment encouraged in ways compatible with fiscal constraints and incentives (Pisani-Ferry 2014). However, if we are to tinker with fiscal instruments we should create the right incentives for long-term stability at the same time. The use of fiscal instruments opens up the perspective of promoting sustainable growth by shifting taxation onto inefficiencies (pollution), and away from taxing productive factors (labour). This requires in turn enough coordination among states to forestall a race to the bottom on corporate taxation, which in the last 20 years has hollowed out the tax base across European states (Piketty 2014). Also, subsidies like the ones on coal and other fossil fuels should be abolished as they encourage their use, which is in conflict with trying to curb CO2 emissions besides increasing budgetary expenditures and distorting incentives and competition (IEA 2014). Moreover, astute regulation can foster private green investments without incurring fiscal expenditure and provide a push for EU green innovation and cost-efficiency. The circular economy package – an approach to resource use that builds-in recovery, recycling and regeneration as fundamental components of economic management – is a case in point where demanding EU regulation can promote innovation and cost efficiency and hence growth and employment creation rather than red tape (EEA 2015). Unfortunately, it seems that the new Commission has scrapped this package at least for the time being. Similarly, the EFSI's results (and impact on EMU's sustainability) will depend on whether the projects are chosen for their contribution to long-term sustainable growth.

As the integrated economic coordination framework has barely advanced, the Five Presidents' report (Juncker *et al.* 2015b) proposes to underpin national reform efforts via competitiveness authorities at the national level and, in a second phase, through a legal base for commitments. While these could help, the Europe 2020 Strategy (not mentioned in the report) ought also to be revived, especially in view of its prescription for long-term competitiveness alongside long-term environmental and social concerns. But much will depend, as so often, on the approach adopted to competitiveness. The proposal by the Five Presidents that commitments should become binding in the second phase suggests that they have little faith in the delivery of national structural reform through non-binding coordination. It remains to be seen whether such a binding character is compatible with the kind of democratically sustainable character of reform discussed above.

The model of conditionality could be complemented with an integrated economic policy framework (Sapir and Wolff 2015). Such an alternative is not without risks because European institutions may be perceived as inflicting austerity and discouraging growth, a narrative that has often been heard in Greece, though also elsewhere. However, it would in turn strengthen ownership of structural reforms and new institutions by the public that reflect the need for 'multiple but connected national politics' to manage more fruitfully the democratic interdependence stemming from monetary union (Nicolaïdis 2013, 352). They can also increase the acceptance of economic reforms against the background of wider benefits from EU integration.

5. Conclusion: Towards EU Sustainable Integration?

The sovereign debt crisis has exposed flaws in the governance framework of EMU that were partially remedied, most emphatically in the area of banking union, arguably reducing the risk of future crises and strengthening the capacity for crisis management. The principal challenges now to sustainable integration are, on the one hand, to strengthen economic coordination of the structural reforms needed to render EMU more resilient and to restore growth to the top of the political agenda; on the other, for integration to be sustainable, citizens have to be convinced that EMU is working for them.

A lack of national ownership and the conditionality of structural reforms have led to greater politicization, putting into question the collective acceptance hitherto of their redistributive implications. Political protests and institutional conflicts have marked the Eurozone in the last five years. Those frictions offer the EU an opportunity to address what we consider to be its greater challenge: pursuing a path of sustainable integration, grounded in enhanced societal capacity and propensity to act for the long term.

The sustainable integration paradigm offers a long-term vision for the EU integration project in the crisis context and beyond. To kick-start it, sustainable growth can be the basis for an exit strategy from the crisis in the shorter term (complementing the financial integration discussed by Jones 2015), and a prerequisite for a smooth functioning of EMU in the long term which would bring about wider benefits from EU integration for EU citizens. But there is a long way to go. The EU approach to sustainable growth is piecemeal and driven by the artificially separate realm of 'climate policy', with a recent boost under the heading of the Energy Union. As yet, it falls short of a coherent development strategy for sustainable growth.

Within such a sustainable integration logic, EU actors must engage in a continuous discussion on the relationship between short-term actions and long-term objectives. This process, if properly implemented, and aligned with citizens' priorities can contribute not only to the sustainability of EMU per se, but to the wider political sustainability of the European integration project as a whole.

Acknowledgements

We would like to thank an anonymous referee, seminar participants at earlier presentations in Oxford and London, and, particularly, Paul De Grauwe, Erik Jones, Russell Kinkaid, Benedicta Marzinotto, Waltraud Schelkle and Max Watson, for very valuable comments and discussions. Of course, the usual disclaimer applies.

Disclosure statement

No potential conflict of interest was reported by the authors.

Funding

Iain Begg is grateful for financial support under the Horizon 2020 research programme for the FIRSTRUN project, grant agreement number 649261.

Notes

1. Negative spillovers were rooted in factors such as unsustainable debt paths, inadequate national financial supervision, the feedback loop between weak banks and over-indebted sovereigns, and lower growth potential associated with insufficient modernization of national economies.
2. The objective of sustainable development was not well integrated in the Lisbon Strategy on growth and employment. The Europe 2020 strategy's green growth objective is based on climate targets (the 2007–2009 climate energy package), which have become insufficiently ambitious to promote innovation and investment with the crisis-induced downturn in economic activity.
3. De Wilde and Zürn (2012) suggest that crises have a strong bearing on the acceptability of greater politicization in EU integration.

References

Bini Smaghi, Lorenzo. 2013. *Austerity: European democracies against the wall.* Brussels: Centre for European Policy Studies.

Bini Smaghi, Lorenzo. 2015. Governance and Conditionality: Toward a Sustainable Framework? *Journal of European Integration* 37, no. 7: 755–68.

Blyth, Mark. 2012. *Austerity: the history of a dangerous idea.* Oxford: Oxford University Press.

Bongardt, Annette, and Francisco Torres. 2012. The lisbon strategy. Chapter 33 in *The handbook on the European Union*, eds. Erik Jones, Anand Menon, and Stephen Weatherill, 469–83. Oxford: Oxford University Press.

Bongardt, Annette, and Francisco Torres. 2013. Economic governance and sustainability chapter 8. In *Mapping European Economic Integration*, eds. V. Amy and T. Alfred, 146–67. Basingstoke: Palgrave Macmillan.

Claeys, Grégory. 2015. Juncker plan: the EIB in the driver's seat. *Bruegel Blog.* 1 July.

De Wilde, Peter, and Michael Zürn. 2012. Can the politicization of European integration be reversed? *JCMS: Journal of Common Market Studies* 50, no. 1: 137–53.

De Grauwe, Paul. 2013. *Design failures in the Eurozone: can they be fixed?* LSE 'Europe in Question' Discussion Paper Series no. 57/2013.

De Grauwe, Paul, and Yuemei Ji. 2015. Correcting for the Eurozone Design Failures: The Role of the ECB. *Journal of European Integration* 37, no. 7: 739–54.

Draghi, Mario. 2015. *Structural reforms, inflation and monetary policy.* Introductory speech, ECB Forum on Central Banking, Sintra. 22 May.

Eichengreen, Barry 2014. *The Eurozone crisis: the theory of optimum currency area bites back.* Notenstein Academy White Paper Series.

European Central Bank. 2015. Progress with structural reforms across the Euro Area and their possible impacts. *Economic Bulletin* 2. Frankfurt: ECB, 59–71.

European Commission. 2010. *Towards a single market act. For a highly competitive social market economy.* Communication from the Commission to the European Parliament, the Council, the economic and Social Committee and the Committee of Regions, Com (2010) 608 final. Brussels. 27 October.

European Commission. 2012. *A blueprint for a deep and genuine economic and monetary union launching a European debate.* Commission Communication, COM(2012) 777 final, 28.11.2012. Brussels.

European Environment Agency. 2015. *European environment state and outlook.* Copenhagen: EEA.

Fay, Marianne, Stéphane Hallegatte, Adrien Vogt-Schilb, Julie Rozenberg, Ulf Narlock, and Tom Kerr. 2015. *Decarbonizing development: three steps to a zero-carbon future.* Washington, DC: World Bank.

Giavazzi, Francesco, and Charles Wyplosz. 2015. EMU: Old Flaws Revisited. *Journal of European Integration* 37, no. 7: 723–37.

Gaspar, Vitor. 2015. The Making of a Continental Financial System: Lessons for Europe from Early American History. *Journal of European Integration* 37, no. 7: 847–59.

Hallegatte, Stéphane, Geoffrey Heal, Marianne Fay, and David Tréguer. 2011. *From growth to green growth: a framework*. NBER Working Paper 17841. National Bureau of Economic Research.

IMF. 2015. Where are we headed? Perspectives on potential output. Chapter 3 in *World economic outlook: uneven growth — short- and long-term factors*. Washington, DC: International Monetary Fund (April), 69–110.

International Energy Agency. 2014. *World energy outlook 2015*. Paris: IEA.

Jones, Erik. 2015. Getting the Story Right: How You Should Choose between Different Interpretations of the European Crisis (And Why You Should Care). *Journal of European Integration* 37, no. 7: 817–31.

Juncker, Jean-Claude, Donald Tusk, Jeroen Dijsselbloem, and Mario Draghi. 2015a. *Preparing for next steps on better economic governance in the euro area*. Analytical Note prepared for the Informal European Council, Brussels. 12 February.

Juncker, Jean-Claude, Donald Tusk, Jeroen Dijsselbloem, Mario Draghi, and Martin Schulz. 2015b. *completing Europe's economic and monetary union*. Brussels: European Commission. 22 June.

Lenschow, Andrea. 2010. Environmental policy. In *Policy-making in the European Union*, eds. H. Wallace, M.A. Pollack, and A.R. Young, 6th ed., 305–30. Oxford: Oxford University Press.

Mongelli, Francesco Paolo, Ettore Dorrucci, Demosthenes Ioannou, and Alessio Terzi. 2015. Responses to the Euro Area Crisis: Measuring the Path of European Institutional Integration. *Journal of European Integration* 37, no. 7: 769–86.

Matthijs, Matthias, and Kathleen McNamara. 2015. The euro crisis' theory effect: northern saints, southern sinners, and the demise of the eurobond. *Journal of European Integration* 37, no. 2: 229–45.

Nicolaïdis, Kalypso. 2010. Sustainable integration: towards EU 2.0? *The JCMS Annual Review Lecture, Journal of Common Market Studies* 48: 21–54.

Nicolaïdis, Kalypso. 2013. European demoicracy and its crisis. *JCMS: Journal of Common Market Studies* 51, no. 2: 351–69.

Nicolaïdis, Kalypso, and Max Watson. 2015. Sharing the Eurocrat's dream: a demoicratic approach to EMU governance. In *The post-crisis and era and the end of the EUrocrat's dream*, eds. Damian Markus Jachtenfuchs Chalmers and Christian Joerges. Cambridge: CUP.

Nordhaus, William. 2006. *The stern review on the economics of climate change*. NBER Working Paper 12741. National Bureau of Economic Research.

OECD. 2015. *Economic policy reforms 2015: going for growth*. Paris: OECD.

Pearce, David, W., and R. Kerry Turner. 1990. *Economics of natural resources and the environment*. Hemel Hampstead: Harvester Wheatsheaf.

Piketty, Thomas. 2014. *Capital in the twenty-first century*. Cambridge, MA: Harvard University Press.

Pisani-Ferry, Jean. 2014. How to climb a mountain with both hands tied. *VoxEU.org*. 7 November.

Randers, Jorgen. 2012. *A global forecast for the next forty years*. White River Junction, VT: Chelsea Green.

Rodrik, Dani. 2011. *The globalization paradox. Democracy and the future of the world economy*. New York: W.W. Norton.

Sachs, Jeffrey. 2012. *The price of civilization*. London: Vintage.

Sapir, André, and Guntram Wolff. 2015. *Euro-area governance: what to reform and how to do it*. Bruegel Policy Brief 2015/01, February.

Schmidt, Vivien. 2013. Democracy and legitimacy in the European Union revisited: input, output *and* 'throughput'. *Political Studies* 61: 2–22.

Schmieding, Holger, and Christian Schulz. 2014. *Euro Pact Plus monitor 2014. Leaders and laggards*. Brussels: The Lisbon Council.

Spence, Michael. 2014. *Growth in the new climate economy*. Project Syndicate. 31 October.

Stern, Nicholas. 2006. *The economics of climate change*, www.hu-treasure.gov.uk.

Stern, Nicholas. 2015. *Why are we waiting? The logic, urgency, and promise of tackling climate change*. Cambridge, MA: MIT Press.

Torres, F. 2009. The Role of Preferences and the Sustainability of EMU Chapter 3. In *The Future of EMU*, ed. Simona Talani, 54–74. Basingstoke: Palgrave Macmillan.

Van Rompuy, Herman. 2012. *Towards a genuine economic and monetary union*. Four Presidents' Report. Brussels: Report by the Presidents of the European Council, European Commission, Eurogroup and the ECB, EUCO120/12. 26 June.

Véron, Nicolas. 2014. *Defining Europe's capital markets union*. Bruegel Policy Contribution 2014/12. November.

Getting the Story Right: How You Should Choose between Different Interpretations of the European Crisis (And Why You Should Care)

ERIK JONES*,**

*Johns Hopkins University, SAIS, Bologna, Italy;
**Nuffield College, Oxford, UK

ABSTRACT The European crisis has many causes. Worse, the different causes are mutually reinforcing. National economies lost competitiveness within the single currency, governments and households lived beyond their means, banks and other financial firms moved capital across borders and then called it back home again in a fit of panic. Europe is suffering as a consequence. European policy-making is suffering as well. With so many 'causes', politicians are dividing their attention across different and at times competing remedies. Europe appears to be 'muddling through' rather than acting decisively as a result. This paper argues that European policymakers should focus their attention on financial causal mechanisms. Although there is some truth to claims about lost competitiveness and excessive borrowing, a close focus on financial markets promises to offer the greatest leverage over the largest number of national economies. A close focus on finance also offers a clear choice between competing policy agendas: Europe's politicians must choose either to accept a renationalization of finance or they must embrace reforms necessary to stabilize international financial market integration. Only once that choice is made, and the necessary policy agendas are put in place, should politicians again turn their focus to issues of second-order (if still significant) importance related to market structural reform, fiscal consolidation, or asset market regulation.

Introduction

The European crisis is over-determined. Although most observers agree that the initial shock emanated from the US, they tend to divide across four different narratives to explain why European countries suffered as much as they have since 2007. There was a design flaw in the euro as a single currency. Governments wasted money and borrowed excessively. Households lived beyond their means. And market participants got startled, lost confidence, liquidated their investments, and retreated within their national boundaries. The contributions to this collection highlight many of these different perspectives.

Worse, the explanations for the crisis are complementary rather than competing. The truth of any one story does not contradict any other; indeed, they are reinforcing. The euro made it easy for governments and households to behave irresponsibly. The symptoms of that financial irresponsibility frightened investors. And the disintegration of European financial markets exposed the deep design flaws in the euro. It does not matter where the story begins because the effects are cumulative.

This over-determination is a problem for analysis. When everything causes everything, it is too easy to find confirmatory data for any part of the story and so to stop data collection prematurely. It is also too easy to gloss over differences between country cases, to exclude cases arbitrarily, and to overlook anomalies. By the same token, it is difficult to distinguish between causes and effects, to recognize where mechanisms start and where they finish, and to assess the relative strength of different influences.

The policy response is underpowered as a result of disagreement among analysts. While the causal mechanisms may be mutually reinforcing, the relevant responses compete for political attention. Politicians are prone to focus on their preferred solution — say fiscal austerity or household deleveraging — rather than weigh an alternative approach. The distribution of adjustment costs only reinforces any divisions. The policy that shunts the burdens of adjustment elsewhere seems the most 'logical' to adopt.[1]

This disagreement creates the impression that European policymakers are muddling through rather than acting decisively. They have initiated policy changes on multiple fronts and yet failed to gain much traction in finding an effective solution. Along the way, mistakes have happened like the near exit of Cyprus from the euro, key actors like the European Central Bank (ECB) have run out of room for maneuver, and structural damage in the form of widespread bankruptcies and long-term unemployment has accumulated. European growth potential is diminished as a consequence and the risks of secular stagnation have increased.

This paper argues that a financial interpretation of the crisis deserves policy priority.[2] The claim is not that this interpretation offers the 'one true narrative'; rather it is that a financial explanation offers the greatest influence over events. Once European politicians have forged a coherent response to their financial challenges, they can afford to give attention to less pressing and yet still vital longer-term considerations.[3]

A Strategy for Choice

European policymakers are not unique in facing a problem of over-determination. Most crises have more than one cause and many of the mechanisms at work are tangled together. Hence, methodologists have developed techniques or strategies for untying the causal knots. The strategy sketched here is based on Miller's (1988) *Fact and Method*.

Miller's approach places causality at the center of explanation; to understand a thing, you have to know what brought it into being. Such explanations look like correlations — if A, then B — but they may only work once, under the unique circumstance of the case at hand. Then, he offers some simple rules for recognizing the 'depth' or significance of the correlations that are the building blocks of causal mechanisms. These rules are similar to the falsifying tests at the heart of Popper's scientific realism, but the goal of applying the rules is to qualify rather than eliminate a possible explanation. Finally, Miller provides a technique for comparing and so 'confirming' causal mechanisms — called 'fair causal comparison'.

These three elements can be combined in a two-step strategy for untangling an over-determined situation. The first step is to focus on the most obvious correlations in order to see which is likely to have the greatest causal significance using the rules for causal depth — necessity, sufficiency, and priority. A necessary correlation occurs in all cases; a sufficient correlation always results in the same effect (which may also arise independently); and a prior correlation can give rise to a variety of symptoms which should be discounted in terms of their own causal significance.

The second step is to link the most relevant correlations together into standard causal patterns or mechanisms. These patterns link correlations of different kinds into narratives that describe how the event came about. These narratives compete insofar as they assign different roles to any observed correlations — sorting out necessity and sufficiency as well as cause and effect. Hence what matters is the structure of the argument, meaning how it starts, progresses, and ends.

An explanation is superior to its closest rival when the causal pattern helps us to understand the greatest scope of the event with the least complexity. This implies a trade-off along Occam's Razor, where the simplest explanation is preferred when all things are equal and yet a more complicated explanation can be warranted when the increase in complexity is more than offset by the greater scope it has to offer on the event. In other words, the better explanation is neither the simplest nor the most complete; it is the explanation that offers the most leverage. Moreover, the standard for 'leverage' is not solely analytical. The best explanation does not have to be the one that offers the greatest understanding; instead it may be the explanation that offers the best prospects for control.[4]

Three Tests for Causal Depth

Correlation is not causation, but causation is a kind of correlation. This correlation happens over time — meaning first one thing, then another; it is preceded and followed by other events; and it may never be repeated. Moreover, to the extent to which there is a material connection between the one thing and the other, that mechanism is going to be difficult if not impossible to observe directly. We can get closer and closer to the actual connection, and so peel off layer upon layer of observed correlations, but we are unlikely to get all the way down to the bottom. The challenge is to find the right depth. That is why Miller (1988) proposes a few simple rules to guide analysis. He focuses on 'necessity' and 'priority' in *Fact and Method*; I have added 'sufficiency' as a third rule implicit in his argument.

These three measures of causal depth make it possible to start sorting out the correlations observed in the recent European crisis. The building blocks for the different explanations are euro membership, government borrowing, household balances, and investor or market confidence. And the relevant questions are whether these things were present in each of the countries that were affected by the crisis (necessity), whether countries were affected by the crises whenever these things were present (sufficiency), whether these things emerged before or after the crisis had effect, and whether there is some other factor that could be responsible for both sides of the correlation (priority).

None of the building blocks used in the predominant explanations for the European crisis is necessary for a country to get into trouble. Great Britain, Iceland, Hungary and Latvia all experienced profound effects of the crisis without being members of the euro area. Moreover, these countries have little in common in terms of exchange rate policy or relative size and importance of the national currency. Neither Ireland nor Spain had excessive government borrowing before the crisis; the ratio of public debt to gross domestic product (GDP) in Portugal was higher, and yet little different from France or Germany.[5] As for leverage, households in Italy and Greece were not hugely indebted. The ratio of household debt to disposable income increased in both countries in the decade prior to the crisis, but it remained low relative to other countries; this is even truer for the ratio of household debts to assets.[6] Market confidence is harder to assess because of the dangers of tautology linking crisis and confidence. A sudden drop in confidence will trigger a crisis but a crisis will also trigger a sudden drop in confidence. Hence this correlation is always likely to be present and must be sorted out in terms of sequencing or priority rather than necessity in assessing its causal depth.

None of the obvious correlations were sufficient to ensure the onset of a crisis either. Countries like Luxembourg and Malta belonged to the euro area without suffering as a consequence. Belgium managed to avoid scrutiny for its high public debt burdens. There was a time when the markets worried about the failure of Belgian politicians to form a government, but that concern abated once Elio Di Rupo announced his coalition and despite continued pressure on public finances.[7] Meanwhile, the two European countries with the highest ratios of household leverage — Denmark and the Netherlands — managed to escape some of the worst of the crisis. Finally, the Belgian case shows that it is possible to recover from a loss of market confidence even as successive Vienna Initiatives to stabilize financial markets in Central and Eastern Europe illustrate a more general dynamic within which a loss of investor confidence can be managed (Epstein 2014).

The question of priority is complicated because it implies a more precise definition of 'the crisis' in order to establish both sequencing and the influence of common factors. We can narrow the crisis down to balance of payments financing without having to revisit the tests for necessity or sufficiency above. Those tests work as well with this narrower definition as with a broader sense of the crisis as a combination of economic problems. Moreover, by focusing on the balance of payments we can isolate a precise temporal landmark while at the same time creating a break in the cumulative causal chain described in the introduction.

The question of priority also requires precision in how we look at the correlations. Consider the problem of euro membership. The challenge is to transform a design flaw in the euro into an appropriate trigger for a crisis in the balance of payments. Changing from non-member to member is unlikely to be adequate, because virtually all of the membership decisions took place before the crisis. Therefore, we need an intermediate correlation. The most obvious would be an increase in a country's current account deficit. The argument is that membership gradually eroded the international competitiveness of some participating countries while at the same time preventing them from using the nominal exchange rate to facilitate adjustment. At some point, market participants question the sustainability of accumulated net foreign liabilities. Hence, the relevant question is whether current account deficits increased or decreased prior to sudden capital outflows from banks or sovereign debt markets.

The need for precision also applies to government borrowing and household balances. Under normal circumstances, these are slow moving variables and so the level of indebtedness and government borrowing tends to look much the same from one period to the next. The focus for attention, therefore, should not be on the levels but on any changes. Specifically, it is worth looking to see whether a sudden increase in borrowing by either governments or households precedes a balance of payments crisis.

Finally, it is worth considering whether the analysis should be reversed. In this case, the question is whether whatever is happening in the balance of payments will undermine international competitiveness, government borrowing, or household finances.

The sequencing of events varies from one place to the next. Moreover, the pattern is often counter-intuitive. For example, Ireland experienced shortfalls in its balance of payments (as measured by Ireland's position in the real-time gross settlement system used by euro area central banks — called TARGET2) against a backdrop of shrinking current account deficits (2008) and rising current account surpluses (2010).[8] Greece experienced a balance of payments shortfall when the Greek government announced a small upward revision in the size of its deficit in October 2008 but not at all when successive Greek governments announced much larger upward revisions in October 2009; capital flowed out of the country during the first instance and into the country during the second (Merler and Pisani-Ferry 2012). The Italian government experienced its balance of payments crisis in July 2011 even as it agreed to a new fiscal adjustment program; meanwhile, Italian household borrowing contracted.[9]

In order to show how a balance of payments crisis impacts on other domestic variables, it is useful to focus on the sudden outflow of capital from a country's banks or sovereign debt markets. The shock of such an outflow to interest rates and credit availability had an impact on international competitiveness because it raised the cost and cut the supply of working capital. The sudden capital outflow also raised government outlays on debt servicing and welfare assistance while lowering revenues accrued from income or value-added. For their part, households found it difficult to make ends meet and while many tried to restrict new borrowing (or found themselves cut off from access to new credit), they also struggled to pay existing debt; the result was that household leverage increased.

This sequencing suggests that any causal account should center on a flight of capital from a country's banks and sovereign debt markets. It also suggests that some prior influence — like the US financial crisis — will have greater causal significance than any correlations with euro membership, competitiveness, government borrowing, or household debt levels. However, in order to translate that suggestion into an argument, it is necessary to flesh out competing narratives as causal patterns and to see which offers the most leverage in understanding and dealing with the crisis.

Fair Causal Comparison

The four competing narratives are easy to sketch. Moreover, they contain many of the same elements. Where they differ is in the ordering and importance assigned to different correlations. They also differ in terms of their logical entailments about the sequence in which different correlations appear.

We can start with a financial pattern that centers on a flight of capital. This financial interpretation of the crisis is called a 'sudden stop' in development economics (Calvo 1998). The standard account begins with a capital account liberalization resulting in a gradual increase in cross-border capital inflows. The capital that flows into the country accumulates as a stock of net foreign liabilities (seen from a domestic perspective). Then there is a shock to the confidence of foreign investors who seek to liquidate and repatriate their assets. The liquidation of assets depresses domestic asset prices and stresses the balance sheets of domestic banks; the repatriation of capital triggers a balance of payments crisis. Firm, household and government finances are all damaged in the wake of the capital outflow.

The 'sudden stop' has few contextual requirements. It can take place under any exchange rate regime. It does not require a particular kind of banking system or configuration of asset markets. There is no necessary accumulation of government or household indebtedness. It does not require that the country experience a current account deficit or savings-investment imbalance prior to the crisis. And there is no need to specify what causes the shock to confidence. All that matters is that foreigners are able to stockpile assets after the liberalization of capital markets that they can liquidate and repatriate once their confidence is lost.

The 'competitiveness' story is the easiest to treat next because many of the elements were presented above. To make the story comparable, however, it is useful to anchor the causal pattern with the same correlation used in the sudden stop account by starting with capital market liberalization and ending with a balance of payments crisis. The liberalization of capital flows make it possible for domestic residents to gain access to foreign credit, either directly or indirectly. They use this access to increase consumption of both traded and non-traded goods. The consumption of traded goods lowers the current account balance; the consumption of non-traded goods raises inflation. In turn, the accelerating rate of inflation lowers the real interest rate and places upward pressure on wages. This reinforces efforts to borrow for current consumption and it results in an increase in relative real unit labor costs. Both the additional consumption and the relative wage growth put downward pressure on the current account balance. This process continues until foreigners become unwilling to extend further credit because they fear that country will not be able to honor its net foreign liabilities. Once the confidence of foreigners breaks, the country experiences a crisis on the balance of payments (Hancké 2013).

The 'competitiveness' story has some contextual requirements. To begin with, the story works best in the context of fixed or managed exchange rates, otherwise a realignment of the nominal exchange rate can compensate for movements in relative prices. That is why the problem of 'competitiveness' is so closely associated with euro membership. A competitiveness story also needs a mechanism to link prices to wages and to wage growth across the traded and non-traded sectors of the economy. Finally, there should be some connection between the loss of competitiveness and the loss of foreign investor confidence. Investors take fright and withhold balance of payments financing because they are concerned about the accumulation of current account deficits.

The 'government finances' and 'household debt' stories can also fill in the gap between capital market liberalization and a balance of payments crisis. In these accounts, the liberalization of capital flows makes it possible for governments and households to borrow more cheaply and to service larger volumes of debt. The accumulation of debt continues until foreign investors begin to question the stability of government or household balances. What differentiates these 'government finances' and 'household debt' accounts from either the 'competitiveness' story or the more general 'sudden stop' is that they focus attention on particular agents in the domestic economy. Governments are to blame in one account; households in the other. By contrast, the 'competitiveness' story focuses attention on wage negotiators and a more general 'sudden stop' account is neutral with respect to who should hold responsibility.

Sudden Stops vs. Competitiveness

The starting point for comparing the 'sudden stop' and 'competitiveness' accounts is to admit the anomalies and irregularities. The Irish example is a case in point. Ireland has flexible labor market institutions and accumulated only a modest cumulative current account deficit (worth about 13 per cent of gross domestic product, or GDP) during the period from the start of the euro in 1999 to the onset of the crisis in 2007. Moreover, as mentioned, the correlation between Irish current account performance and capital outflows is counter-intuitive. Hence Ireland looks more like a sudden stop than a case of lost competitiveness. The question is whether Ireland is an exception.

The Italian case suggests it is not. Although Italy has notoriously rigid labor market institutions, its cumulative current account deficit over the 1999–2007 period is just 5 per cent of GDP. Moreover, a close examination of Italy's export performance suggests it is surprisingly competitive (Tiffin 2014). Italian firms succeed not only in holding onto world export manufacturing shares but also manufacturing employment.[10] This is curious insofar as there is evidence of a progressive appreciation of Italy's relative real effective exchange rate since the onset of the euro.[11] For the competitiveness account, Italy is another exception.

Greece is also a problem case. Unlike either Ireland or Italy, Greece ran up massive current account deficits in the period from 1999 to 2007 — more than 101 per cent of GDP. But the mechanism at work behind this deterioration is hard to connect to Greek 'competitiveness' for at least three reasons. First, Greek real effective exchange rates appreciated by less after it joined the euro than they did beforehand. The explanation is that euro membership brought Greek price inflation under control — eliminating a threat to competitiveness that consistently outran any advantages to be had from nominal currency depreciation when Greece retained the drachma.[12] Second, Greece added manufacturing employment during its first eight years in the euro; this suggests that manufacturing workers were not 'too expensive'. Indeed, Greek real unit labor costs declined by 1.7 per cent relative to the country's main trading partners during the 1999–2007 period even as total factor productivity increased by 15.5 per cent. Third, Greece retained its tiny share of world export markets while moving up the value chain in the composition of exports within Europe. Between 2001 and 2007, fruits and vegetables, vegetable fats, wool, textiles and clothing all declined in importance as a share of Greek exports while pharma, plastics, metals, machinery, and road vehicles all increased.[13]

These three anomalies should not lead us to reject the competitiveness argument altogether. Arguably it does have some role to play in Spain and Portugal. It may be important elsewhere as well. However, the existence of such anomalies inside the euro area make it challenging to argue that 'competitiveness' is comparatively the most useful lens through which to interpret the European crisis (Cecchetti *et al.* 2012). The existence of anomalies outside the euro area makes the situation even more problematic. Here it is worth focusing on three aggregates of roughly equal importance for world trade: Germany, the five peripheral countries of the euro area (PC-5, meaning Greece, Ireland, Italy, Portugal and Spain), and a clutch of northern European countries that choose not to join the euro area (United Kingdom, Switzerland, Denmark, Norway, and Sweden). The presumption in the competitiveness argument is that the PC-5 should lose more export market share and manufacturing employment than either Germany (inside the euro area) or USDNS (outside). The reality is that for the period from 1999 to 2007, the PC-5 do much better that expected.[14]

These patterns in manufacturing employment and export markets shares are inconsistent with the 'competitiveness' story but they are irrelevant if we privilege a financial interpretation that centers on 'sudden stop' dynamics. Moreover, the financial interpretation will make it possible to explain why capital flowed out of Denmark and Sweden at the start of the crisis only to flow back in once the economic situation in the euro area periphery worsened. The financial interpretation also explains how the UK got into trouble (and the pound depreciated strongly) when there was a run on its banks and why small countries like Switzerland and Norway suffered from flights to safety by international investors. In other words, the financial interpretation has fewer anomalies and explains more variation than a 'competitiveness' interpretation of the crisis.

Sudden Stops vs. Government Finances

The weakness of a financial interpretation of the crisis is that it requires a trigger to set off the movement of capital across borders. Hence it is worth asking whether the trigger or the mechanism warrants greater attention. This question is implicit in the comparison between a financial interpretation of the crisis and one that centers on government finances. The financial interpretation is almost purely mechanistic insofar as it invokes 'market actors' as an obscure kind of agency that loses confidence and moves assets. The government finances interpretation is more concrete as a trigger because it focuses on policy action. Governments behave recklessly and eventually get their comeuppance.

This comparison of the two interpretations draws on three country cases — starting with Greece. The first point to note is that Greece maintained a roughly constant ratio of sovereign debt to GDP during the period from 1999 to 2007 and the spread between Greek and German long-term sovereign debt instruments was roughly constant from the time Greece joined the euro in 2001 until the onset of the crisis. This spread began to change with the revelation of (yet another round of) Greek fiscal accounting irregularities in spring 2008, which was around the same time that the US investment bank Bear Sterns got into trouble. Market participants began to liquidate their exposure to Greek assets and the spread between Greek and German sovereign debt instruments suddenly increased. This is consistent with a 'government finances' interpretation. The next jump occurred in October 2008. Soon after the collapse of Lehman Brothers, the Greek government announced a modest revision in its deficit figures and market actors again responded by liquidating their positions. Capital flowed out of the country and the spread between Greece and Germany again increased. Moreover, the pressure continued into the early months of 2009. It peaked only when then German finance minister Peer Steinbrück made it clear both to the German business community and the financial press that no euro area country would be allowed to go bankrupt (Benoit and Barber 2009). From that point onward, the pressure on Greek sovereign debt instruments diminished (Figure 1).

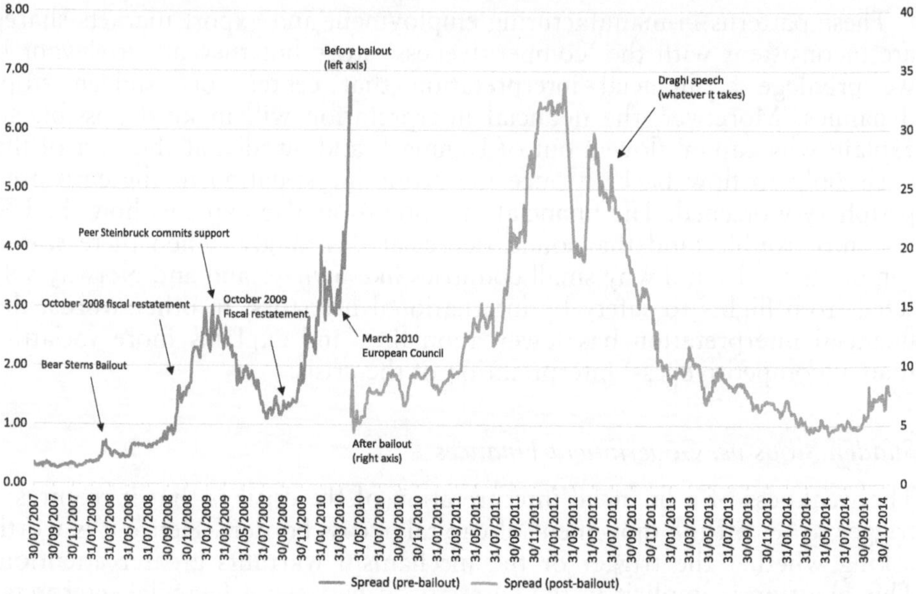

Figure 1. Greek-German 10-year spread (before and after bailout)

That pressure only increased again once a change in German political leadership abandoned the commitment to bailout Greece. In this account, it remains true that the accumulation of Greek sovereign debt was a necessary condition. But the agency behind the 'trigger' is German and not Greek. If the German government had remained committed to bail out the Greek state, the situation might have been different. A government finances account is consistent only with the interpretation that some crisis was inevitable even with a German guarantee; a sudden stop account is consistent with either counterfactual alternative depending upon whether market actors lose confidence or regain it for any number of reasons.

The Italian case shows how market actors can suddenly lose confidence. Superficially, the story looks like Greece insofar as both countries have very high and persistent public debt to GDP ratios. Nevertheless, the two cases are different. Italy has high quality public accounting statistics, excellent treasury operations and sovereign debt management, and it had the euro area's largest primary surplus — meaning excess of public revenues over receipts, net of debt servicing requirements. Italy also benefits from a large and very liquid secondary market for its sovereign debt instruments. Hence for much of the early phase of the financial crisis, market actors viewed Italy as a relative safe source of yield on their investments. Up until June 2011, Italy not only ran a surplus on its Target2 position with the rest of the euro area but the foreign holdings of Italian sovereign debt instruments increased.

This situation changed suddenly in late June and early July of 2011 as negotiations over a second Greek bailout raised concerns among international investors that the principal in their Italian sovereign debt holdings might also be at risk. Market actors began selling out their positions and repatriating their capital; the spread between Italian and German bonds suddenly increased and Italy's Target2 position with the rest of the euro area moved sharply into deficit. Moreover, no change in domestic policy, government, or institution could restore market confidence. This only changed as a result of external intervention by the ECB in July 2012. By that point, however, the damage to Italian economic performance was sufficient to raise questions about the country's long-term debt sustainability. This is more consistent with a sudden stop interpretation of the crisis than with a government finances account.

The Belgian case is another illustration of how market sentiments can swing free of government finances. Prior to the crisis, the Belgian state engaged in almost two decades of fiscal consolidation, bringing the debt-to-GDP ratio down from a peak of 135 per cent in 1993 to a low of 86.9 per cent in 2007. The collapse of Dexia and Fortis coupled with the need to prop up other banks in 2008 and 2009 erased a chunk of the progress that had been made and the debt-to-GDP ratio began growing again. Then the May 2010 elections resulted in a hung parliament and more than 550 days of fractious coalition negotiations — the longest in European history. Market participants followed the story only sporadically until the onset of the Italian crisis in July 2011 — then the pressure on Belgian sovereign debt yields launched upward. The Belgian spread over Germany was 107 basis points on 30 June 2011; it was 366 basis points by 25 November. The pressure was enough to convince Di Rupo and his negotiating partners to hammer out an overnight agreement. By the time the government was invested on 6 December, the spread was already down to 214 basis points.

The contrast between the Belgian and Italian cases is important because it reveals the fickle assessments of market actors. Both countries went through a change of government in late 2011. Belgium received a lopsided coalition with a growing regionalist opposition; Italy received a technocratic administration headed by a former European Commissioner, Mario Monti, with a strong reputation for sound economic management. Belgian sovereign debt markets stabilized quickly with the formation of the new government despite the fact that the underlying sources of political instability remained acute, the banking system continued to need state resources, and public debt continued to accumulate. Italian sovereign debt markets enjoyed a brief honeymoon under Monti only to continue their deterioration. If there is an explanation for this pattern, it is more likely to be idiosyncratic than to be determined by government finances per se. In that sense, both cases fit more easily within a financial interpretation of the crisis.

Sudden Stops vs. Household Balances

The 'household balances' account is like the 'government finances' interpretation in the sense that it privileges a particular agency; households live beyond their means and get into trouble, non-performing loans accumulate in the domestic banking sector, the state has to step in to shore up domestic banks, and international investors take flight from both sovereign debt markets and the domestic banking sector. Often the story involves the emergence and implosion of domestic asset bubbles in real estate, commercial property, asset-backed securities, or domestic equity markets. There are many uses of household leverage beyond consumption. Hence the point is simply that private actors are responsible for taking on unsustainable levels of debt.

The anomaly that Europe's most indebted households in Denmark and the Netherlands were not hardest hit by the crisis has already been noted. Moreover, the household balances pattern does appear to be relevant in the cases of Ireland, Spain, and, to a lesser extent, Portugal. It could also apply to Hungary and Latvia outside the euro area. The absolute levels of household indebtedness in these countries were not excessive but the exposure of households to foreign-currency denominated debt was problematic. Finally, the same pattern would fit the United Kingdom and even the US (Mian and Sufi 2014). This broad range of diverse cases gives the household balances interpretation considerable traction in public debate.

The question is whether the household balances interpretation of the crisis adds much analytical leverage to the more general financial interpretation based on sudden stop dynamics. The answer depends upon how much autonomy households have in taking on foreign-financed debt, including debt in foreign currency. If households have considerable autonomy, then the appropriate policy response is to structure incentives to hold down household leverage. If households are likely to get into trouble whatever the mix of financial incentives, then a household balances interpretation of the crisis does not add much to the more general case.

Unfortunately, the mix of incentives is unlikely to have a decisive impact. It can change how credit is deployed and where leverage is concentrated, but it is unlikely to eliminate the accumulation of unsustainable imbalances. This is true because it is so much easier to make a country borrow than to make a country lend. Foreign investors searching for high yields can purchase sovereign debt instruments or other marketable securities including corporate bonds, equities, or derivatives. They can penetrate the domestic banking system directly by setting up branches or acquiring subsidiaries, or indirectly through purchases of secured or unsecured bank debt, by making deposits, or by participating in interbank markets. Such transactions not only increase the volume of liquidity in the economy but also crowd out domestic savings that will look for a suitable yield with a traditional home bias. The effect will be to price new domestic borrowers into the market for loanable funds. These will be new customers for lenders, who not only struggle to deploy the liquidity at their disposal but also to differentiate between good and bad customers. By implication, these lenders are likely to experience an adverse selection bias as much of the credit extended to participants only recently priced into the market for loanable funds will end up underperforming expectations (Martin and Taddei 2013).

Putting Finance First

A financial interpretation of the crisis does not exclude the possibility that there were countries affected by a loss of competitiveness, irresponsible government finances, or households living beyond their means. Such factors were present in different European cases to a greater or lesser extent. Moreover, each is important in revealing particular dimensions of the crisis as it unfolded. In that sense, a financial interpretation of the crisis should not obscure the valuable insights that other interpretations have to offer on specific cases. It should not downplay the importance of giving attention to longer-term sustainability either (see, e.g. Begg *et al.* in this volume).

Nevertheless a financial interpretation of the crisis does yield specific clusters of policy recommendations. To the extent to which these recommendations come into conflict with remedies specific to other interpretations of the crisis, the financial policies should be given priority. They offer the most general solution to the problem at hand and hence the greatest leverage in stabilizing European economic performance.

The financial interpretation suggests two competing agendas, focusing on different ends of the initial correlation. One agenda attempts to limit the impact of capital market liberalization; the other attempts to mitigate the possibility that international market actors will suddenly take fright and liquidate their domestic positions in order to repatriate their investments.

The agenda to limit the impact of capital market liberalization seeks to restore domestic policy autonomy even at the expense of sacrificing many of the benefits of financial market integration. Within this agenda, governments should restrain the growth of household leverage, they should run conservative fiscal balances, they should place brakes on asset price growth in real estate markets, they should limit the dimensions of domestic financial institutions to a size that can be resolved without straining national resources, and they should discourage excessive cross-border exposure to wholesale markets or currency mismatches. Such an agenda amounts to a renationalization of finance within integrated capital markets. Ironically, it is also the symptom of the current crisis elevated to a 'new normal' status. ECB President Mario Draghi (2013) warned in the immediate aftermath of the crisis in Cyprus that European policymakers would have to accept this renationalization of finance if they were to resist empowering common institutions; many European policymakers including Eurogroup President and Dutch Finance Minister Jeroen Dijsselbloem seemed to argue that this renationalization of finance would be preferable to the alternatives (Spiegel 2013).

The agenda to stabilize integrated financial practices focuses on a wider array of measures to build investor confidence and to channel any flights to liquidity or quality in ways that do not drain resources from individual national economies. Within this agenda, the ECB plays the role of lender of last resort (above and beyond the role of the European Stability Mechanism) by placing a floor under sovereign debt markets through the promise to make direct purchases of unlimited amounts of distressed country sovereign debt instruments with relatively short residual maturity in secondary markets. This agenda also includes the European banking union with the ECB as a single supervisor using a common rulebook, the promise of a common resolution authority with pooled resolution financing, and the prospect of some kind of common deposit insurance mechanism including both comparable standards for insurance and coverage and adequate funds to cover contingent liabilities (Howarth and Quaglia 2013). This banking union is unlikely to be as comprehensive in practice as it could be in theory; by adopting a financial interpretation of the crisis, European policymakers would see good reasons to be more ambitious.

There are other elements that emerge in an agenda to stabilize European financial market integration. The capital markets union project being developed by incoming European Commission President Jean-Claude Juncker and his team promises to sketch many of the key technical components (Hill 2014). Nevertheless, there is one feature that has been on the table since November 2011 — and that is the mutualization of at least some share of European sovereign debt in a common Eurobond or similar instrument (European Commission 2011). This instrument would not only provide a reservoir large enough to absorb any flight to liquidity or quality in the event of a crisis of confidence, but it would also do so without necessarily pulling investment capital across national boundaries. The reason is that Eurobonds would trade freely in each of the participating countries much as US treasury instruments trade freely across the various US states. Banks and firms could use these Eurobonds for their treasury operations, pension funds and insurance companies could hold them as their principal long-term assets, and household could rely upon them to safeguard their savings. In times of distress, a flight into Eurobonds would strengthen rather than weaken the balance sheets of those who hold them.

If policymakers can maximize their leverage over the crisis by focusing on creating a banking union, a capital markets union, and ultimately a Eurobond, then they should give those projects priority consideration. Such measures are likely to provide the greatest support to the largest number of cases. That is the best rule of thumb for dealing with an overdetermined crisis like the one European policymakers currently face. The alternative of trying to pursue multiple, overlapping, and contradictory agendas is less attractive because it is likely to prove less effective.

Acknowledgement

The author would like to thanks Francisco Torres, Kalypso Nicolaidis, Daniel Ottolenghi, Biswajit Banerjee, and Boštjan Jazbec for their very generous support and comments related to earlier drafts of this paper.

Disclosure statement

No potential conflict of interest was reported by the author.

Notes

1. The point I am making here connects to a large literature on the role of ideas in policy-making and during the current crisis in particular. In the interests of space, we pick up those connections in the introduction to this collection rather than developing them in this contribution.
2. My interpretation hews closest to De Grauwe and Ji in this collection; see Vines for a contrasting view.
3. Begg *et al.*, in this volume focus on these longer-term considerations. They also make the important point that any reforms introduced during moments of crisis should take longer-term impacts into account.
4. Again, see Vines in this collection for a contrasting view.
5. Unless noted otherwise, references to comparative data are drawn from the Annnual Macroeconomic Database (AMECO) of the European Commission, which is available on-line at http://ec.europa.eu/economy_finance/db_indicators/ameco/index_en.htm. The data code for debt to GDP ratios is UDGGL. In 2007, Portugal's debt to GDP ratio was 68.4 per cent, France's was 64.2 per cent, and Germany's was 63.5 per cent.
6. This data is taken from the OECD and is available on-line at http://www.oecd.org/std/fin-stats/. The trend analysis refers primarily to Italy; the data for Greece is a point level for 2007.
7. This point would be explored in greater detail below. The data for market pressure are the spread on long-term sovereign debt yields between Belgium and Germany. I have based my analysis on daily market data for bid-yields provided by IHS Global Insight. As that is a proprietary database, I do not include a URL.
8. The data for Target2 balances is available on-line at http://www.eurocrisismonitor.com/. The data for current account balances is from AMECO. The relevant code is UBCA.
9. The ratio of Italian household debt to gross disposable income was 83.3 per cent in 2010 and 82.9 per cent in 2011; the same ratio in Denmark was 300.2 in 2010 and 297.8 in 2011. Again, these data are from the OECD.
10. The AMECO code for world export market shares is AXGT and for manufacturing employment is NETM.
11. The AMECO code for relative real effective exchange rates is XUNRQ.
12. The argument here is based on an analysis of the decomposition of the relative real effective exchange rate (XUNRQ) into a relative nominal effective exchange rate (XUNNQ), a relative movement in GDP price deflators (PVGDQ), and a relative movement in real unit labor costs (QLCD). Those data lines are all reported separately in AMECO.
13. This analysis is based on analysis of Greek export composition with the rest of the EU-27 using two digit SITC codes as reported by Eurostat.
14. These data are from the AMECO database and can be made available upon request.

References

Begg, Iain, Annette Bongardt, Kalypso Nicolaïdis, and Francisco Torres. 2015. EMU and Sustainable Integration. *Journal of European Integration* 37, no. 7: 803–16.

Benoit, B., and T. Barber. 2009. Germany ready to help Eurozone members. *Financial Times* (18 February).

Calvo, G.A. 1998. Capital flows and capital market crises: the simple economics of sudden stops. *Journal of Applied Economics* 1, no. 1: 35–54.

Cecchetti, S.G., R.N. McCauley, and P.M. McGuire. 2012. Interpreting Target2 balances. *BIS working papers (No. 393)*. Basle: Bank for International Settlements (December).

Draghi, M. 2013. *Introductory statement to the press conference (with Q&A)*. Frankfurt: ECB (4 April).

Epstein, R.A. 2014. When do foreign banks 'cut and run'? Evidence from west European bailouts and east European markets. *Review of International Political Economy* 21, no. 4: 847–77.

European Commission. 2011. *Green paper on the feasibility of introducing stability bonds*. Brussels: European Commission, COM (2011) 818 Final (23 November).

Hancké, B. 2013. *Unions, central banks, and EMU*. Oxford: Oxford University Press.

Hill, J. 2014. *Capital markets union: finance serving the economy*. Brussels: European Commission, SPEECH-14-1460 (6 November).

Howarth, D., and L. Quaglia. 2013. Banking union as holy grail: rebuilding the single market in financial services, stabilizing Europe's banks and 'completing' economic and monetary union. In

The JCMS annual review of the European Union in 2012, eds. N. Copsey and T. Haughton, 103–23. London: Wiley.

Martin, A., and F. Taddei. 2013. International capital flows and credit market imperfections: a tale of two frictions. *Journal of International Economics* 89: 441–52.

Merler, S., and J. Pisani-Ferry. 2012. Sudden stops in the Euro area. *Bruegel policy contribution No. 6*. Brussels: Bruegel (March).

Mian, A., and A. Sufi. 2014. *House of debt: how they (and you) caused the great recession, and how we can prevent it from happening again.* Chicago, IL: University of Chicago Press.

Miller, R. 1988. *Fact and method: explanation, confirmation, and reality in the natural and social sciences.* Princeton: Princeton University Press.

Spiegel, P. 2013. Cyprus rescue signals new line on bailouts. *Financial Times* (25 March).

Tiffin, A. 2014. European productivity, innovation, and competitiveness: the case of Italy. *IMF working paper (WP/14/79)*. Washington, DC: International Monetary Fund (May).

At Cross-purposes: Commercial versus Technocratic Governance of Sovereign Debt in the EU

ZSÓFIA BARTA* & WALTRAUD SCHELKLE**

*Rockefeller College of Public Affairs & Policy, State University of New York, Albany, USA;

**European Institute, London School of Economics and Political Science, London, UK

ABSTRACT The governance of EMU was premised on the idea that market discipline, informed by fiscal surveillance, supports the building of a hard currency union. Theory would lead us to expect that the international–commercial and the supranational–technocratic assessments of sovereign debt are fairly aligned. But they were not. We show that credit rating agencies and Eurostat have rather different assessments of what certain policies mean for sovereign debt. These assessments reveal divergent institutional logics of market actors and regulators. Private agencies are prone to conformism and herding behavior, allowing for little consistent discipline, while the public agency follows a bureaucratic imperative of accountability and transparency, which gets in the way of evolving policy priorities. Our findings thus shed light on the difficulties of fiscal governance by regulation only but they also suggest that reforms at the EMU level do not provide quick fixes.

EU Fiscal Governance and the Lack of Support by Market Discipline

The articles in this special issue identify the most important institutional shortcomings and design flaws of EMU and provide plenty of ideas on how they could be amended. *Giavazzi and Wyplosz*, for instance, set off with a systematic and honest assessment of whether a similar analysis in 1998 stood the test of time; *De Grauwe and Ji* and *Begg et al.* discuss more recent lessons from the crisis. While there is no complete agreement, nobody proposes that EMU governance should leave more room for market discipline. How times change.

Fiscal surveillance in the euro area was premised on the idea that if it would signal the right information to market observers, their reactions would support the building of a hard currency union. Already the Maastricht convergence criteria invited market forces to sit on the judging panel to decide who was 'fit' for EMU: Convergence of interest and inflation rates could not be simply manipulated by authorities. Yet, far from disciplining budgetary policies, capital flows financed deficits at historically low interest rates. It is safe to assume that the EU's fiscal rules could have been more easily enforced if financial market actors had supported the Commission's fiscal surveillance and, for instance, credit rating agencies (CRAs) had downgraded the bonds of offending member states reliably and investors imposed rising risk premia accordingly.

Some economists warned of the lack of market discipline (Faini 2006; *Jones*). They could point to the convergence of government bond spreads of member states despite different or deteriorating fiscal positions. Yet, those who believed in market discipline could point out that this might be due to diminishing exchange rate risks, leaving only liquidity and default risks to price (Manganelli and Wolswijk 2007: 10–11, 24–25). The empirical evidence before the 2007–2008 crisis suggested that bond spreads reflected different ratings but the methodology used could obviously not quantify whether the pricing was correct. Moreover, expansionary fiscal policy by a member state seemed to spillover into the average level of interest rates, suggesting that fiscal rules were needed additionally to prevent this externality (Faini 2006: 464, 469). The regulation of credit ratings was briefly discussed in Europe after the Asian crisis and the Enron scandal but was resisted by international business and banks which depended for their investments and also their own ratings on a sovereign benchmark (Abdelal 2007: 175).

The lack of support for EU surveillance from CRAs should come as a surprise even to those who do not believe that efficiency is an inherent feature of financial markets. After all, sovereign credit rating is a multi-billion dollar business, dominated by three agencies (Fitch, Moody's, and Standard & Poor's) that constantly provide information to markets about the credit risk of government bond issues. By mid-2010, Standard & Poor's (S&P) rated 125 governments, the other two over a 100 each (IMF 2010: 87). This makes reputation for accurate ratings extremely valuable. Moreover, there should also have been incentives for the monitoring of these monitors. Credit ratings were built into the regulation of financial institutions, in that the risk weights of the assets could be based on such credit ratings and thus determine the capital requirements under Basel II (IMF 2010: 91–92). Since highly rated bonds of OECD countries carried a zero risk weight and were therefore very attractive to meet capital requirements, it should at the same time have given independent financial regulators considerable incentive to make sure that the ratings of government bonds signaled problems of fiscal sustainability accurately. Last but not least, the

European Central Bank (ECB), like other central banks, used these credit ratings in refinancing operations: In return for central bank credit, banks had to put up collateral that met a certain credit rating standard in order to be acceptable to the ECB. In sum, both financial and institutional incentives for reputation of commercial and technocratic monitors of public finances should have been aligned.

These considerations can be supported by at least two conceptualizations of the European integration project. There is, first, the interpretation of the EU as a regulatory polity that suggests that it constitutes a 'fourth branch of government' for supranational economic regulation (Majone 1993, 1996). This theory seeks to explain why sovereign governments delegated considerable regulatory powers to independent bodies, such as the Commission or the ECB. In this view, delegation of policy-making powers guards against well-known failures of democracy to either represent the majority or to consider the legitimate interests of outsiders of national democratic processes, be it foreigners or future generations. In the medium-to-long run, these failures impoverish countries and the interdependence of economies makes national democratic failure a problem for other countries. Hence, governments agree on supranational institutions as restraint on destabilizing macroeconomic policies. The analogy of the regulatory polity and the institutionalization of CRAs as regulators is striking: Governments, not only in Europe but internationally, gave self-regulatory authority to financial markets they had liberalized and the markets ceased some of their power to the agencies (Abdelal 2007: 165). Far from privatizing regulatory authority, CRAs seemed to fit into an innovative approach of non-politicized regulation of global markets in which sovereigns could not claim privileges.

At the opposite end of this functionalist view of EU policy-making is a constructivist interpretation that sees European economic integration as putting into practice neo- or ordoliberal ideas. This followed the perceived German success story at a time when Keynesian interventions seemed to fail (McNamara 1998). A singularly independent central bank and fiscal rules were introduced to tie governments' hands. The recent failure of financial markets on a colossal scale did not end the neoliberal reign, on the contrary, an 'austerity delusion' has taken hold of EU policy-makers that is manifestly counterproductive for economic recovery (Blyth 2013: ch.3). In this view, the fiscal surveillance process can be seen as directly feeding financial investors with data, inviting them to sanction government behavior that would prioritize domestic redistribution and stimulus over the repayment of bonds. The role of credit ratings in the Basel II framework of financial regulation is further evidence for a close alignment of business interests and neoliberal ideas of government. CRAs invented 'a common language of credit risk' and governments proceeded to make 'the bond market's private authority public' (Abdelal 2007: 174).

The empirical corollary of these theories is that the international–commercial assessments of sovereign creditworthiness and the supranational–technocratic surveillance of budgets should be fairly aligned. Prospective bond buyers had in the Commission a potential ally and the regulatory/neoliberal polity in fiscal policy should have directly fed into the assessment of sovereign creditworthiness by rating agencies. The commercial agencies' interest in the probability of sovereign default can be seen as a specification of the EU's interest in externalities of public debt accumulation, such as higher interest rates and inflationary pressures.

For our study of rating agency behavior, we concentrate on Standard and Poor's, which is the most active and influential agency in sovereign credit rating (De Haan and Amtenbrink 2011: 5, 9). We rely both on publicly available data by analyzing the content of Rating Methodologies and individual rating reports for individual countries issued by S&P and on interview evidence.[1] For the study of technocratic fiscal surveillance, we analyze the ways in which Eurostat's statistical accounting translates data on pension savings and banking rescues into information about fiscal sustainability. So we turn the theoretical puzzle into the empirically researchable question: Why do market actors and a supranational economic bureaucracy have different assessments of these government interventions?

We have chosen pension reforms and bank rescue programs because they have strong fiscal consequences in contrast to, for instance, cuts in unemployment benefits.[2] They also have sufficiently rich and complex budgetary effects so that their assessment is a non-trivial task. Their long-term effects can be different from the short-term. Pensions have been a construction site of reforms over several decades now, while systemic bank rescues in developed countries took government watchers by surprise. This allows us to see how commercial and technocratic monitoring of sovereign debt interpret complex data and construct information about fiscal sustainability or sovereign creditworthiness, respectively.

The next three sections analyze the rating and statistical accounting of the two policy measures as well as recent changes to the approach of CRAs and to fiscal surveillance in the wake of the economic and financial crisis. In the section before the conclusions, we discuss our findings and we try to answer the overall question of why EU fiscal governance by regulation only is so unsatisfactory, both from the point of view of those who are concerned about high debt and those who are concerned about constraints on fiscal stimulus. Our conclusions argue that markets and distributional conflicts can overstretch governments' capacity to control their budgets.

Pension Reforms

The increasing pension liabilities of governments have bothered EU fiscal surveillance for some time. Member states must provide estimates of the evolution of age-related contingent liabilities over a rolling 50-year horizon in their annual stability programs. There are dedicated publications, such as the tri-annual Ageing Reports and the Fiscal Sustainability Reports, in which the European Commission regularly quantifies the effects of aging on the ratios of workers to pensioners, on government expenditure, and on debt. In the country-specific recommendations issued under the European Semester, the Commission urges pension reform, notably increasing the retirement age, reducing public pension entitlements, and introducing mandatory personal pensions, in more than half of the member states (SPC 2008).

However, despite these revealed concerns about the demographic drivers of sovereign debt, the statistical accounting for pensions has not managed to incorporate the issue in a way that provides incentives for the recommended pension reforms. Eurostat is quite explicit about the difficulties to account consistently for the various tiers or pillars of old age security. The 'Manual on Government Deficit and Debt' notes, with an undertone of regret, that there is an inconsistency in the accounting between pension obligations from funded and from unfunded schemes (Eurostat 2013: 144): the obligations under the latter obligations are not counted as debt and become visible only as they arise in future expenditure.

One consequence of these accounting rules is that pension liabilities can be made to disappear by transferring them from a funded occupational scheme to a public pay-as-you-go scheme. This is a live issue in the 'cleaning out' of state-owned enterprises before privatization (Eurostat 2013: 142), namely to assume debt or obligations that could scare off prospective investors. The clean out typically requires a one-off payment from the company as compensation for the government taking over all or part of the liabilities. Pensions for employees are typically the most relevant issue. Debt assumption and the one-off payment could be timed such that it helps the government to enhance its budget balance at a convenient moment. Eurostat (2013: 142–143) accepts the lump sum payment to the government as deficit-decreasing revenue. This revenue will be offset by future payments of pensions that increase the deficit. However, if the lump sum or one-off payment does not match the actuarial value of the obligations, the difference must be recorded as a deficit-increasing capital transfer if the lump sum is too low, while it must be recorded as a deficit-neutral 'withdrawal of equity' (switch of public asset composition) if it is too high (Eurostat 2013: 143). This asymmetry means that the accounting rule penalizes debt assumption by government but does not reward implicit taxation of investors in privatization.

Thus, rather than shifting from public unfunded to private or collective funded schemes, there are incentives to move in the opposite direction. In this European accounting sense, the move to a funded public pension pillar is therefore not made attractive for any administration currently in power.

The commercial rating of pension liabilities shows other signs of inconsistency. The stance of S&P on pension reforms evolved in a curious fashion over time. In its rating methodologies issued in 2006 and 2008, S&P emphatically warned of the risks to fiscal sustainability that aging would bring and warned that sovereigns that fail to address age-related spending pressures might be downgraded in the medium term (S&P 2006: 10; S&P 2008). Country-specific rating reports also repeatedly brought up the issue of the risk of age-related spending increases. Austria, Belgium, France, Germany, and Italy were frequently urged to address their vulnerabilities in this regard.[3] In other countries, the absence of rising pension liabilities was stressed as a factor that leads to stronger ratings. Favorable demographics and prefunding were mentioned as important strengths in Ireland, a fully funded and sizeable second tier propped up ratings for Denmark, whereas the UK was commended for its largely private pension provision.[4] Since the start of the crisis, however, S&P has put much less emphasis on pension reforms. Compared to the alarmist tone in earlier methodologies, the revised methodologies issued in 2011 and 2013 explicitly downplay the aging-related risks to sovereign creditworthiness and emphasize that in many cases, there is still sufficient time to address these issues (S&P 2011: 26 and S&P 2013: 26). In line with this change of methodologies, the individual country reports have become mostly oblivious of the issue of aging and of pension reforms.

In sum, commercial rating and supranational surveillance go into opposite directions as regards their assessment of reducing public pensions. Eurostat flags up the issue but consistency of statistical rules prevents it from accounting for the contingent pension liabilities in public budgets in the headline fiscal indicators, the debt- and deficit-to-GDP ratios. As indicated, fiscal surveillance has found other venues, such as the European Semester and the regular stability programs, to drive home the message. S&P issued warnings that it would initiate downgrades if a government failed to deal with age-related expenditures but hardly ever acted on it. More recently, this CRA has backtracked on pension reforms considerably. There is certainly no alignment in this policy area.

Crisis Management: Economic Stabilization and Bank Rescues

The financial and economic crisis since 2007–2008 forced governments to temporarily set aside fiscal rigor in an effort to prop up their ailing economies with stimulus measures. It also pushed governments into bank rescues on a truly astounding scale, for fear that otherwise the banks' struggle for survival would bring down the economy and inflict unacceptable social disruption on core constituencies. Governments guaranteed banks' liabilities, took over their bad assets or temporarily nationalized insolvent financial institutions. How much leeway did the two forms of fiscal monitoring provide to governments in those testing times?

EU fiscal rules that guide surveillance arguably prioritize prudent public finances over the stabilization of the economy; the accounting principles to generate the underlying information are designed accordingly. As far as bank rescues are concerned, Eurostat put out extensive communications since the start of the financial crisis to clarify the rules and made decisions on the treatment of 'financial defeasance structures', as bad banks are called in official language. These ensure that costs incurred and liabilities assumed by governments cannot be kept off the books unless there is a very strong chance that they either will not materialize or that they can be turned into profitable investment in the future. The most important principles distinguish the various rescue measures. Capital injections in 'too big to fail' entities are grants that are deficit-increasing (Eurostat 2013: 112, 120). By contrast, government guarantees of a bank's liabilities, notably savings deposits, affect neither debt nor deficit and only once the guarantee is called, does it increase the deficit (Eurostat 2013: 188, para 33). If the guarantee keeps a unit alive that is not really active in markets any more, Eurostat (2013: 188) puts down criteria for financial defeasance that national accountants can use to establish whether it has actually turned into a vehicle to wind down some of the former business. This is the case for instance, if the guaranteed bank is closed to new deposit taking or lending. In other words, only guarantees that do not meet the criteria for financial defeasance are below the line of relevant fiscal items in the Commission's surveillance.

Furthermore, the transfer of bank assets and liabilities is subject to asymmetric valuation principles. If a bank or some of its assets and liabilities become part of a defeasance structure, the difference between the transfer value of the assets and the market or fair value is a capital transfer to the debtors (banks) of the defeasance structure that increases the deficit (Eurostat 2013: 183–186). In a crisis, this difference and hence the effect on government deficits are likely to be overstated because market or fair values tend to be unduly low in distressed markets. Revaluation of the assets later, for instance due to rising prices for real estate, is not taken into account for the net lending or borrowing of the government (Eurostat 2013: 184, para 19; 185, para 21; 187, para 30). The assets and liabilities of a bad bank also come on the government books; hence, (gross) debt of general government increases. These accounting rules generate considerable penalty for bank rescue measures in the European system of fiscal surveillance.

S&P's approach creates even greater difficulties for governments in trying to deal with economic and financial crises. Since the start of the crisis, S&P has aggressively downgraded previously high-rated countries — like Ireland and Spain — for disappointing growth prospects and for assuming large liabilities in bailing out troubled banks. The current heavy-handed response stands in marked contrast with the leniency exercised before the crisis. From the mid-2000s, S&P had voiced concerns about an overheating economy (Ireland), excessive private sector indebtedness (Ireland and the UK), bubbles on the real estate markets, and the possibility of sharp corrections (Ireland, Spain, and the UK).[5] Although all of these factors foreshadowed problems with growth and the banking sector, the agency did not consider a downgrade or even a negative credit watch back then. Since the start of the crisis, however, rating methodologies have been updated to put more emphasis on growth prospects and the stability of the banking sector.

S&P downgraded governments for bank rescues irrespective of whether they took the form of guarantees, capital injections, or nationalizations. For example, Ireland — which still received a clean bill of health as late as November 2007[6] — was issued a negative outlook in January 2009 after its government issued guarantees to seven national banks. It was then downgraded six times in the following 3 years as the massive costs of those guarantees materialized.[7] Importantly, once the scope of the banking crisis became clear, S&P did not restrict itself to rate explicit government measures but sought to provide forward-looking evaluations by carrying out in-house modeling of the further costs of saving banks.[8] In none of the successive rating reports was there allowance for the beneficial effect bank rescues might have for the health of the banking sector and the economy in the longer term. Spain's experience was similar. On three occasions, downgrades were prompted by S&P's progressively worsening forecasts of the likely costs of government involvement in saving the banking sector (S&P Sp2010Apr28, Sp2011Dec5, Sp2012Apr26). Efforts to restore a viable banking industry came into consideration only as a downside risk for public finances.

In sum, the two systems of surveillance also display considerable differences. The SGP has an escape clause to allow for suspending fiscal rules in times of recession, although the Commission and the Council opted for not using it. In the handling of bank rescues, Eurostat aims at maximum accounting accuracy and transparency by differentiating between the different instruments governments use for bank rescues and by only recording the actual costs of a transaction once financial defeasance materializes. By contrast, S&P assesses bank rescues indiscriminately (negatively), and it has sought to adopt a proactive approach by penalizing government involvement in the troubles of the banking sector even before the costs of government intervention can be known with a reasonable degree of certainty. For S&P, weak growth is a main reason for downgrading countries.

Changes in Fiscal Monitoring in the Wake of the Crisis

Our comparison between fiscal surveillance by a deliberately technocratic body and credit rating by a commercial agency shows noticeable differences between the two ways of fiscal monitoring. The recent responses to the crisis by Eurostat, on the one hand, and by S&P, on the other, confirm and reinforce this finding. While Eurostat has sought to emphasize the continuity of the principles of the European System of Statistics, S&P has gone out of its way to demonstrate that it has incorporated into its methodologies and assessments the most important lessons of the crisis.

Although Eurostat naturally had to respond to new issues as a result of the crisis, it sought to address these issues emphatically through the continuation, or 'clarification', of existing principles. For example, when it upgraded its Manual on Government Deficit and Debt in 2013, only one of the three new chapters related to the crisis. This chapter dealt with new 'European entities related to the Euro Area sovereign debt crisis', i.e., the emergency fund, the European Stability Mechanism with its predecessor EFSF, which provide credit to governments under attack in bond markets. All other issues raised by the crisis, like financial defeasance or the capital injections on an unprecedented scale in the case of Ireland, did not make Eurostat invent new accounting devices but issue 'clarifications'. There are no significant changes to the recording of the other two policy areas analyzed above, pensions and privatizations.

Eurostat also stresses the consensual character of its decisions concerning issues emerging from the crisis. The new Manual refers to wide-ranging consultations on the clarifications and refinements of existing principles: 'It is the result of a collective work, co-ordinated and animated by Eurostat, by experts in Government Financial Statistics and national accounts representing EU Member States, the Commission (the Directorate General for Economic and Financial Affairs) and the ECB' (Eurostat 2013: 1).

The attempt to uphold continuity and transparency in the European System of Statistics is based on a conspicuous consensus among national and international experts, thus fending off criticism and interventions by some treasuries.

By contrast, S&P has emphasized change, adaptation to shifting conditions, and the incorporation of new lessons into assessments of creditworthiness. Since the start of the crisis, S&P issued three new methodologies, in 2008, 2011, and 2013. These successive iterations of methodologies integrate new issues and discuss old ones in more detail than before. All three policy areas discussed above have been subject to considerable revisions. The urgency of pension reform is now explicitly downplayed, as already indicated (S&P 2011: 26 and 2013: 26). Privatization and structural reform also receive much less emphasis. Accordingly, these issues literally disappear from individual country reports. Contingent liabilities generated by an unstable banking sector are discussed in much greater detail than before (S&P 2011: 28–30 and 2013: 28–30). Growth prospects also become a central issue, and a long section is dedicated to explaining how they are assessed (S&P 2011: 17–18 and 2013: 17–18).[9] These new issues affected the ratings of a host of countries besides Ireland and Spain. Growth concerns led to falling ratings in Greece, Italy, and Portugal, whereas problems with the banking sector contributed to downgrades of Belgium and potential banking problems cost Austria its AAA rating.[10] An important new issue in focus is crisis management or, more specifically, the ability of governments to respond to economic and financial shocks (S&P 2011: 13 and 2013: 13). Finally, the constraints on policy adjustment in countries that are members of monetary unions are mentioned for the first time in the two latest methodologies (S&P 2011: 34–35 and 2013: 34–35). The new focus on the latter two issues motivated an unprecedented collective rating report issued in January 2012, which simultaneously reviewed existing ratings for all euro-members in response to what was seen as weak crisis management at the European level, by the Commission and the ECB.[11]

The reforms in rating methodologies and profound changes in the rating approach indicate that credit ratings do not have a consistent methodological basis to make them usable for regulatory purposes. Instead, ratings focus on current issues that are of most interest to market investors at any given moment. This explains both why S&P placed such emphasis on privatizations and pension reforms before the crisis, even though these issues have only a tenuous relationship to the probability of sovereign debt default, and why it was so willing to disregard these issues once the crisis threw up others. This approach stands in marked contrast with Eurostat's insistence on maintaining continuity and consistency despite the extraordinary times.

Two Different Logics

Our take on these findings is that they support neither the regulatory polity interpretation, which sees the EU as a fourth branch of government for supranational economic regulation, nor the neoliberal project view, which construes EU fiscal governance as an institutionalized practice of neoliberal ideology. The differences in the approaches Eurostat and S&P charted in the previous sections reveal that the two types of monitoring do not complement each other well enough to allow either for effective fiscal discipline or to generate consistent neoliberal pressure on policy-making.

To start with the latter, S&P cannot be classified as truly neoliberal and its interaction with Eurostat does not lead to a persistent advancement of a neoliberal policy agenda. Rather than dependably pushing for coherent policy choices, S&P is transparently opportunistic in that it tries to speak to market concerns about the risk-return prospects in sovereign credit. The concern post-crisis is low growth that can lead to adverse income flow and debt stock dynamics even when the fiscal headline figures are improving. Downgrading countries for low growth prospects is rational but procyclical, pushing governments in difficulties into more difficulties. Privatization of pensions and of public assets were put on the backburner at a time when households are financially overstretched and financial institutions reluctant to invest in illiquid assets. The fact that a CRA partly anticipates and partly follows investor interests as they perceive them does not make it neoliberal.

Eurostat's independent effect on policy is not unambiguously neoliberal either. For example, accounting rules do not give governments a straightforward incentive to retrench public provisions or to privatize pensions. On the contrary, Eurostat's rules make public finances look better if the government takes over pension liabilities from state-owned enterprises into a pay-as-you-go system in return for a lump sum payment.

The regulatory polity theory would require that European fiscal surveillance provide fiscal discipline that reconciles dependable rigor with the collective interests of member states. A supranational regulator is required to solve this collective action problem, namely not to overuse the common resource of a stable currency. If one considers this to be the prime problem of a monetary union, as the architects of the euro area certainly did, then the regulatory polity theory has some evidence on its side. S&P's manifest failure to exert consistent pressure for fiscal restraint on countries supports the view that enforcing discipline cannot be left to the markets and a supranational public agency is required instead.

It is debatable, however, whether European fiscal surveillance manages to further collectively desirable policies while regulating budgets in this way as the theory requests. Eurostat's striving for stability of rules and its ostentatious reliance on international expert consensus is consistent with the role of a supranational regulator. Yet, being bound so tightly by its own statistical rules can also come into conflict with policy priorities evolving during a crisis for which these rules were not written. Bank rescues are a case in point (Mabbett and Schelkle 2014: 15–22). Under Eurostat rules, all measures aimed at consolidating banks affect public finances negatively, except for guarantees. This fiscal accounting gave European governments no incentives to pursue bank recapitalizations and restructuring. The revealed, if contingent liabilities urge governments to prioritize budget consolidation, not for fear of an EDP but for fear of market panic. Ireland, Italy, and Spain were in this situation. National banking systems then survive mainly because the ECB throws them a lifeline, by offering banks very low refinancing in the hope that they earn higher returns and recapitalize themselves out of the margin.[12] However, this means that Eurostat's rules contribute to perpetuating a regime that is in the short-term interest of national democracies but not conducive to what is officially considered good governance of the union.

The observed divergence between monitoring and responses to the crisis shows the difficulty of a purely regulatory approach to fiscal governance. Without a budget that could provide incentives for compliance or fill the gaps left by member states, regulation by supranational bureaucracies will be imperfect even if they seek to enlist the help of market actors. The Commission, in the guise of Eurostat, follows a bureaucratic imperative of continuity, accountability, and transparency, whereas monitoring by CRAs is driven by market opportunism and herding behavior. Neither is fully justifiable on economic grounds, especially not under the circumstances of a crisis. They are driven by institutional logics, of an administration, on the one hand, and of commercial firms, on the other. This is not by mistake but an inherent trait of each.

Rating agencies insist on their assessments being fundamentally different from regulatory purposes and now object to the regulatory role ascribed to them. This view is clearly expressed by the Chief Risk Officer and Chief Credit Officer at Moody's: 'The growing use of ratings in regulation had given rise to three potentially adverse industry dynamics: (i) the substitution of regulatory demand for investor-driven demand for ratings, (ii) the growing perception that ratings were something more than an opinion as a result of their official recognition by regulators, and (iii) a vicious circle of intrusive regulation to induce ratings and rating agencies to behave in line with regulatory needs, potentially changing the nature of ratings'. (Cantor 2013: 27). In an interview, a senior decision-maker at S&P expressed similar reservations against their regulatory role. CRAs define their role as service providers to the financial industry, not as actors outside or beyond that industry. They stress that what they offer is an opinion on creditworthiness meant to help investors in their own decision-making process rather than authoritative assessments of credit quality to be used for regulatory purposes. Key in this distinction is the room for qualitative, subjective assessment that is recognized as such.

This emphasis on 'opinions about creditworthiness' might be self-serving, namely to limit legal liability and defending their autonomy. But it is still an insight that needs to be heeded by those who hope that a tightened fiscal surveillance regime and new rules for sovereign credit rating can do the trick for EU fiscal governance. New regulation on the rating business came into force on 20 June 2013, seeking to make it more transparent, more predictable, and more accountable.[13] However, such rules have little chance of transforming CRA activities as desired by the regulator if CRAs and the regulator disagree about what rating agencies do.

Concluding Remarks

Market discipline, even if it reliably existed, is not a natural ally of prudent regulation. When markets become a binding constraint on government finances, they usually trigger a crisis that, for better or worse, nobody is prepared to simply let run its course. The EU approach of regulating governments into ever more transparency and accountability is prone to distort the lessons to be drawn from any of these financial crises. It always starts and ends with holding governments accountable, regardless of whether sovereign debt is the cause in the first place.

This bias reveals a view of governments as potentially effective actors who can control their budgets if only given the right incentives. When they fail to do so, then it must be out of opportunism, notably to raise their reelection chances. Such a view cannot account for what happened to all governments in this crisis: they were pushed by market failure into huge deficits or at least high contingent liabilities. Certainly, some governments were ill-prepared for such a fiscal shock because they did not have their budgets under control before the crisis: Greece, the euro area's weakest link, therefore broke first. Unresolved distributive conflicts in many countries make budgetary policy the overstretched guarantor of fragile compromises (Barta 2011). Stabilization may therefore be delayed even if it is a negative sum game — a situation that Alesina and Drazen (1991) captured in the stylized notion of a war of attrition that fiscal authorities are too weak to end.

For the recasting of integration and governance of EMU, our findings imply that there are limits to institution building. Reformers and their academic advisors should acknowledge that it is sometimes the vulnerability of governments and not their strength and activism that is the problem. Exposing them to market pressures, through transparency and other devices of social engineering, cannot force governments to do the right thing; it just shows their vulnerability. No institutional fixes at the EMU level can solve the distributive conflicts inside member states. This precludes the more maximalist solutions like a central budget for the foreseeable future, unless one wants to risk a political backlash reversing integration. The US dollar union was not built in just 5 years (*Gaspar*). Hamilton's reforms were all undone in the following century, including political union with the secession of Southern states. To this very day, a no bail-out regime for states and municipalities is in place that is harsher than present EMU practice. An insolvency law for sovereign debtors might be a more constructive way forward, not least because it could discipline financial markets.

Acknowledgments

We are grateful to Dermot Hodson, Deborah Mabbett (both Birkbeck, University of London), James Savage (University of Virginia), and Wolfgang Streeck (MPI Köln) for most helpful comments.

Disclosure statement

No potential conflict of interest was reported by the authors.

Notes

1. The textual evidence is based on 267 country reports between 1999 and 2012 and four different editions of rating methodologies (2006, 2008, 2011, and 2013). The content of all of these documents were systematically analyzed using the Nvivo software. Reports specifically referenced in this text are specified by country acronym and publication date. The interview evidence is drawn from a telephone interview conducted in November 2013 with one of S&P's four primary analysts in the sovereign rating group.
2. An earlier version looked at the privatization of state-owned enterprises, left out for reasons of space. We found that despite the general agreement between EU authorities and S&P about the desirability of privatization in principle, the tangible incentives that the supranational and commercial channels of surveillance provided were quite different. European statistical rules encourage privatization to reduce current debt, thus allowing governments to prettify their fiscal performance. But Eurostat has also been at pains to ensure that some of the hidden losses entailed in the sale of government assets are recorded transparently (Savage 2005: 81–89). S&P, on the other hand, did not acknowledge costs of privatization. Apart from the occasional warning that one-off measures to decrease the deficit should be greeted with caution, the reports do not take into consideration that privatization deals may be myopic and reduce future revenues.
3. S&P Au2000June13, Au2003May21, Be1999Feb1, Be2002Feb18, Be2003Mar18, Be2004Jan23, Fr2001Jan24, Fr2002Jan28, Fr2003Mar19, Fr2004Jan20, Fr2006Feb28, Ge2002Dec10, Ge2003May6, Ge2005Mar1, Ge2005Nov16, Ge2006Dec19, It1999May27, It2000Apr19, It2001Oct26, It2003Jan15, It2006Oct19.
4. S&P Dk2001Feb27, Dk2002Mar26, Dk2003Apr9, Dk2004Aug26, Dk2005Sep30, Dk2006Sep25, Dk2007Sep26, Ir1999Aug13, Ir2000Oct3, Ir2001Oct3, Ir2002Sep5, Ir2003Oct30, Ir2004Dec23, Ir2005Dec20, Ir2006Dec21, Ir2007Nov23, UK2003June24.
5. S&P Ir2004Dec23, Ir2005Dec29, Ir2006Dec21, Ir2007Nov23, Sp2004Dec13, Sp2005Nov28, Sp2006Nov28, Sp2007Nov26, UK2005Mar31, UK2006Nov10.
6. The 2007 November credit report contended that 'Ireland's extremely strong [AAA] credit standing should remain secure against most foreseeable downside economic, political, and financial risks' (S&P Ir2007Nov13: 3).
7. S&P Ir2009Mar30, Ir2009June8, Ir2010Aug24, 2010Nov23, Ir2011Feb2, Ir2011Apr1.
8. Examples of the type of independent assessment of the costs of banking crisis can be found in the March 2009 and the April 2010 rating reports on Ireland (S&P Ir2009Mar30: 2–3 and Ir2010Apr8: 2–3).
9. Interestingly, the new methodologies explicitly promise to avoid the mistake that S&P committed when not acting upon asset bubbles and credit-fueled growth in Spain and Ireland before the crisis: 'A sovereign's economic score would be one category worse than the initial score, when GDP growth seems to be fueled mostly by a rapid increase in banking sector domestic claims on the private sector, combined with a sustained growth in inflation-adjusted asset prices, indicating vulnerability to a potential credit-fueled asset bubble'. (S&P 2011: 17, a similar paragraph can be found in S&P 2013: 16).
10. S&P Au2012Jan13, Be2011Nov25, Gr2010Apr27, Gr2012May2, It2011Sep19, Pt2010Apr27
11. In this collective rating action, nine sovereigns were downgraded, whereas the ratings of seven others were affirmed (S&P 2012).
12. The number of banks that are thus kept alive is much higher than the indicator of defeasance structures all over Europe shows. The ECB is forced to keep many banks on its list of monetary and financial institutions with access to the discount window. If they were declared part of defeasance structures, the ECB could not support them with its liquidity measures as this would fall under the prohibition of monetary financing of governments (Mabbett and Schelkle 2014: 19–20).
13. The new rules mandate CRAs to set up a calendar indicating when they will rate Member States and to rate sovereigns at least every 6 months, but not more often than three times a year. They also stipulate that rating changes may only be announced on Fridays after close of business to allow governments to react to the news before markets can move. They require CRAs to make their methodologies public and invite comments from stakeholders. They also demand that CRAs

disclose the assumptions that their assessment is based on. They seek to create greater accountability by making CRAs liable for errors caused by 'gross negligence'. (see: http://europa.eu/rapid/press-release_IP-13-555_en.htm?xrs=RebelMouse_tw accessed on 29 December 2014).

References

Abdelal, R. 2007. *Capital rules. The construction of global finance*. Cambridge, MA: Harvard University Press.

Alesina, A., and A. Drazen. 1991. Why are stabilizations delayed? *American Economic Review* 81, no. 5: 1170–81.

Barta, Z. 2011. *Flirting with disaster: explaining excessive public debt accumulation in Italy and Belgium*. Unpublished Ph.D. thesis. London: London School of Economics.

Blyth, M. 2013. *Austerity: the history of a dangerous idea*. Oxford: Oxford University Press.

Cantor, R. 2013. Ratings and regulation. In *Sovereign risk: a world without risk-free assets? Proceedings of a seminar on sovereign risk*, Basel, 8–9 January 2013. BIS Papers No 72.

De Haan, J., and Amtenbrink, F. 2011. *Credit rating agencies*. DNB Working Papers No. 278, Amsterdam: De Nederlandsche Bank.

Eurostat. 2013, 2014. *Manual on government deficit and debt: implementation of ESA95*. Luxembourg: Eurostat.

Faini, R. 2006. Fiscal policy and interest rates in Europe. *Economic Policy* (July): 443–89.

IMF. 2010. The uses and abuses of government bond ratings. In *Global financial stability report*, ed. International Monetary Fund, ch.3, Washington DC: IMF.

Mabbett, D., and W. Schelkle. 2014. *Searching under the lamp-post: the evolution of fiscal surveillance*, LEQS Paper 75/2014. London: London School of Economics.

Majone, G. 1993.*The European Community: an independent 'fourth branch of government'?* EUI working paper SPS no.93/9. Florence: European University Institute.

Majone, G. 1996. *Regulating Europe*. London: Routledge.

Manganelli, S., and G. Wolswijk. 2007. *Market discipline, financial integration and fiscal rules — What drives spreads in the euro-area government bond market?* ECB Working Paper No. 745. Frankfurt a.M.: European Central Bank.

McNamara, K.R. 1998. *The currency of ideas. Monetary politics in the European Union*. Ithaca: Cornell University Press.

Savage, J.D. 2005. *Making the EMU: the politics of budgetary surveillance and the enforcement of Maastricht*. Oxford: Oxford University Press.

SPC. 2008. *Privately managed funded pension provision and their contribution to adequate and sustainable pensions*. Brussels: The Social Protection Committee.

Standard and Poor's. 2006, 2008. *Sovereign credit ratings: a primer*. www.standardandpoors.com/ratingsdirect (accessed January 2010).

Standard and Poor's. 2011, 2013. *Sovereign government rating methodology and assumptions*. www.standardandpoors.com/ratingsdirect (accessed June 2012 and February 2014).

Standard and Poor's. 2012. *Standard & Poor's takes various rating actions on 16 Eurozone Sovereign governments*. www.standardandpoors.com/ratingsdirect (accessed June 2012).

The Making of a Continental Financial System: Lessons for Europe from Early American History

VÍTOR GASPAR

International Monetary Fund, Washington, DC, USA

ABSTRACT Alexander Hamilton was the first US Treasury Secretary from 1789 to 1795. When he started, the federal government was in default. During his tenure, US Treasuries became the ultimate safe asset. He successfully managed expectations, achieved debt service reduction, and stabilized financial panics. He delivered sound public finances and financial stability. In the end, the US possessed a modern financial system able to finance innovation and growth. At a time when Europe is working its way out of the sovereign debt crisis and implementing banking union and financial union, it is worthwhile to search for lessons from early US history.

I. Introduction

In the autumn of 2009, the global financial crisis mutated in Europe into sovereign debt crises in several countries of the euro area. Financial market participants were desperately seeking access to liquidity and safe assets. Credit risk became a relevant consideration for hitherto considered safe sovereign debt. The prospect breakdown of the euro area was a present threat for investors and populations. The situation started stabilizing only after political commitment to deeper integration was achieved in the European Council of June 2012. That was followed by the announcement of the Outright Monetary Transactions Program by the ECB in September 2012. One year after, in the summer of 2013, euro area fragmentation appeared to no longer be a relevant consideration in the financial calculations of international investors.

The history of financial politics in the early stages of US history can provide insights into what can be done to build a robust and resilient European financial system and to establish the credibility of sovereign debt as safe assets. The US federal government has never defaulted on its debt and the US is a well-integrated monetary union of continental dimension. Alexander Hamilton was the first secretary of the US Treasury, from 1789 to 1795. He managed successfully the transition from a bankrupt federal government to a situation where the US Treasury became the issuer of the ultimate safe asset. In the process, Alexander Hamilton laid the foundations for a modern financial system able to finance innovation and growth.

Alexander Hamilton appears as a rare combination of theoretical and practical reason; strategic and tactical thinking; and of audacity and realism. Building a Continental financial system in the aftermath of sovereign debt crises in the euro area is a priority in Europe. The aim of this article was to find out whether we can learn Hamilton's recipe for building a continental financial system in Europe.

The comparison of the challenges of Europe today and the early US is the theme of Thomas Sargent Nobel Lecture (Sargent 2013) that provided the inspiration for this article. Sargent draws on the general lessons from US financial history, focusing on two episodes: the origin of the US fiscal constitution in the late 1780s and the state debt crisis of the 1840s. James (2015) and Kincaid (2014) also interpret a much longer period of US financial history. This article instead concentrates on a very specific period from late 1789 to early 1795 and looks at broader dimensions of finance. By concentrating on a briefer period, it is possible to examine in more detail how it was done. The paper closest to this one in scope is Sylla (2014).

The Hamilton moment illustrates the very strong threefold cord constituted by politics, fiscal policy, and financial activities. As emphasized by Sargent (2013), it took a political transformation to make it possible to ground public finances on solid fundamentals. More generally, it is important to realize that changing policy outcomes systematically requires changing the rules and incentives of politics. For Europe, a crucial question is: How can we (Europeans) design institutions in Europe so as to align political incentives with macroeconomic stability and financial integration? The experience of the first US Secretary of the Treasury offers some inspiration.

Alexander Hamilton himself poses and answers some fundamental questions:

- Why is it important to honor public credit? Why not repudiate debt?
- By what means can public credit be maintained? How to ensure public credit? How to promote a smooth and quick transition?
- How to restore financial stability in the face of financial panic?

These answers are fundamentally relevant for Europe today. That much was clear from the summary presentation of the euro area crisis in this

Introduction. The euro area and its member states are struggling to find timely answers. Those answers matter. They influence growth and employment prospects and the lives of millions of people. But there is onc aspect that is crucial to stress. The only answers that can be relevant in the real world are political answers. Public finance and the financial system are part of a system of institutions in the political realm. Those institutions shape the relevant incentives and determine a set of possible outcomes. To repeat: the fundamental question is political: How can the rules of the political game, in Europe, be shaped in order to improve outcomes?

The article has a narrow focus. As already said, it looks at a well-determined episode: the experience of Alexander Hamilton as first secretary of the Treasury, from late 1789 to early 1795. The episode does not exhaust lessons from the US for European financial integration. For example, the importance of politics in shaping the financial system is clear from the coalition between rural debtors, incumbent bankers, and state governments that led to a fragmentation of the US national banking system through a myriad of local monopolies (see Calomiris and Haber 2014).

The article is organized around the answers to the questions above. The history of the United States, in its early years, illustrates the importance of political institutional building. The replacement of the articles of the Confederation by the American Constitution of 1788 offers a perfect illustration. The history of subsequent decades also shows what institutional designs proved robust and which were not able to withstand political pressure.

The remainder of the article is organized as follows: Section II looks at constitutional politics in the US in the 1780s. Section III presents Alexander Hamilton's vision of a modern financial system. Section IV argues that the initial conditions were, according to standard indicators and analysis, very difficult. Sections V and VI discuss specific actions by Hamilton. We discuss public debt management and crisis management, respectively. In Section VII, we conclude.

II. Changing the Rules of the Political Game

The challenge of building up US public finances was daunting. Thc main problem was to ensure the service of debt accumulated during the War of Independence. At the end of 1789, total debt in the US (federal and state) amounted to about $80 million (about 40 percent of GDP). Roughly speaking, about one-third was States' debt and the remainder federal. In his *First Report on Public Credit*, Alexander Hamilton estimates the contractual interest rates as amounting to $4.6 million. Such amount compares with total operating expenditures of federal government estimates at $0.6 million.

In 1789, the US was, in fact, in default. Bonds were perpetual debts (called consols). Therefore, default corresponded to the accumulation of interest arrears. Principal debt corresponded to bonds called 'continental certificates', while accumulated interest arrears were named 'indents'. In 1789, these bonds traded at heavy discounts. At the lowest point, the market value was about 20 percent for continental certificates and 12.5 percent for indents. To have a term for comparison, the minimum market value for Greek 10-year bonds, in mid-2012, was about 15 percent. During the War of Independence, Congress also issued paper currency. Credibility was further undermined by the dramatic depreciation of paper money.

The situation in the 1780s still reflected the experience under the Articles of the Confederation. Congress had the authority to incur debts. And, as explained in *Federalist 30*, the means to service these responsibilities were supposed to be provided by the States. However, the requests from Congress were left unfulfilled. The system in place was not effective. No state met its obligations in full; some did not comply at all or nearly so; and there is even at least one example of explicit refusal to comply (New - Jersey). It was also the case that the attempt at reaching agreement for Congress to launch general taxation failed. The specific proposal was to launch a general import duty, whose revenue would be fully devoted to debt service. The proposal to amend the Articles of the Confederation for this effect failed (first in 1781, vetoed by Rhode Island in 1782, and, second in 1783, vetoed by New York). The proponent of these initiatives, Robert Morris, eventually resigned in 1784. Hence, it was clear at the launch of the Pennsylvania Convention that the framework of the Articles of the Confederation left the debt accumulated during the War of Independence, for all practical purposes, unfunded. Congress did not have the power to tax. The inability to mobilize adequate revenue, to ensure debt service, translated into the deep discounts reported above.

The problem was political *and* financial. As much is clearly stated in *Federalist 30*:

> Money is with propriety considered a vital principle of the body politic (...) From a deficiency in this particulars, one of two evils must ensue: either the people must be subject to continual plunder (...) or the government must sink into fatal atrophy and in a short course of time must perish (...)
>
> (...) to depend upon a government that must itself depend upon thirteen others for the means of fulfilling its contracts, when once its situation is clearly understood, would require a degree of credulity, not to be often met in the pecuniary transactions of mankind, and little reconcilable with the usual sharp-sightedness of avarice.

The political solution involved having the 1788 Constitution substituting for the Articles of the Confederation. The US Constitution:

(1) Strengthened the ability of federal government to tax; and confirmed the ability of federal government to use public credit (Article 1, Section 8, Clauses 1 and 2).
(2) Gave the central government exclusive competence to regulate external trade and interstate commerce (Article 1, Section 8, Clause 3; 'the commerce clause').

That was appropriate from the viewpoint of public finances as government revenue was — in the late eighteenth century — dominated by tariffs. To use an expression of Richard Sylla's, the 1788 Constitution created the 'Constitutional Theater' where Alexander Hamilton acted as first US Treasury Secretary. The Constitution made available the tools that would later be used by government (Sargent 2013). The way this was done is the subject of what follows. Before doing so, next section will characterize Hamilton's financial program.

III. Alexander Hamilton's Financial Program

Sylla (2011) and Sylla, Wright, and Cowen (2009) characterize a modern financial system as having six main elements:

> First, stable and sustainable public finances and competent public debt management;
> Second, a stable currency;
> Third, a central bank;
> Fourth, a banking system;
> Fifth, securities markets; and
> Sixth, a process for incorporation of financial and non-financial businesses.

Sylla (2014) refers that these components were in place in the Dutch Republic early in the seventeenth century and that England introduce them shortly after the Glorious Revolution of 1688. These examples were known in the US, Alexander Hamilton referred to them with some frequency.

Sylla (2011) also documents that all of this information is contained in three letters that Hamilton wrote: two in 1780 (Robert Morris and James Duane, 1780a, 1780b) and 1781 (again to Robert Morris). These letters reveal a profound knowledge of financial history and institutions. According to the biography written by Chernow (2004), Hamilton studied numerous authors including William Blackstone, Thomas Hobbes, Hugo Grotius, Samuel Pufendorf, John Locke, Malachy Postlethwaite, David Hume, Richard Price, and Adam Smith. It is clear from those writings that he was as impressed with the successful Dutch and British financial revolutions as he was with the demise of John Law's schemes in France. The latter experience may have been decisive for the First Treasury Secretary's acute sense of the importance of trust and stability in finance. From all of this, Hamilton concluded that finance was key to state power and economic prosperity. The quote above clearly illustrates the link between public finances and state power. The importance of finance is made clear in the *Third Letter:*

> Most commercial nations have found it necessary to institute banks; and they have proved to be the happiest engines that ever were invented for advancing trade. Venice, Genoa, Hamburg, Holland, and England are examples of their utility. They owe their riches,

commerce, and the figure they have made at different periods, in a great degree to this source.

When Alexander Hamilton started his tenure as Secretary of the Treasury, none of the six elements, used by Sylla and co-authors to characterize a modern financial system, was in place. As we have seen in Section II, the Treasury was bankrupt. When he left the Treasury, all six components were in working order.

Rosseau and Sylla (1999) report estimates of average annual growth in per capita GDP, in the US, in the period 1790–1806 that of about 1.5 percent. This result must be put in perspective. First, it is important to recall that growth rates in per capita income before 1800 were about zero. Second, growth in per capita income in the US has been persistently on a positive trend from 1790 onwards. The authors argue for a causal link between finance and growth in early US history. In Rosseau and Sylla (2001), they widen the analysis to a panel of seventeen countries, in the period from 1850 to 1997. They especially examine the examples of the Dutch Republic, England, France, Germany, and Japan. The authors suggest the possibility that both growth and globalization may have been 'finance led'. That would be in line with Hamilton's claim about: 'banks ... as the happiest engines ever invented to advance trade'.

IV. A Challenging Beginning: Why Pay for Public Debt?

The Treasury Department was created in September 1789. It immediately got a mandate from Congress to prepare proposals to restore and maintain public credit. The urgency is clear; the *First Report on Public Credit* was presented in January 1790. One crucial first question was: Why pay for the public debt? Why not default?

The answer can be given at various levels. They are all present in different forms in the first *Report*.

First, at a very general level, public credit is a cornerstone of public finances and of financial development. Hence, it is vital for political government. It is also key for economic activity, that is for trade, manufacturing, and farming, and, therefore, for economic prosperity. These points were systemically articulated. The structure of the argument is very close to that followed in recent research by Christoph Trebesch and co-authors (e.g., Trebesch 2011; Cruces and Trebesch 2013).

Second, the debt was accumulated to finance the War of Independence. From the viewpoint of the United States, that was clearly a common good. Today, we would label it a pure public (or collective) good. Therefore, the case for honoring the debt was strong on grounds of political (collective) cohesion.

Third, Hamilton was persuaded that the political coalition necessary to foster financial development involved the state and moneyed people. The latter were the main creditors of Congress. The viability of political support required an outcome compatible with the interests of creditors.

In Section II, we have already documented that the US Constitution provided the federal government with the powers necessary to fund public debt. Congress immediately approved a national tax, along the lines of the proposals that were blocked under the Articles of the Confederation. Nevertheless, the starting conditions were dire.

In *The First Report on Public Credit*, the interests due (annually) under contractual arrangements were estimated at $4.6 million. In 1790, the first complete year of operation of the new Constitution, total tax revenues came in at $1.64 million (Sylla 2011). Total operating expenses of the government amounted to $0.825 million. So it turned out that tax revenues, while about twice operating expenditures, were only about one-third of interest payments due. We have already reported that when Hamilton took office, the US was in default in its internal and international debt. It was accumulating interest arrears. Sylla (2011) further reports that in March 1790, Alexander Hamilton informed the President that the US Treasury did not have enough funds to honor current expenditures and interest payments on Dutch loans. Authorization for a new $100,000 loan was sought. Within two days, Washington authorized the loan. The federal government was, in 1790, operating hand-to-mouth.

In these conditions, it was very difficult to establish trust and credibility. Nevertheless, from September 1789 when he took office, to March 1790 when the Dutch loan was obtained, the second market quote of Continental certificates and indents recovered substantially. The increase was from about 0.25–0.40 for the Continental certificates and from about 0.15–0.30 for indents. The secondary market discounts quickly diminished after that. How did he do it?

V. Hamilton's Debt Management Strategy

Hamilton's debt management strategy aimed, first and foremost, at expectations' management. It was based on two main elements: a market-based debt service reduction scheme (see Garber 1991) and a Sinking Fund.

US debt was dominated, as was frequently the case in the eighteenth century, by consolidated perpetual annuities (consols). These bonds paid a percentage of their face value forever. The government, however, had the option to redeem, at any time, the consol at face value. That allowed the government to benefit from falling interest rates. If success in generating expectations of falling interest rates (increasing bond prices) was obtained, he could implement his market-based public debt reduction scheme. The idea is that by paying more than expected on existing debt, he would generate prospective savings that would more than compensate the costs.

Hamilton proposed to pay foreign debt in full. Surprisingly, this was not controversial. However, as Garber reports, even in the case of foreign debt, he did not allow for compound interest to apply to interest rate arrears. According to estimates in Garber (1991), the value saved as of 1 January 1790 represented about 2.3 percent of the total of foreign debt. The payment of external creditors made it possible for the US to tap European bond markets. As described below, European finance played an important role in Hamilton's market-based strategy, through the use of the Sinking Fund.

For internal debt, the proposals and debated options were much richer (see Sylla [2011] for a summary presentation and Garber [1991], for the details). In the end, the Funding Act, of August 1790, provided that domestic debt could be converted, under prescribed conditions, into new domestic debt instruments. The new bonds were 6 percent coupon bonds (the 6s); 6 percent coupon bonds with interest payments deferred 10 years (the deferred) and 3 percent coupon bonds (3s). The new bonds paid interest quarterly. The conversion offer treated principal and interest differently. For the principal, the offer was conversion at par into two-thirds 6s and one-third deferred. For interest arrears, the conversion was at par into 3s. There were specific provisions for the conversion of the debts of the states. The details are of no particular relevance for the line pursued in this article.

Garber documents that the market value of the offer was significantly below par. Hence, there was a substantial reduction in net present value of US Treasury liabilities. On the same vein, Sylla shows that interest payments were reduced from about \$4.6–\$3.6 million. This was a substantial reduction.

The operation was very successful. At the end of 1794, when Hamilton was close to depart from the Treasury, 98 percent of domestic debt had been voluntarily converted. However, the take up was gradual over time. By September 1791, only about \$30 million in bonds had been converted. The response in bond market prices was much quicker.

The second important element of the plan was the *Sinking Fund*. The Fund was entitled to revenue generated by the operation of the Post Office. In the *First Report on Public Credit*, this revenue is estimated at \$100,000. It was further asserted that the sum was likely to considerably grow over time. Hence, the Fund benefited from an important and reliable source of funding. The main ostensive argument for the Sinking Fund was the need to repay (to extinguish) public debt. However, the *Sinking Fund* could also use loans. That provided the Fund with considerable flexibility.

Therefore, the Sinking Fund was able to play three very important (and related) roles: first, to anchor expectations on a regime where Treasuries were properly funded; second, to accelerate the transition (increase) in bond prices to their new fundamental value ('true standard'); and, third, to provide the Treasury with an effective instrument for bond market stabilization in case of disturbances. The latter role was not yet made explicit. It became clear through the actions of the Sinking Fund in stopping the financial panics of 1791 and, more clearly and importantly, 1792.

VI. How did Hamilton Restore Financial Stability in the Face of Financial Panic?

The success of the plan and the rapid development of financial markets and financial organizations led, in 1792, to a dangerous threat to financial stability. In a letter to William Seton, in early 1792, Hamilton expresses his grave concern with developments observed in securities' markets: 'these extravagant sallies of speculation do injury to the government and to the whole system of public credit'. Given that bond prices peaked in February 1792, a few weeks after the letter was written, the episode testifies how closely and accurately Hamilton observed financial market developments. Already in 1791, there had been a financial disturbance in August–September. The 1791 disturbance was associated with speculation in banks' stock. In that context, the *Sinking Fund* was used to stabilize bond markets.

However, it is the panic of 1792 that provides the paradigmatic example. Sylla, Wright, and Cowen (2009) argue that these actions anticipate the classical lender of last resort doctrine.

The classical function of lender of last resort was articulated by Thornton (1802) and Bagehot (1873). An excellent presentation is Humphrey (1992). The lender of last resort function aims at protecting the financial system as a whole. It does not aim to save individual organizations. Only illiquid but solvent corporations are eligible for lender of last resort assistance. Insolvent entities should fail. The balance sheet and financial integrity of the liquidity provider are protected by adequate collateral. According to the doctrine liquidity, through the lender of last resort function, should be available only at penalty rates.

In letters to William Setton, Hamilton defends the provision of very large amounts of liquid funds. Those liquid funds should be made available against the pledging of good collateral. The cost of funding suggested was 7 percent (that was the ceiling fixed in usury laws). Hence, the interpretation of Sylla et al. that Hamilton was an early practitioner of the lender of last resort doctrine.

But there is an interesting question. What assets were identified as sound collateral? In the letter quoted in Sylla, Wright, and Cowen (2009), Hamilton lists the 6s, the 3s, and the deferred as the appropriate assets for the purpose. He suggests that the 6s should be accepted as collateral at par, the 3s should be accepted at 50 percent of nominal value, and the deferred at 60 percent. These values are below but close to the market prices that were to prevail in April 1792 (but clearly below those that had prevailed in early March). Sylla et al. also quote a remarkably clear message to William Seton where he urges the Bank of New York to ponder 'how much more can be done in favor of parties who can pledge *Public Stock* as collateral security. This security of credit you are sure is a good one'. It is hard to think how a case for US Treasuries as safe and liquid assets could be made more emphatically. Perceptions of what are safe and liquid assets act as cornerstones in financial structures. Perceptions and expectations of assets as safe are shaped under financial stress. Hamilton used the 1792 crisis to promote the emergence of US bonds as the ultimate safe and liquidity asset: a safe haven in times of distress.

There is another important point worth repeating. Alexander Hamilton was concerned with the stability of the system. Financial instability threatened the whole edifice that was being built. The economic consequences of financial instability are so far-reaching that they fundamentally influence the effects of financial systems on economic performance. These effects, in turn, have broader political consequences.

VII. Lessons for Building a Continental Financial System in Europe

The first lesson to be drawn is that politics, finance, and fiscal policy are co-determined and co-evolutionary. The process must be conceived and executed in a systemic way. What can be achieved in one dimension is determined simultaneously with the other two.

The US is a monetary union backed by a well-integrated financial system and federal public finances. The euro area is an international monetary union backed by national (political) responsibility for fiscal sustainability. In the sovereign debt crisis in the euro area, financial fragmentation substituted for financial integration. Since mid-2012, the trend of financial disintegration was inverted. Europe is on its way to creating a banking union and a financial union.

The process of European integration has been driven to a very large extent by economic integration. The single market and the single currency are its most emblematic realizations. The European Union provides a pole of attraction and a role model favoring peace, democracy, and human rights. Specifically, it shows the possibility of effective application of international law.

The second lesson is that there is a case to give priority to public credit; a case that is based on political, public finance, and also on broader economic and financial arguments. The arguments put forward by Hamilton are in line with the implications of recent empirical research by Christoph Trebesch and co-authors. Alexander Hamilton managed to establish public credit while ensuring debt service at favorable terms.

To my mind, this lesson is very general. It applies at the national level. It is also a precondition for successful financial integration.

The third lesson is that the fundamental foundation of public credit requires fiscal sustainability. In the US, that required the US Constitution to substitute for the Articles of the Confederation.

In the euro area after the failure of euro area governance to prevent the crisis, very significant progress was achieved. First, the fiscal governance of the euro area has been strengthened through the adoption of important EU legal acts (the six pack and the two pack). Second, and more importantly, in parallel, member states have also adopted the fiscal compact. Broadly speaking, the rules in the Fiscal Compact are in line with the six pack.[1] The important difference is that the Fiscal Compact aims at internalizing the European constraints into national governance frameworks. This aspect is decisive. In Europe, politics are dominated by the fundamental principle of the dominance of the national dimension of politics. Hence, European rules can only be fully effective once subsumed in the national frameworks. *Giavazzi and Wyplosz* (2015) also underscore that, to be effective, institutions for fiscal discipline must be well adapted to political institutions.

The European rules prescribe a fiscal position close to balance or in surplus over the medium term. The effective operation of such rule ensures a slowly declining public debt to GDP ratio (assuming positive nominal growth of GDP over the medium term). Fiscal sustainability is guaranteed by compliance with European rules. Nevertheless, it is sobering to recall that government default in the early years of the US had, at its root, political behavior not in line with the letter of the Articles of the Confederation. At the end of the day, the responsibility has to be national: in accordance with the principle of the primacy of the national dimension of politics.

Clearly it is possible to deny the primacy of the national dimension of politics and to advocate centralization. However, it seems to me that centralization is neither politically desirable nor politically feasible.

The fourth lesson is that smooth and quick transition requires active and skillful management. This is particularly so given the importance of perceptions and expectations. The transition must be so managed that perverse equilibrium paths are avoided.

In Europe, financial support has been made available in diverse forms. The European Central Bank (ECB) has signaled that 'Within our mandate, the ECB is ready to do whatever it takes to preserve the euro' and Mario Draghi, the President of the ECB added, 'and believe me it will be enough'. The ECB announcement came in July 2012. One month after, heads of state or government reached a political agreement on deeper economic and monetary union. Since August 2012, quick progress has been achieved. In the autumn of 2013, the catastrophic risk associated with euro area fragmentation was no longer a salient concern for global investors. Nevertheless, a transition is never complete before the new framework is capable to prevent accidents and to minimize their effects in case they occur.

That leads to the *fifth lesson*, given that it is always possible that accidents will happen, public finance and the financial system must be robust and resilient. The institutional framework underpinning budgetary discipline and financial stability must be designed so as to be able to stem episodes of financial panic and to exclude perverse self-fulfilling equilibria. Alexander Hamilton proved more than equal to the task during the financial panic of 1792.

In 2009–2010, the euro area was not prepared for sovereign debt crises. The euro area was unable to prevent financial fragmentation and negative sovereign-bank credit risk feedback loops. Much progress has been made. But the job is not yet done. The priority, also emphasized by *Jones* in his chapter, is the realization of the banking union complemented by the integration and development of financial markets. The credibility of the banking union requires the existence of financial backstops of sufficient capacity to break the vicious sovereign-bank links and, hence, to ensure robust and resilient financial integration. These elements are discussed in greater detail by *Kincaid* and *Watson* 2015.

It is also important to bear in mind that financial transitions are dangerous moments. Liberalization and opening of financial systems is often associated with exuberance and excess. The local connection between politics and finance adds up complexity. Financial crises, especially when associated with balance sheet vulnerability, have very long-lasting consequences, spanning generations. Therefore, the ability to maintain financial stability is key for the long-run consequences of financial architectures. Transition risks have also to be pondered. This is particularly important when building continental financial systems.

In the end, it is clear there is no recipe for baking a continental financial system. Institution building requires deep understanding of the specifics of the particular case.

To conclude: For Europeans, the most inspiring message may well be:

> Whoever considers the nature of our government with discernment will see that though obstacles and delays will frequently stand in the way of the adoption of good measures, yet when once adopted, they are likely to be stable and permanent. It will be far more difficult to *undo* than *to do*. *Gazette of the United States,* September 1, 1790.

Paraphrasing Thomas Sargent: That may well have been true of the US then and it is certainly true for Europe now.

Acknowledgements

The views expressed in this article are the sole responsibility of the author and should not be attributed to the International Monetary Fund, its Executive Board, or its management. The article benefited from comments, corrections, and suggestions from Guillermo Calvo, Zsolt Darvas, Roger Gordon, Stephanie Hare, Heinz Hermann, Russell Kincaid, Sixten Korkman, Harold James, Johannes Lindner, Silvia Luz, Hans-Helmut Kotz, Maria Eugénia Mata, Laura Jaramillo Mayor, Yves Mersch, Ricardo Reis, André Sapir, Richard Sylla, Francisco Torres, Shahin Valée, Max Watson, Thomas Wieser, Guntram Wolff, and Michael Woodford and participants in seminars at Bruegel, Brussels, at St. Anthony's College, Oxford, at the ECB, Frankfurt, at CFS, Frankfurt, at Columbia University, New York, and at a Conference at Eltville organized by the Bundesbank, the Bank of Japan, the Institute for Monetary and Financial Stability and the University of Hamburg.

Disclosure statement

No potential conflict of interest was reported by the author.

Note

1. The fiscal governance framework in the euro area has also become more complex, which gives rise to a number of other challenges (see Eyraud and Wu 2014).

References

Bagehot, W. 1873. *Lombard Street.* London: H.S. King. In *The collected works of Walter Bagehot,* volume nine, eds. N. St. John-Stevas. London: The Economist.

Calomiris, Charles, and Stephen Haber. 2014. *Fragile by design: the political origins of banking crises and scarce credit.* Princeton, NJ: Princeton University Press.

Chernow, Ron. 2004. *Alexander Hamilton.* New York, NY: Penguin Books.

Cruces, Juan J., and Christoph Trebesch. 2013. Sovereign defaults: the price of haircuts. *American Economic Journal: Macroeconomics* 5, no. 3: 85–117.

Eyraud, Luc, and Tao Wu. 2014. *Euro area policies: 2014 Article IV consultation selected issues*. IMF Country Report No. 14/199. Washington, DC: International Monetary Fund.

Giavazzi, Francesco and Charles Wyplosz. 2015. EMU: Old Flaws Revisited. *Journal of European Integration* 37, no. 7: 723–37.

Garber, Peter. 1991. *Alexander Hamilton's market based debt reduction plan*. NBER Working Paper 3597, January.

Hamilton, Alexander. 1780a. Letter to Robert Morris, *First letter*, Available from Alexander Hamilton. 1904. *The works of Alexander Hamilton*, volume III, ed. Henry Cabot Lodge (Federal Edition). New York: G.P. Putnam's Sons.

Hamilton, Alexander. 1780b. Letter to James Duane, dated September 3, *Second letter*, Available from Alexander Hamilton. 1904. *The works of Alexander Hamilton*, volume I, ed. Henry Cabot Lodge (Federal Edition). New York: G.P. Putnam's Sons.

Hamilton, Alexander. 1781. Letter to Robert Morris dated April 30, *Third letter*, Available from Alexander Hamilton. 1904. *The works of Alexander Hamilton*, volume III, ed. Henry Cabot Lodge (Federal Edition). New York: G.P. Putnam's Sons.

Humphrey, T. 1992. Lender of last resort. In *The new Palgrave dictionary of money & finance*, eds. P. Newman, M. Milgate, and J. Eatwell, 571–4. London: Macmillan.

James, Harold. 2015. U.S. Precedents for Europe. In *Current federal reserve policy under the lens of economic history*, ed. Owen Humpage, 174–93. New York, NY: Cambridge University Press.

Kincaid, Russell. 2014. Comments on Vitor Gaspar's paper. *The making of a continental financial system: lessons for Europe from early American history*. Washington, DC: International Monetary Fund. (unpublished).

Kincaid, Russell and Max Watson. 2015. Avoiding Another Crisis in the EuroArea: Public and Private Imbalances and National Policy Responses. *Journal of European Integration* 37, no. 7: 785–801.

Rosseau, Pierre and Richard Sylla. 1999. *Emerging financial markets and early U.S. growth*. NBER Working Paper 7448, December.

Rosseau, Pierre and Richard Sylla. 2001. *Financial systems, economic growth and globalization*. NBER Working Paper 8323, December.

Sargent, Thomas. 2013. United States then, Europe now. *Nobel lecture*. Chapter 10 in Thomas Sargent. *Rational expectations and inflation*, third edition. Princeton, NJ: Princeton University Press.

Sylla, Richard. 2011. Financial foundations: public credit, the national bank, and securities markets. In *Founding choices: American economic policy in the 1790s*, eds. Douglas Irwin and Richard Sylla, 59–88. Chicago, IL: University of Chicago Press.

Sylla, Richard. 2014. Early U.S. struggles with fiscal federalism: lessons for Europe? *Comparative Economic Studies* 56, no. 2: 157–75.

Sylla, Richard, Robert Wright, and David Cowen. 2009. Central banker: crisis management during the financial panic of 1792. *Business History Review* 83, Spring: 61–86.

Thornton, H. 1802. *An enquiry into the nature and effects of the paper credit of Great Britain*. F. von Hayek (ed.). London: George Allen & Unwin, 1939.

Trebesch, Christoph. 2011. Sovereign default and crisis resolution. Ph.D. dissertation. Free University of Berlin, Berlin.

[illegible], 2014. [illegible] *Country Report No. 14/*[illegible]. Washington DC: International Monetary Fund.

[illegible] 2015. [illegible]

[illegible], 1991. [illegible] *Working Paper* [illegible]

Hamilton, Alexander, [illegible]. Letter to Robert Morris, [illegible]. Available from: [illegible] 1961. *The Papers of Alexander Hamilton, Volume II*, [illegible] Harold C. Syrett, [illegible] Columbia University Press.

Hamilton, Alexander, 1790. [illegible] Available from: [illegible] *The Papers of Alexander Hamilton*, [illegible] Harold C. Syrett. New York: Columbia University Press.

Hamilton, Alexander, [illegible] *The Papers of Alexander Hamilton*, [illegible] Harold C. Syrett, [illegible] Columbia University Press.

[illegible] London: [illegible]

James, Harold, 2012. [illegible]

[illegible]

[illegible] unpublished.

[illegible] and Mark Watson, 2015. [illegible]

[illegible]

[illegible] Working Paper [illegible]

Sargent, Thomas, 2012. [illegible] Princeton University Press.

Sylla, Richard, 2014. [illegible]

[illegible] University of Chicago Press.

[illegible]

Wills, [illegible]

[illegible]

Impossible Macroeconomic Trinity: The Challenge to Economic Governance in the Eurozone

DAVID VINES*,**,***,****,*****

*Economics Department, Balliol College, Oxford University, Oxford, UK;
**St Antony's College, Oxford University, Oxford, UK;
***Institute for New Economic Thinking (INET), Oxford University, Oxford, UK;
****Crawford School of Public Policy, Australian National University, Canberra, Australia;
*****Centre for Economic Policy Research, London, UK

ABSTRACT Europe now faces a new impossible macroeconomic trinity: it is no longer possible to combine monetary union, German political requirements and coherent economic analysis. Economic analysis shows that there must be more inflation in Germany, a significant fiscal expansion in Germany, a significant easing of austerity in the GIIPS countries and a write-down of much of the debt of southern European sovereigns. These changes will be resisted by Germany. But they are necessary if the monetary union is to survive.

The ideas of economists ..., both when they are right and when they are wrong, are more powerful than is commonly understood. Indeed the world is ruled by little else. Practical men, who believe themselves to be quite exempt from any intellectual influence, are usually the slaves of some defunct economist. (John Maynard Keynes, General Theory, Chapter 24)

Introduction: A New Impossible Trinity

The 'impossible trinity' of international macroeconomics states that a country cannot have a fixed exchange rate, open international capital markets and an independent monetary policy. This is why members of the European Monetary Union all share the same monetary policy, carried out by the European Central Bank. It is my belief that Europe now faces a new impossible macroeconomic trinity: it is no longer possible to combine European Monetary Union, German political requirements and coherent macroeconomic analysis.

Europe has resolved this contradiction by choosing incoherent macroeconomic analysis.[1] German political requirements have made it necessary to demand that the GIIPS[2] countries: (i) deflate their costs and prices as much as is necessary to restore their competitiveness; (ii) live within the constraints imposed by the Stability and Growth Pact (SGP) and by Europe's new Imbalances Procedure; and (iii) honour their sovereign debt obligations. But these objectives cannot be achieved. Any analysis which suggests that these things are possible is incoherent.

Europe has chosen incoherent macroeconomic analysis for powerful reasons. It is important for those Europeans who live within the Eurozone to show a continuing loyalty to the monetary union project, as part of the ongoing process of European integration. The abandoning of monetary union would be very costly in many ways. And it is important for Europeans to respect what is politically possible in Germany. Germany has found itself with responsibilities, as the new European hegemon,[3] which go well beyond its own national borders. But Germany's political imperatives are nationally driven, and they are constrained by a national sense of what is necessary and appropriate.[4] As a result of these two strong forces, Europe now finds itself between a rock and a hard place.

I am not the first to identify an impossible trinity within the Eurozone.[5] But the impossible macroeconomic trinity which I describe goes deeper than that examined by other authors. The reforms which they propose, although both important and necessary, will not produce an acceptable outcome unless they are accompanied by the three necessary changes in macroeconomic policy-making outlined in this article: more inflation in Germany; significant fiscal expansion in Germany combined with an easing of fiscal austerity in the GIIPS countries; and forgiveness of much of the debt of southern European sovereigns. German economists and politicians have made it clear that each of these three things will be resisted. If these three policy changes are not achieved, however, I forecast a slow motion train-crash: endangering not just of Greece's membership of the Eurozone, but also Italy's, Spain's and Portugal's. And, agonisingly, we will also watch France trapped in the wreckage.

The challenge of economic governance within the Eurozone is now to ensure that these three policy changes are brought about. And the intellectual challenge facing those who live within the Eurozone is to create a climate of opinion, in Germany and elsewhere, which sees the incoherence of the current policy stance and accepts that changes are necessary. This is a challenge as large as that thrown down by Keynes in his *General Theory*.

We know from history that incoherent macroeconomic analysis leads to crisis. Think about the collapse of the gold standard in 1931, recall the disintegration of the Bretton Woods system in 1971, and remember the ending of the East Asian Miracle in the East Asian Financial Crisis of 1997. In each case, the macroeconomic policy regime in place in the run-up to the crisis was underpinned by an analysis which now seems incoherent. It is true that, in each case, crisis came slowly. In each case, it was always possible to argue that the macroeconomic policy regime was sustainable — and people did argue this. But then crisis came. I believe that, if there is no change in the set of ideas underpinning the EMU policy framework, and if German politics does not accept such a change, then Europe will face the collapse of its entire Monetary Union project.

This crisis in the Eurozone began at the end of 2008 when the global financial crisis struck the world. In Europe, as everywhere, there was a massive downturn in aggregate demand. By early 2010, it had become very clear that the GIIPS were vulnerable because they had over-borrowed extensively, and were therefore in an uncompetitive position. In particular, these countries had become *fiscally* vulnerable. The collapse in output hit fiscal revenues everywhere, but in the uncompetitive GIIPS countries, it became clear that fiscal debts might never be repaid. As a result, Europe faced a number of sovereign debt crises. Previously, such crises were only found in emerging market economies: Latin America (1981), East Asia (1997), Russia (1998) and Argentina (2001). Suddenly, these crises came to Europe.

The Eurozone survived the initial onslaught, and in the summer of 2012 Mario Draghi announced that the European Central Bank would do 'whatever it takes'. By the end of 2013, there was general optimism. But now that optimism is completely gone.

How the Eurozone was Meant to Work

When the Eurozone was created, the overall objective was to create a region in which inflation would be under control, countries would be appropriately competitive vis-a vis each other, capital would be able to flow to whatever part of Europe in which it would best be used and governments would not over-borrow. Macroeconomic policy-making was designed to bring this about and was based on a very clear assignment of responsibilities. An understanding of who was meant to do what can help us recognise why things went so badly wrong.

Monetary Policy: The ECB

Monetary policy was given the task of macroeconomic stabilisation (i.e. managing aggregate demand) within the Eurozone region as a whole. This task was to be carried out by the ECB, which was to operate an inflation-targeting regime *for the Eurozone as a whole*. This was a well-defined task, and its workings were well understood.[6] The ECB was to raise the interest rate when inflation was above target, or when aggregate demand was excessive, and to lower the rate when inflation fell below target, or aggregate demand became too low. Such an assignment of a particular instrument — the interest rate — to a particular target — the rate of inflation — was a set-up which meant that fiscal policy would not be required to play a significant part in the stabilisation of the European economy. The ECB would — on its own — carry out monetary policy in such a way as to bring about the appropriate level of inflation, and aggregate demand, for the Eurozone as a whole.

Wage and Price Setting: National Actors' Responsibilities

It was believed that wage bargaining, and price setting, within each country in the Eurozone would be conducted by people who recognised the discipline which had been imposed on them by their membership of a monetary union. It was believed that wages and prices in each country *should* be set in the knowledge that the country needed to remain appropriately competitive, relative to the other members of the Union, so as to prevent the emergence of inter-country imbalances. This belief also involved an assignment of responsibilities. It was believed that wages and prices in each country *would* be set in this way. Otmar Issing explained this requirement very clearly in an important paper published in 2006.[7] It was also suggested that the Lisbon process, which was set up after the launch of EMU, might play a part in helping the necessary behaviour to emerge. It was thought that this process might help to bring pressure on uncompetitive regions to adjust their costs and prices in an appropriate manner. However, it was never made clear how the Lisbon process might help this to happen more effectively in some countries than in others.

Financial Liberalisation: Light-touch Regulation at the National Level

It was also believed that the financial integration brought about by the Single European Market could be carried much further after the Eurozone had been created, leading to a more integrated, and more competitive, European financial system. As a result, capital would flow to the European South, enabling rapid growth there, bringing better welfare for Europe as a whole. Currency risk for the separate countries within the Eurozone would disappear. And there would be no default risk for the separate sovereigns, since sovereign states would be bound together by the SGP (as described below). As a result, interest rates in the different countries within the union would converge. In such a stable European financial system, financial regulation could remain safely delegated to the separate nation states and assigned to the authorities in each state, who would manage financial supervision. They would also provide lender-of-last resort financing to banks headquartered within their country, when necessary, and be responsible for bailing out any failing banks within their country.

Fiscal Discipline: To be Administered Nationally

Fiscal policy was assigned the task of stabilising public debt, something which had been severely out of control in Europe in the 1980s and 1990s.

Article 104c [Article 126 TFEU] of the Maastricht Treaty stipulated that public deficits were not to exceed 3 per cent of GDP, except in exceptional circumstances, and that public debt was to be gradually reduced towards a target level of 60 per cent of GDP.[8] In 1997, there was a further agreement, based on a proposal by the German Government, to reinforce the fiscal provisions of Article 104c. The Stability and Growth Pact, or SGP, as this agreement came to be called, provided a commitment by EMU countries 'to respect the medium-term budgetary objective of positions close to balance or in surplus'.[9] Fiscal policy was assigned to this task only. In contrast with ideas from Keynesian economics, fiscal policy would pay no role in helping to stabilise the European economy.

What Went Wrong

During the first decade of the Euro's existence, two fundamental things went badly wrong. There emerged a competitiveness problem and an over-borrowing problem. European Monetary Union will only survive if the implications of these two problems are dealt with.[10]

The Competitiveness Problem: Ill-disciplined Wage and Price Setting

Wages and prices did not remain in check as Otmar Issing had told us so clearly was necessary. In Europe, the Great Moderation produced a Great Divergence. There was a lack of appropriate responsiveness of prices and wages, which were not adjusted smoothly across products, sectors and regions (European Commission 2008; Sapir 2012). Real exchange rates (i.e. relative unit labour costs) moved cumulatively upward in the GIIPS countries relative to those in Germany, while France was in the middle. This led to a loss of competitiveness. The amount of movement was very large — approximately 40 per cent in Greece, 35 per cent in Ireland and 30 per cent in Italy, Portugal and Spain.[11]

It is important to understand why this failure was allowed to arise.

The Over-borrowing Problem: Ill-managed Financial Liberalisation

Financial liberalisation was badly managed: The understanding of what would happen financially within the Eurozone, following greater financial integration within Europe, was initially correct. However, there was undisciplined over-lending to the GIIPS countries by banks within those countries, by northern European banks, and by global banks. As a consequence, these countries over-borrowed. Experience should have been a good guide here. Something very similar happened with the liberalisation of East Asian capital markets during the East Asian Miracle in the run-up to the East Asian financial crisis. And it had happened before that in Mexico, just after Mexico joined NAFTA. In each case, it suddenly seemed to players that policy risk had fallen. As a result, too many people thought that they had to get in on the act, lending an excessive amount. Just as in Thailand, Korea and Mexico, the players said 'this time is different' (Reinhart and Rogoff 2009). But it was not different.

The Eurozone Macroeconomic Policy Regime: Not Fit for Purpose

It is clear from the above review that the macroeconomic management of Europe *as a whole* was successful during the period of the Great Moderation. The ECB ensured price stability, and a stabilisation of output and inflation in the face of Eurozone-wide shocks.[12] The ECB's interest rate policy was of the right type, compared with estimated reaction functions for the US and the UK (see European Commission 2004). The ECB was also relatively 'active', more active than would have been suggested by a commonly used standard of reference — the 'Taylor Rule'. And its reaction function was reasonably symmetric in its operation.[13]

But things were not going well *between* countries.

The Walters Critique

It has become clear to economists that a tendency for costs and prices to diverge is an *intrinsic* problem in a monetary union. This has been widely understood in the UK, since the idea was put forward by Sir Alan Walters in the late 1980s. Walters was the economic adviser to Prime Minister Thatcher, and was rightly critical of the UK's membership of the European Monetary System. According to the 'Walters critique', as the European financial system integrated, interest rates in peripheral economies would converge on those in the north of Europe. But if the peripheral countries experienced a boom and higher inflation then this would cause its real interest rates to fall. This is exactly what happened in the GIIPS countries after the formation of EMU. In Spain and other GIIPS countries, real interest rates were around 300 basis points lower than in Germany for a period of nearly 10 years.[14] Walters said that such lower real interest rates would stimulate booming economies, exacerbating the inflation problems there. He thought that, as a result, the EMU system would actually become unstable.[15]

This set of issues is analysed carefully in Allsopp and Vines (2007, 2008), Allsopp and Vines (2008) and Kirsanova *et al.* (2007).The authors show that the instability described in the previous paragraph is a likely outcome, even although the booming economy becomes less competitive and suffers from declining net exports. Crucially, their research finds that stability of an economy in a monetary union can be assured only if wage and prices setters look forward in the way that Issing said was necessary. But the facts show that this did not happen.[16] It now appears unlikely that an economy belonging to a monetary union will actually be stable unless some other policy dampens the effects of asymmetric shocks which occur in that country but not in the union as a whole.

Destabilisation of the SGP

In the situation described above, fiscal policy could have played the necessary stabilising role (Allsopp and Vines 2007). However, such a policy was ruled out of court by the SGP.

Numerical simulations of the stabilising effects of such a policy are set out in Kirsanova *et al.* (2007) and Allsopp and Vines (2008). The detail of what was necessary was carefully explored in a paper (European Commission 2006) reporting on the work of a team led by the late Max Watson.[17] That team recommended that the SGP be amended to make countercyclical policy possible, and they further urged that such a policy be adopted. However their recommendations were ignored.

Furthermore, the effect of the SGP was actually destabilising. The SGP was to actually encourage fiscal loosening in the GIPPS countries during their boom, as can be seen from a description of what happened in Spain. High growth in domestic demand there during the mid-2000s led to inflation and to a worsening current account position. But it was not allowed to lead to a greater fiscal surplus so as to dampen the spending boom. Instead the Spanish government spent most of the extra revenues, meaning that fiscal policy actually supported the boom. It augmented the destabilising effects outlined in the Walters critique, rather than seeking to dampen them. The SGP positively encouraged pro-cyclical behaviour.

Conversely, the effect of the SGP in Germany was to support the tightening of domestic spending. Low growth of aggregate demand during this period led to lower fiscal revenues, and the effect of this was over-rued by further fiscal consolidation, under the influence of the SGP.[18] The tighter fiscal position further dampened German demand, augmenting the destabilising effects identified by the Walters critique. In Germany, higher real interest rates than in the South caused growth to lag. Fiscal tightening in Germany augmented this effect, rather than seeking to offset it.

In sum, the macroeconomic regime in Europe was not fit for purpose. As a result of the inflation differential between North and South, real interest rates diverged, leading to expenditure decisions which served to further magnify the inflation differential. And fiscal policy actually augmented these difficulties, rather than dampening them.

A Failure to Understand What Went Wrong

During the Great Moderation, many people were pleased with the ongoing integration of European economies. When shown pictures of the widening divergence of costs and prices between countries, many economists justified what was happening by saying that higher inflation in costs and prices was to be expected in the European periphery, since the GIIPS countries were integrating more closely with Northern Europe, and would be able to pay higher wages as they incorporated more modern methods of production. This view now looks wildly over-optimistic.

Unfortunately, such over-optimistic views remain commonplace today amongst those in authority in the Eurozone. For instance, consider the position of Pierre Moscovici, the European Union's Commissioner for Economic and Financial Affairs, in charge of the DG-ECFIN, the Directorate General for Economic and Financial Affairs. In a recent speech on the future of the Eurozone, given at the Bruegel Think Tank in Brussels, Moscovici walked right past the problem outlined above (Moscovici 2015). In his speech, he asked why the Eurozone had become vulnerable by 2008. The answer which followed was a surprising single sentence: ... 'Structural reform did not deal with this [problem]'. This response raises the question:

are there *structural* reforms which would have dealt with the *macroeconomic* problem which I have described? The answer is, of course, no. What is needed is a *macroeconomic analysis* of what went wrong — an analysis of the kind outlined above. Moscovici did not provide this. His failure to do so is symptomatic of the general outlook of those who work in DGECFIN.

The Onset of the Crisis

Suddenly, at the end of 2008, the global financial crisis struck. In Europe, there was a massive downturn in aggregate demand. Macroeconomic management of Europe by the ECB was initially successful. Interest rates were cut to very low levels to help mitigate the downturn, and liquidity was injected as needed. This monetary action was coupled with a highly expansionary fiscal policy, a policy which deliberately overrode the SGP. That is why the European crisis took more than a year to arrive after the onset of the GFC at the end of 2008.

However, by early 2010, it was clear that the uncompetitive GIIPS countries had become vulnerable. In particular, as already noted, these countries became *fiscally* vulnerable. This happened *not* because the fiscal authorities had over-borrowed but because of over-borrowing by the private sectors in these countries. The resulting collapse in private expenditure led to a collapse in output and income, and in fiscal revenues. In the uncompetitive GIIPS countries, which were all unable to devalue their currencies, it became clear that the resulting fiscal debts might never be repaid.

As a consequence, Europe faced the prospect of a sovereign debt crisis. What then happened was the result of a lack of policy clarity. The emergence of a default risk for peripheral sovereigns raised the interest rates which these sovereigns needed to pay, worsening their default risk and creating a vicious circle. In addition, this sovereign default risk increased the vulnerability of banking systems in GIIPS countries because those banks held so much of their own country's sovereign debt. However, because national sovereigns were still the guarantors of the banks within their countries, vulnerability was created in the banking systems of many peripheral countries, leading to a further tightening of the vicious circle. Furthermore, currency risk emerged, as it ceased to be clear that the Eurozone would survive, causing yet more tightening of the circle. A self-fulfilling bad outcome had become a distinct possibility.

What will it *Really* Take?

Mario Draghi's statement in 2012 — 'We will do whatever it takes' — put a temporary end to the situation described above. But now, three years later, it is clear that the dangers have not disappeared. We need to consider carefully the meaning of 'whatever it takes'.

The analysis which follows is not, of course, uncontentious. However, it is an analysis to which many in the economics profession now subscribe. Articulate expositions of this analysis, designed to be read by non-economists, may be found in pieces in the *New York Times* by the

Nobel-Prize-winning macroeconomist Paul Krugman and in Simon Wren-Lewis's blog called Mainly Macro.[19]

Adjustment of Costs and Prices

I have described above how, in 2008, costs and prices in Southern Europe were of the order of 30 per cent out of line with those in Northern Europe. There has been some movement to correct this position since 2008. But what has happened has been much less than what is needed.

How might the large remaining differences in unit labour costs be adjusted? After the East Asian financial crisis, Thailand, Korea, Indonesia and Malaysia were able to devalue their exchange rates by the same order of magnitude — 30 to 40 per cent — and to begin their recovery through export-led growth. Of course, this option is not available in Europe. Europe thus requires the GIIPS countries to have 4 or 5 per cent inflation less than Germany for four or five years.

There are two ways of achieving this objective.

One solution would be for there to be a period of sustained deflation in the GIIPS countries. However, we have known, ever since Britain rejoined the gold standard at an overvalued rate in 1925, that deflation like this is hard to bring about. It takes time, and, as in Britain in the late 1920s, the outcome may not be successful.[20] Furthermore, during the lengthy adjustment process, it will be difficult for growth to resume in the GIIPS countries. Even productive firms will find it difficult to borrow in such circumstances and bankruptcies will occur. Consumers will suffer from debt deflation in the way described by Irving Fischer. It is hard to imagine political support for such a strategy being sustained in the GIIPS countries.

Adjustment would be considerably easier to achieve if Germany were to share the burden, by allowing a much higher rate of German inflation. However, the behaviour of German representatives at the ECB has revealed an unwillingness to allow this. This explains why, in late 2014, the ECB was so unwilling to take decisive action to prevent inflation from falling well below the 2 per cent target. German resistance to quantitative easing (QE), early in 2015, can be seen in this light. Furthermore, it is possible to interpret much recent discussion of fiscal policy within Germany as suggesting that such a policy should actually be tightened, to help keep a lid on German inflation.

Thus, the necessary adjustment of costs and prices looks difficult, largely because Germany has ruled out what is necessary. As a result, 'whatever it takes' appears to be hard to achieve.

Revision of the SGP and the Imbalances Procedure

The SGP has been tightened since the crisis of 2008[21] and has been accompanied by the Macroeconomic Imbalances Procedure. These policy changes have been introduced in a set of policy moves known as the 'six pack' and the 'two pack'. But I would argue that these changes in regime are part of the problem, not part of the solution.

As described above, the SGP forced Germany to follow excessively tight policies during the Great Moderation but allowed excessive laxity in the GIIPS countries. Now, however, the SGP is imposing overall fiscal deflation in Europe — that is a policy of fiscal constraint the North, coupled with austerity in the South. This is a recipe for low growth. Numbers presented in the OECD (2014) suggest that output in Europe is 3 or 4 per cent lower than it would have been without such fiscal austerity.

The Imbalances Procedure is adding to the difficulty of adjustment, rather than helping with it. How is it that this procedure imposes surveillance on all countries with a deficit of more than 4 per cent of GDP, forcing them to curtail fiscal deficits, but allows countries with surpluses of up to 6 per cent to escape surveillance, rather than forcing them to expand fiscally? And why is it that Germany, with a surplus of nearly 8 per cent, is escaping surveillance and pressure to expand, and that Holland is doing the same, with an even greater surplus?

With such a combination of discipline and asymmetry, the only way that demand can begin to grow again in Europe is through growth in net exports. And the only way to achieve this is through currency depreciation, brought about by QE. Such an approach to macroeconomic management for Europe has been described as 'currency warfare', and can be seen as contributing to global instability (Vines 2015).

I would argue that the current fiscal position in Europe must change: there must be a significant fiscal expansion in Germany combined with an easing of fiscal austerity in the GIIPS countries. And, in future, the fiscal framework within the Eurozone must allow fiscal policy to play a part in countercyclical stabilisation. There have been many descriptions of what is required.[22] The implication for European governance is that German officials and politicians must come to understand that membership of Monetary Union requires Germany to do two things: to expand fiscally now and to agree to an overall change in the European fiscal-policy framework.

'Whatever it takes' includes such fiscal changes.

Writing Down European Sovereign Debt

I have left until last what has been most in the news — the prospect that the sovereign debt of the GIIPS countries will need to be written down.

In considering this issue, it is helpful to recall the Latin American debt crisis of 1981. The move to debt relief took eight years — Latin America's 'lost decade' — because the necessary debt reduction was resisted for many years both by US banks and by the US government. A similar write-down is inevitable in Europe, and is being resisted by Germany.

In Ireland, in late 2010, the European Central Bank and the European Commission prevented the Irish Government and the Irish Central Bank from imposing losses on bond holders who had invested in Irish banks which had become bankrupt. Such debt relief — worth perhaps 6 or 7 per cent of GDP — would have greatly eased the debt burden which has fallen on Irish tax payers.

The case of Greece is much more serious. Greek debt should have been written down in 2010. Instead, an extremely harsh austerity programme was imposed on Greece. The debt was partly written down in 2011, but by an inadequate amount. Now in 2015, a further write-down has become inevitable. There is widespread German opposition to such a write-down, as became evident the first part of 2015 (Stark 2015). Furthermore, writing down the debt has also become more difficult that it was in 2010, when much of it was held by the banks in Northern Europe and the US, who had over-lent to these countries in the first place. In the intervening years, these banks have been able to pass on their debt, first to the IMF and then to the ECB and to the European Stability Mechanism (ESM). Writing down the debt held by the ESM will be politically difficult.

It is true that the ESM has reduced the interest rate which Greece — and other Southern European countries — must pay on their debt. Estimates suggest that this figure for Greece may be as much as 4 per cent (or 400 basis points). The ESM has also enabled Greece and other countries to extend the period of their low-interest loans, thereby greatly reducing their effective debt burden. But this will almost certainly not reduce the debt enough to enable the fiscal position of Greece and of the other GIIPS countries to be sufficiently relaxed. And as has already become evident in the case of Greece, it is politically unlikely that the electorate in these countries will be willing to allow a debt overhang to remain, even if the effective repayment obligations have been substantially written down. At some stage, this debt will need to be forgiven, just as happened in Latin America.

Until this occurs, uncertainty will cast a shadow over the ability of the GIIPS countries to return to growth. 'Whatever it takes' must include a write-down of debt, sooner rather than later.

A Failure to Understand the Need for a Reformed Macroeconomic Policy Regime

In the speech referred to above (Moscovici 2015), Commissioner Moscovici failed to understand that a new macroeconomic policy regime is required within the Eurozone. Instead he argued for a number of *supply side* reforms. These reforms are important. But they will be inadequate unless Europe also makes changes to its macroeconomic policy regime. The same criticism can be levied at the other proposals put forward in this Journal.

Conclusion: The Political Vulnerability of the Euro Project

It is apparent that German officials and politicians do not agree with my analysis (see Stark [2015], for a clear statement of German reasoning). In the view of these people, the maladjustment of costs and prices which led to the Eurozone crisis arose as a result of a lack of discipline. And to them, what is now needed is for GIIPS countries to accept the kind of discipline which Germany regards as appropriate: deflation, fiscal discipline and a plan to honour debt obligations. In this article, I have provided an analysis of why these three things cannot be achieved. That is the reason for the trilemma which I identify in the title of my article.

Are we confident that such a German-led approach will be successful? This approach says: 'We may be near the edge of crisis, but in the end we will impose the necessary discipline'. But political processes in the GIIPS countries — not just in Greece — are increasingly revealing that the citizens of these countries are unwilling to submit to German discipline. It is often said that no rational member of a GIIPS country would wish to leave the Eurozone — the costs would be too great. In the end — it is said — GIIPS countries will come to realise what they need to do. My belief is that this calculation is changing. The costs of leaving the Eurozone would be very great. But for these countries, the costs of remaining within the Eurozone are also enormous. And politicians in the GIIPS countries are coming to realise that the German discipline which leads to these costs is based on incoherent economic analysis.

The Eurozone may survive. But for this to happen, policy will need to change. And for that to happen, the macroeconomic analysis which underpins the EMU Project will need to change. Keynes was right about the importance of ideas.

Acknowledgements

I am grateful to Christopher Allsopp, Lukas Freund, Wendy Carlin, Russell Kincaid, Klaus Regling, Peter Temin and Guntram Wolff for helpful discussions. An anonymous referee has made a number of helpful suggestions. And I am especially indebted to the late Max Watson who, over many years, helped me to think more clearly about European issues.

Disclosure statement

No potential conflict of interest was reported by the author.

Notes

1. I deliberately use the phrase 'incoherent macroeconomic analysis', rather than using Keynes' language.
2. Greece, Italy, Ireland, Portugal and Spain.
3. I use this word to refer to a set of privileges and obligations which I do not discuss here.
4. See Stark (2015), for a very clear exposition of the German position. My article focuses on the position taken by Germany. It is correct that a change in the German position on these matters may not be sufficient to lead to an acceptance the reforms which I propose. But a change in the German position is necessary. That is why I focus on Germany.
5. Sapir (2012) identifies an inconsistency between free capital movements, financial stability and national financial supervision within a monetary union. Pisani-Ferry (2012) finds a contradiction between the no-monetary financing rule, the absence of a banking union and the fact that there is no co-responsibility for public debt. Bibow (2012) identifies an impossible trinity for the German nation: perpetual export surpluses, a no transfer/no bailout monetary union and a 'clean', independent central bank.
6. An arrangement of this kind — very different from what might have been contemplated for economic policy in the 1950s or 1960s — was already conventional by the time that EMU was established. Such an arrangement had already been established, with some difficulty, in the US, the UK, Australia, Canada and New Zealand, during the 1980s and 1990s. See Woodford (2003) and Allsopp and Vines (2000).
7. See also Issing (2002).
8. This Article demanded that 'Member States ... avoid excessive government deficits'. It called upon the 'Commission [to] monitor the development of the budgetary situation and of the stock of government debt in the Member States with a view to identifying gross errors', i.e. substantial

excesses over 'reference values' (3 per cent of GDP for the deficit and 60 per cent for the debt) specified in the protocol on the excessive deficit procedure annexed to the treaty. Article 104c foresaw the Council being able to impose sanctions if a Member State persisted in failing to correct its situation.

9. This would allow EMU countries to deal with normal cyclical fluctuations while keeping their government deficit below the reference value of 3 per cent of GDP. In essence, the SGP was designed to transform the 3 per cent reference value specified in the treaty, which remained untouched, into a hard ceiling.
10. Erik Jones, in Chapter 7 below, agrees with this identification of the Eurozone's problems, but nevertheless offers a 'solution' which does not address them. He instead argues for financial reforms, because 'a close focus on financial markets promises to offer the greatest leverage over the largest number of national economies'. This is clearly a non-sequitur.
11. See Temin and Vines (2013, Chapter 5) for a plot of these cumulative divergences, which remorselessly built up over a period of nearly 10 years.
12. Such a two-for-one feature results from the fact that the trade-off between inflation and unemployment is only a short run trade-off (see Alesina *et al.* 2001).
13. 'The ECB aims at inflation rates of below, but close to, 2 per cent over the medium term'.
14. See Temin and Vines (2013, Chapter 5).
15. It is clear that the real interest rates which emerge in this way do not respect the Taylor principle, which requires that real interest rates rise as inflation rises (see Woodford 2003).
16. A country in a monetary union is more likely to have a stable economy if the private sector in such an economy is also forward looking in its expenditure decisions; see Allsopp and Vines (2008) and Kirsanova *et al.* (2007). But this additional point seems rather unimportant in the light of our experiences in the GFC.
17. Watson was then Economic Adviser to the Director General of the Directorate General for Economic and Financial Affairs (DG-ECFIN).
18. The SGP was violated during this period, for which Germany is often criticised. But if the SGP had been respected, German fiscal policies would have been even tighter.
19. Some of the papers in this Journal consider some of the reforms which I propose, in particular Chapters 1, 2, 5 and 7. But these reforms need to be located within a changed macroeconomic framework of the kind which I describe.
20. Britain's overvaluation in 1925 was less than half of what there is in Europe at present, and yet adjustment proved to be impossible.
21. This statement is correct even although there have been repeatedly extended extensions of deadlines.
22. For a discussion of how this needs to be done, see Allsopp and Vines (2005, 2007, 2008), HM Treasury (2003), Kirsanova *et al.* (2007), Kirsanova, Stehn, and Vines (2005), Leith and Wren-Lewis (2004), Pisani-Ferry (2002), Swedish Government (2002), Westaway (2003), and Wyplosz (2005).

References

Alesina, A., O. Blanchard, J. Gali, F. Giavazzi, and H. Uhlig. 2001. *Defining a macroeconomic framework for the euro area.* London: CEPR.

Allsopp C.J., and D. Vines. 2000. Macroeconomic policy. *Oxford Review of Economic Policy* 16, no. 4: 1–32.

Allsopp, C.J., and D. Vines. 2005. The macroeconomic role of fiscal policy. *Oxford Review of Economic Policy* 21, no. 4: 485–508.

Allsopp, C., and D. Vines. 2007. Fiscal policy, labour markets, and the difficulties of intercountry adjustment within EMU. In *The travails of the Eurozone*, ed. D. Cobham. London: Palgrave.

Allsopp, C., and D. Vines. 2008. *Fiscal policy, intercountry adjustment and the real exchange rate.* Chapter 13, European Commission.

Bibow, J. 2012. *The euro debt crisis and Germany's euro trilemma.* Working Paper No 21. Levy Economics Institute, Bard College.

European Commission. 2004. *EMU after 5 years.* European Economy, Special Report. Brussels: European Commission.

European Commission. 2006. *Adjustment dynamics in the euro area.* The EU economy 2006 review. Brussels: European Commission.

European Commission. 2008. *EMU@10: successes and challenges after ten years of Economic and Monetary Union*. European Economy, Brussels: European Commission.
HM Treasury. 2003. *Fiscal stabilisation and EMU: a discussion paper*. London: HM Treasury.
Issing, O. 2002. On macroeconomic policy co-ordination in EMU. *JCMS: Journal of Common Market Studies* 40, no. 2: 345–58.
Issing, O. 2006. *The euro: a currency without a state*. BIS Review 23. Basel: Bank for International Settlements.
Kirsanova, T., M. Satchi, D. Vines, and S. Wren-Lewis. 2007. Optimal fiscal policy rules in a monetary union. *Journal of Money, Credit and Banking* 39, no. 7: 1759–84.
Kirsanova, T., J. Stehn, and D. Vines. 2005. The interactions between fiscal policy and monetary policy. *Oxford Review of Economic Policy* 21: 532–64.
Leith, C., and S. Wren-Lewis. 2004. *Fiscal stabilisation in EMU: a survey of policy and design issues*. March. London: Draft Report prepared for HM Treasury.
Moscovici, P. 2015. *Deepening economic and monetary union*. Speech given at Bruegel in Brussels on 19 January, 2015.
OECD. 2014. *Economic outlook*. November. Paris: OECD.
Pisani-Ferry, J. 2002. Fiscal discipline and policy coordination in the eurozone: assessment and proposals. In *Budgetary Policy in E(M)U*. the Hague: Ministerie van Financien.
Pisani-Ferry, J. 2012. *The euro crisis and the new impossible trinity*, http://www.bruegel.org/publications/publication-detail/publication/674-the-euro-crisis-and-the-new-impossible-trinity/.
Reinhart, C., and K. Rogoff. 2009. *This time is different: eight centuries of financial folly*. Princeton, NJ: Princeton University Press.
Sapir, A. 2012. Europe after the crisis: less or more role for nation states? *Oxford Review of Economic Policy* 27, no. 4: 608–19.
Stark, J. 2015. The historical and cultural differences that divide Europe's union. *Financial Times*. February 11.
Swedish Government. 2002. *Stabilisation policy in the monetary union: summary of the report*. The commission on stabilisation policy for full employment in the event of Sweden Joining the Monetary Union. Swedish government Official Reports SOU 2002:16. Stockholm: Swedish Government.
Temin, P., and D. Vines. 2013. *The leaderless economy: why the world economic system fell apart and how to fix it*. Princeton, NJ: Princeton University Press.
Vines, D. 2015. On concerted unilateralism: raising the global growth rate through macroeconomic policy coordination. Forthcoming in T. Bayoumi, S. Pickford, and P. Subacchi. *Managing complexity: economic policy cooperation after the crisis*. Washington, DC: Brookings Institution.
Westaway, P. 2003. Modelling shocks and adjustment mechanisms in EMU. London: HM Treasury.
Woodford, M. 2003. *Interest and prices*. Princeton, NJ: Princeton University Press.
Wyplosz, C. 2005. Fiscal policy: institutions versus rules. *National Institute Economic Review*. 191: 64–78.

Using Interdisciplinary Analysis to Shape a Policy Agenda

ERIK JONES*,** & FRANCISCO TORRES***,****

*Johns Hopkins University SAIS;
**Nuffield College, Oxford, UK;
***European Institute, London School of Economics and Political Science, London, UK;
****European Studies Centre, St. Antony's College, Oxford University, Oxford, UK

ABSTRACT This conclusion uses an interdisciplinary approach to the crisis to contribute to the debate on EMU governance and EU institutional reform. It begins with stocktaking based on the Five Presidents Report (2015). It then identifies policy priorities for the short and medium term. It uses these priorities to shape a longer term agenda for a sustainable Europe. And it concludes with suggestions for further research. If any economics window on an interdisciplinary crisis may shed some light, perhaps a political science window could shed more.

This collection of essays came together alongside two developments that will have a lasting impact on the euro area — the 'Five Presidents Report' (2015) on 'completing Europe's economic and monetary union' and the events surrounding the end of Greece's participation in the second bailout program. These developments underscore why we believe the crisis in the euro area can only be understood at the juxtaposition of insights from different disciplines. They also illustrate why we chose to highlight themes related to multilevel governance, policy ideas, distributive bargaining, and popular legitimation in our introduction. The goal of the 'Five Presidents Report' is to strengthen the European Union by drawing the right lessons from the crisis and then implementing them in a manner that will reinforce action taken at the member state level while shoring up popular support for European integration. The situation in Greece, even if it is a rather particular case among all Eurozone countries, suggests that we are still far from achieving that objective.

The purpose of this short conclusion is to show how the essays in this collection can move us in the right direction. Along the way, we hope to underscore what useful progress has been made and where more attention should be directed. As we announced in the introduction, this is not a definitive exercise. Often we can only point to problem areas or raise useful questions. That is useful nonetheless. When we say European integration is a work in progress, we should probably underscore the importance of 'work' as much as 'progress'. Much remains to be understood and then put into action before anything substantial can be accomplished.

This conclusion has three elements. It starts with an assessment of where things stand based on the analysis provided in the preceding essays. The second section looks at priorities for action. Here we admit that there is room for contestation, even among our own contributors. The third section extends those immediate priorities into a longer term agenda. The final section offers suggestions for further research based on this analysis.

Taking Stock

The recent events in Greece have cast a pall over the European project. The details have been widely reported in the media. A bare-bones outline might go like this. Negotiations between Greece and its creditors dragged on for months after the election of a Syriza-led coalition government. During the period of uncertainty that surrounded those negotiations, the Greek economy continued to contract and the balance sheets of the Greek banks worsened. Events came to a head toward the end of the second bailout program in June 2015. Nevertheless, the Greek government and its creditors could not come to agreement. Instead the Greek government called for a yes-or-no referendum on whether to accept the terms offered by its creditors (even though that offer lapsed in the interim). The situation with the banks continued to worsen and the Greek government had to impose capital controls as a consequence. This forced the Greek economy into an even deeper contraction. The Greek people rejected the offer made by Greece's creditors and yet the Greek government had few alternatives to stabilize public finances or the country's banks. As a result, it agreed to enter into negotiations over a new bailout program that was at the same time more generous (because it involved larger sums of assistance) and more rigorous (because it placed greater constraints on Greek policy-makers).

This situation is revealing because it shows the tensions built into Europe as a multilevel governance framework. As Mongelli and his colleagues reveal, there has been much progress made on many different dimensions of the European project. Nevertheless, important gaps remain. Some of these gaps, like a lender of last resort facility for governments and sovereigns, have long attracted attention from the community of policy analysts. That is the point that Giavazzi and Wyplosz make. Nevertheless, the framework remains dangerously inadequate. Although the EU has put together some institutions to act as a firebreak in the event of crisis, it continues to underestimate the fragility of the European financial system and so it continues to overburden the European Central Bank. This point is underscored by De Grauwe and Ji. It is also central to the Jones essay.

The European framework lacks two things in particular. One is a pre-established mechanism (and formula) for distributing adjustment costs in the event of a sudden crisis. This point is stressed by De Grauwe and Ji but also by Bini Smaghi. The other thing lacking is an institutional framework for exercising discretion in times of need. This is a concern raised by Gaspar. Without those two elements, it is almost certain that any significant shock will give rise to distributive bargaining (if not conflict). That is why large macroeconomic imbalances are so threatening, as outlined by Kincaid and Watson. Unfortunately, however, there is little political will to resolve this dilemma. The most powerful member states show no desire to build up large centralized financial arrangements or to establish automatic lender-of-last resort facilities. On the contrary, they are more concerned to emphasize national responsibility and to prevent moral hazard. Some of these inclinations arise from economic models that are popular in these countries. That is the point made by Vines in his essay. Some, however, stems from a more general unwillingness to share resources across national boundaries (to which the amount of resources transferred to Greece by all the other Eurozone members, including poorer member states, has contributed) — a point made by Kincaid and Watson but also De Grauwe and Ji.

The political requirements to overcome this reluctance have not been met and are unlikely to develop spontaneously. The European Union is a single framework for multilevel governance but it contains a multitude of discrete political communities. Begg and his colleagues make that point clearly. The implication is not that European integration is doomed from the outset or that political union will remain forever beyond reach. Rather it is that political community building is a slow-moving process that requires constant nurturing. Unfortunately, the tensions that emerged at the end of the second Greek bailout program are pushing in the opposite direction. This is not a new phenomenon. The European Union has been struggling to forge a closer political community at least since the early 2000s. That is why the European Council issued its Laeken Declaration in December 2001. What the political crisis around Greece reveals is that little progress has been made in the interim; indeed, Europe may have moved in the opposite direction.

Priorities for Action

The Five Presidents Report is well timed in this respect. The report calls for action across four dimensions — economic union, financial union, fiscal union, and political union. The economic challenge is to create markets that are both efficient and convergent but also to reconcile growth, employment, and competitiveness with the sustainability of EMU, while avoiding negative spillovers across national borders. The financial challenge is to strike a balance between systemic stability and moral hazard. The fiscal challenge is to share risks as well as resources in the face of oversized external shocks. And the political challenge is to establish the legitimacy of these new arrangements in order to shore up popular support. The Five Presidents report makes suggestions for policy in each of these areas. The problem is that Europe's heads of state and government are unlikely to be able to tackle all of these agendas at once. Hence they will need to establish clear priorities. The contributions to this collection have a number of suggestions.

For Vines, the emphasis must be on competitiveness and hence the establishment of efficient and convergent markets. The reason traces back to the original literature on optimum currency areas. It is also reinforced by the experience of large macroeconomic imbalances, as per Kincaid and Watson. It is hard to see how a single currency can be sustainable if national economies interact in a destabilizing manner through movements in relative prices and national savings. Therefore, it is essential that European leaders work to reform their market institutions. This poses a twofold challenge. To begin with, have to create the space for positive action. That is why Vines places such emphasis on using macroeconomic policy instruments to stabilize aggregate demand. However, the challenge now is to promote growth in a way that is compatible with fiscal consolidation and reduced indebtedness while at the same time ensuring long-term sustainability. As illustrated by the example of Puerto Rico within a financially integrated monetary union, a sustainable growth strategy with structural reforms at the national level seems necessary for a durable recovery.

For Jones, the priority should be completion of Europe's financial union. Again, the goal is to provide sufficient space for policy action in other dimensions. It is not to preclude improvements to competitiveness, but rather to facilitate their achievement over the longer term. The challenge is to provide sufficient resources to shore up European financial institutions — not just in Greece but also elsewhere. This will require moving beyond what is currently available in Europe either in terms of resolution financing or deposit insurance. That message is consistent with arguments made by Giavazzi and Wyplosz. It is also consistent with De Grauwe and Ji. The open question is how such resources will be financed. The answer is not immediately obvious.

For De Grauwe and Ji, the answer is fiscal integration. That answer fits with American experience, which is a point noted both by Gaspar and by Giavazzi and Wyplosz. It is controversial nonetheless. As mentioned above, there is little desire among the wealthier European countries to create a mechanism to transfer resources automatically across national boundaries. If such a mechanism is essential to the smooth functioning of Europe's financial union, then Europe will have to continue to live with a suboptimal institutional arrangement across both dimensions. There are hints of this contradiction in the Five Presidents Report; De Grauwe and Ji place it front and center in their conclusion.

Paradoxically, the argument made by De Grauwe and Ji suggests that the priority for action should lie in efforts to influence the most slow-moving variable — which is the degree of political union or solidarity across countries. This brings us back to the analysis made by Begg and his colleagues. They stress that Europe's peoples will respond to a vision of integration that promises to resolve many problems and not just the current crisis. Articulating this vision is only the first challenge for policy action; building popular trust in such a conception of Europe will require more sustained effort. This is a very different argument from that made by Vines, Jones, or De Grauwe and Ji insofar as it suggests that the immediate priority is also the priority for the longer term. European integration is a political project with economic benefits as well as being an economic project with political implications. Once again we find ourselves looking through a prism with political legitimacy on one end and economic rationality on the other.

Longer term Consideration

To its credit, the Five Presidents Report does not shy away from this longer term political challenge. Hence, while many of the contributors to this volume may disagree with specific recommendations either because of what they put forward or because of what they omit, there is general agreement on the broad thrust of the project. The difficulty lies in implementation.

That implementation requires action on many dimensions. First and foremost, it requires openness to new ideas. Giavazzi and Wyplosz stress the importance of allowing new ideas to penetrate into the policy process; Barta and Schelkle emphasize the penetration of new ideas into the markets; Vines emphasizes the impact of ideas on the world of high politics. These are all areas where Europe has been resistant to change. But the signs are that resistance is diminishing — particularly where the policy process and markets are concerned. The bigger concern is the political arena. Challenging fundamental assumptions is never easy, particularly when those assumptions are underpinned by great wealth and strong economic performance. It is nevertheless essential for Europeans to take a system-wide perspective if they are to tackle system-wide problems. To put not too fine a point on it, Europe cannot prosper as Germany writ large both because such an evolution would impose an unacceptably high cost of adjustment on a number of member states (as per Bini Smaghi) and because it would result in pushing the problem of macroeconomic imbalances to the global level (which is one of the implications of Kincaid and Watson).

Changing ideas is not enough on its own. Those ideas must be translated into functioning institutions for multilevel governance. The work by Mongelli and his colleagues shows us where that institutionalization has progressed and where more work is required. Giavazzi and Wyplosz emphasize that sequencing matters in economic terms. Begg et al. show how sequencing matters in the political process. The implication is that we need to develop ideas not just about what to do but how it should be accomplished. Moreover, these ideas about the content and process of institutional reform must be consistent. This is a point that emerges in Barta and Schelkle. What they show is how difficult it is to achieve such consistency within a multilevel governance framework where the focus is on interaction between states and markets. European leaders have no choice but to rise to the challenge.

Finally, the longer term agenda must tackle other problems that are likely to emerge. This is the point made by Begg et al. It is also the point revealed by Gaspar's more historical analysis. The advantage of the longer view is that it helps to put setbacks into perspective. Even major conflicts or changes in policy, like those experienced in the United States during the nineteenth century, do not have to derail a sound policy agenda — particularly where there is broad-based determination to succeed both politically and economically. The point here is not to suggest that the crisis surrounding Greece, or the political malaise that has affected Europe since the end of the 1990s, compares in any way to the traumas experienced in the United States. Recent events look dramatic but not in anything like the same way. Even so the goal for policy-makers should be to remain fixed on the longer term horizon and to look for opportunities to introduce sound policies or innovations for which there is no support at the moment (or for which there may be outright opposition). The discussion of mutualized sovereign debt instruments (or Eurobonds) falls in this category. Fiscal union may fit in this category as well. These are important innovations that should be kept on the longer term agenda even if the opportunity to implement them may never come.

Suggestions for Research

This allusion to the long term suggests an important research agenda that can be described in terms of the political acceptability of economic integration or the economic possibilities from political integration. The goal of this collection has been to focus attention on both sides of that problem. We have relied on insights from economists that we can make available to a wider community of political scientists or cognate researchers. But that is only half of the wider agenda. It is easy to imagine an exercise that opens the literature in political science to the community of economics. What is clear is that the two communities are addressing the same themes, albeit often with different language and drawing upon contributions from different communities. What is also clear is that the different disciplines of scholarship have a lot to offer one-another. Unfortunately, the barriers to entry in the conversation are so high that it will always be easier to speak within a group than to initiate a dialog across communities. The incentives of academic publishing and career promotion reinforce that tendency. This is bad for policy and bad for Europe. We would not go so far as to argue that such Balkanized scholarship explains the current crisis; but we would not be unfair to suggest that it would explain the next crisis given the many different good ideas for strengthening European integration that are on offer.

Disclosure statement

No potential conflict of interest was reported by the authors.

Index

Note: Page numbers in *italics* represent tables
Page numbers in **bold** represent figures
Page numbers followed by 'n' refer to notes

For Product Safety Concerns and Information please contact our EU representative GPSR@taylorandfrancis.com Taylor & Francis Verlag GmbH, Kaufingerstraße 24, 80331 München, Germany